The Other Sylvia Plath

LONGMAN STUDIES IN TWENTIETH-CENTURY LITERATURE

Series Editor: STAN SMITH,
Research Professor in Literary Studies,
Nottingham Trent University

Titles available:

THE OTHER
SYLVIA PLATH

TRACY BRAIN

Longman

An imprint of **Pearson Education**

Harlow, England · London · New York · Reading, Massachusetts · San Francisco
Toronto · Don Mills, Ontario · Sydney · Tokyo · Singapore · Hong Kong · Seoul
Taipei · Cape Town · Madrid · Mexico City · Amsterdam · Munich · Paris · Milan

FOR SHELLY, LORI, AND IMOGEN

Pearson Education Limited
Edinburgh Gate
Harlow
Essex CM20 2JE
England

and Associated Companies throughout the world.

Visit us on the World Wide Web at:
http://www.pearsoneduc.com

First published 2001

ISBN 0-582-32730-X PPR

British Library Cataloguing-in-Publication Data
A catalogue record for this book can be obtained from the British Library

Library of Congress Cataloging-in-Publication Data
Brain, Tracy
   The Other Sylvia Plath/Tracy Brain
      p. cm. -- (Longman studies in twentieth-century literature)
   Includes bibliographical references (p.) and index.
   ISBN 0-582-32730-X (pbk. : alk. paper)
      1. Plath, Sylvia--Criticism and interpretation. 2. Women and literature--United
States--History--20th century. I. Title. II. Series.

PS3566.L27 Z5827 2001
811'.54--dc21   00-061498

10 9 8 7 6 5 4 3 2 1
05 04 03 02 01

Set by 7 in 11/13 Bembo
Produced by Pearson Education Asia Pte Ltd.
Printed in Singapore

CONTENTS

CONTENTS

LIST OF PLATES

ACKNOWLEDGEMENTS

I am grateful to the British Academy for a generous research grant that allowed me to work in the Plath archives during the summer of 1998. This book owes its existence to the encouragement and sensitive editorial support given by Liz Mann, who commissioned it, to the fine scholarship and advice of Stan Smith as series editor, and to the continued editorial support of Casey Mein, Paula Parish and Katy Coutts. Philip Gross, Gavin Cologne-Brookes and Colin Edwards have given me valuable feedback on drafts of this work. I am grateful to the Humanities Faculty at Bath Spa University College for freeing me from some of my teaching so I could write, and especially to Neil Sammells and Jeff Rodman. Students of my Sylvia Plath course have contributed immeasurably to this book. The Curators and Librarians in Smith College's Mortimer Rare Book Room and Indiana University's Lilly Library offered advice, practical help and kindness that went beyond the call of professional duty. Karen Kukil, Associate Curator of Rare Books at Smith College, deserves special thanks for her time and knowledge. So do Martin Antonetti, the Curator of Rare Books at Smith, and Elizabeth Powers and Helena Walsh at the Lilly Library. Terry Gifford offered unasked-for assistance. Chas was there when this started. Stuart Laing has continued to offer support and encouragement. Richard Kerridge's love, support and intelligence have helped me in so many ways. I could not have done this without my parents; to name the ways they have helped me would take a whole book.

All published materials used in the writing of this book are listed in the Bibliography at the end. Endnotes for each instance of quotation appear at the end of the relevant chapter. I have listed only essential details in each endnote, while making it clear and easy for the reader to consult the Bibliography for fuller publication details. Unless otherwise stated in the endnote, all quotations from Plath's books are from the English editions published by Faber and Faber.

Wherever I have quoted from unpublished sources, the location and bibliographic details appear in the corresponding endnote. Whenever possible, I have indicated the location of omissions in published editions of Plath. By this I mean that if I quote a sentence that Plath cancelled from *The Bell Jar* in a typescript or handwritten draft, I identify the position where the cut would have appeared in the readily available published Faber edition. SMITH stands for the Mortimer Rare Book Room at Smith College; LILLY stands for the Lilly Library at Indiana University: I have followed the individual conventions of the given library for cataloguing and storing the material. T.L.s. in some of the SMITH citations stands for Typed.Letter.signed.; A.L.s. stands for Autographed.Letter.signed.

PUBLISHER'S ACKNOWLEDGEMENTS

We are grateful to the following for permission to reproduce copyright material:

Faber and Faber Ltd for extracts from *THE JOURNALS OF SYLVIA PLATH* 1950–62 ed. Karen V Kukil, London: Faber and Faber Ltd 2000; Faber and Faber Ltd/HarperCollins Publishers Inc for extracts from *THE BELL JAR* by Sylvia Plath, London: Faber and Faber Ltd 1963/Copyright © 1971 by Harper & Row, Publishers Inc; Faber and Faber Ltd/HarperCollins Publishers Inc for extracts from *THE COLLECTED POEMS OF SYLVIA PLATH* edited by Ted Hughes, London: Faber and Faber Ltd 1981/Copyright © 1960, 1965, 1971, 1981 by the Estate of Sylvia Plath. Editorial material copyright © 1981 by Ted Hughes; Faber and Faber Ltd/HarperCollins Publishers Inc for extracts from *JOHNNY PANIC AND THE BIBLE OF DREAMS AND OTHER PROSE WRITINGS*, London: Faber and Faber Ltd 1977, 1979/Copyright © 1952, 1953, 1954, 1955, 1956, 1957, 1960, 1961, 1962, 1963 by Sylvia Plath. Copyright © 1977, 1979 by Ted Hughes and Faber and Faber Ltd/HarperCollins Publishers Inc for extracts from *LETTERS HOME* ed. Aurelia Schober Plath, London: Faber and Faber Ltd 1975/Copyright © 1975 by Aurelia Schober Plath.

Plates 1 to 4 are taken from Sylvia Plath's art scrapbooks and are reproduced courtesy of the Lilly Library, Indiana University, Bloomington, Indiana, and with kind permission of the Estate of Sylvia Plath.

CHAPTER 1

THE OUTLINE OF THE WORLD COMES CLEAR

A poem can't take the place of a plum or an apple. But just as a painting can recreate, by illusion, the dimension it loses by being confined to canvas, so a poem, by its own system of illusions, can set up a rich and apparently living world within its particular limits.

Most of the poems I am going to introduce in the next minutes attempt to recreate, in their own way, definite situations and landscapes. They are, quite emphatically, about the 'things of this world'.[1]

Packaging Sylvia Plath

The packaging and physical design of any book can never be innocent. Books need to be sold, and this is often a much more pressing concern for publishers, agents, and sometimes even for writers, than if – or how – books are subsequently read. With Sylvia Plath's work, these commercial pressures are manifested in unusual ways, and magnified to an unusual degree.

This has been the case from the start. William Heinemann published the first edition of *The Bell Jar* early in 1963, just a few weeks before Plath took her own life on 11 February that same year.[2] Not surprisingly, nothing on the cover of this first edition, no aspect of its packaging, would have made the reader suspect that Victoria Lucas was a pseudonym, much less that the pseudonym was a mask worn by Sylvia Plath. Between *The Bell Jar*'s first edition, and its second (Heinemann's Contemporary Fiction edition of 1964, published one year after Plath's death), something made Heinemann decide that it was necessary to call attention to this pen-name, while explicitly refusing to name the author. This 1964 edition announces on the back of its dust jacket: 'Victoria Lucas is a pseudonym, and we are not in a position to disclose any details of the author's identity'.[3] With hindsight and even a rudimentary knowledge of Plath's work, this is a statement that may well raise goose bumps. At the beginning of the twenty-first century, when most people know very well that Sylvia Plath wrote *The Bell Jar*, it seems almost impossible to imagine a moment where such a lack of awareness was possible. Even as early as 1964, only a year after Plath's death, such a disclaimer would have aroused suspicion and curiosity where before there was none – or at least only a relatively small amount of it. Frances McCullough reminds us that 'everyone in literary London knew Plath was the author'[4] (though it is worth remembering what a tiny population of individuals 'literary London' actually was). The moment of *The Bell Jar*'s initial publication in early 1963 was a moment relatively free of preconceptions about what the novel was 'about'. It was a moment where each element of plot and language was not assumed to refer directly to the writer's life.

At the outset of Plath criticism, before we all knew too much, reviewers were able to discuss her work with originality, responding to what was actually in her books instead of confirming their expectations. 'Few writers are able to create a different world for you to live in; yet Miss Lucas in *The Bell Jar* has done just this',[5] wrote an unnamed critic in the *Times Literary Supplement* three weeks before Plath's death. Two weeks before Plath died, Laurence Lerner observed in *The Listener* that *The Bell Jar* offered intelligent 'criticisms of American society' and managed, unusually, to be both 'tremendously readable' and achieve 'an almost poetic delicacy of perception'.[6] Lerner and the unnamed reviewer react instead of imitate. Such moments have been rare in the history of Plath publishing, and occur only in relation to the two publications that appeared while Plath was still alive, and – outside of poetry circles – little known.

Retrospectively, we can see that like *The Bell Jar*, *The Colossus* marked a moment of relative innocence. The brief biography included in the first American edition of *The Colossus* actually says something helpful and imaginative about Plath's writing, something that has been lost to reviewers and critics since Plath died and her 'own story' became public property. Potential readers are informed that Plath's 'work reflects both her New England heritage and the landscape of England where she now makes her home'.[7] Here, the central thing about Plath's work is seen as geographical and cultural: the presence of two nationalities and two landscapes in her writing. This strand of Plath's thought is every bit as important and prevalent as her alleged obsession with depression and death, yet national identity has all but vanished as a theme that might help us to understand her work. It is a strand to which I will be giving careful consideration in this book.

The back cover of the American first edition of *The Colossus* prints the text of 'Watercolor of Grantchester Meadows', while the inside front cover provides excerpts of notices that are entirely non-personal. These excerpts, like the reference to Plath's landscapes in the brief biography, again suggest ways of reading that have evaporated since Plath's death. The text on the inside of *The Colossus*'s dust jacket begins startlingly. 'Sylvia Plath', we are told, 'is a young American poet whose work has appeared widely in recent years on both sides of the Atlantic'.[8] Again, it is difficult to imagine such a moment: when few knew who Sylvia Plath was, or what her story might be. It was a moment where Plath needed to be introduced to readers in the simplest of terms: when she was 'young', and above all, *alive*. Reviewers got the point, in those too few days before Plath died. They discussed her work in terms, and posed questions, that I want to revisit. To do so, we must try to simulate the vantage point of those early critics, and step outside the shadow cast by Plath's death when we look at her work. First, these initial reviewers of *The Colossus* detected the unstable complexity through which Plath speaks about gender in her writing, the difficulty of pinning down her speakers and tones as purely masculine or feminine. Second, they acknowledged the technical proficiency of her poetry.

The Colossus's inside front cover quotes A. Alvarez's assertion that 'Miss Plath neither asks excuses for her work nor offers them. She steers clear of feminine charm, deliciousness, gentility, supersensitivity and the act of being a poetess.' Some feminist critics might take issue with the implicit disparagement of Alvarez's allusion to 'feminine' qualities. Others might share his appreciation of a woman writer's refusal to be feminine. Whatever political judgement we might make, Alvarez is right to identify the tricks Plath plays with gender, the refusal of so many of her poetic voices to be categorised as either masculine or feminine, their insistence on constantly shifting and surprising and above all challenging the reader. Plath has often been accused of using her writing to express her anger at men, and in particular her resentment of her father and husband. We will see that this is an injustice to her work. Such crude misreading overlooks Plath's concern that men as well as women are put under terrible pressures to comply with the rules and constraints imposed upon them by gender. Another critic quoted inside *The Colossus*'s front dust jacket rightly noted 'a skill with language that is curiously masculine in its knotted, vigorous quality, combined with an alert, gay, sometimes rather whimsical sensibility that is wholly feminine'. In the years since Plath's death, her ability to create voices that might be described as hermaphrodite in their ability to slip between masculinity and femininity, or blend the two, has too often been ignored.

Alvarez goes on to discuss the technical accomplishment of Plath's work. 'She simply writes good poetry', he writes. 'And she does so with a seriousness that demands only that she be judged equally seriously.' Two of the other reviewers quoted on *The Colossus*'s inside front cover praise the book along these same lines. 'The book is a revelation suitcase', wrote a critic from *Poetry Review*, 'bulging, always accurate, humor completely unforced, wresting a certain beauty from the perhaps too-often-preferred ugly, but with a control and power of expression unsurpassed in modern poetry'. A third commentator asserts that 'Miss Plath possesses astonishing skill … She has learnt her craft all the way.'[9] Since her death, the terms by which Plath's work has largely been judged have tended to evaluate her writing with reference to biographical 'fact'. If Alvarez was right in his characterisation of Plath's 'seriousness' about her writing and her wish to produce 'good poetry', as I believe he was, the terms of Plath's later critics are far from those she would have wished for. In the years since Plath died, Plath criticism, reviews and cover blurbs have been increasingly dominated by a vocabulary of confessionality, depression, and the death drive. The first commentaries, however, are distinguished by a very different vocabulary. It is a vocabulary of 'humor', 'control and power of expression', 'astonishing skill', and 'craft'. These are terms against which poetry should be measured, discussed and judged, and Plath's no less than any other. Yet it is a vocabulary that has all but disappeared from Plath criticism. I want to recover this vocabulary, this way of seeing, and develop it further.

Subsequent, posthumous publications of Plath's work have moved forcefully away from the tenor of those early editions of *The Bell Jar* and *The Colossus*, announcing in the bluntest of ways the presence of the book's author, and manipulating the reader's interpretation before he or she can even begin to read. Contrast the reviewers' excerpts printed in the first edition of *The Colossus*, during Plath's lifetime, with the text on the inside front cover of the first English edition of the posthumous *Ariel*. On an otherwise plain design, beneath the book's title and Plath's name, *Ariel*'s cover gives us the beginning of an excerpt from an essay by Robert Lowell that is printed in full as a Foreword. 'In these poems, written in the last months of her life, and often rushed out at the rate of two or three a day, Sylvia Plath becomes herself, becomes something imaginary, newly, wildly and subtly created.'[10] This is continued on the inside front cover of the book, where for Lowell Plath becomes

> hardly a person at all, or a woman, certainly not another "poetess," but one of those super-real, hypnotic, great classical heroines ...
>
> There is a peculiar, haunting challenge to these poems. Probably many, after reading *Ariel*, will recoil from their first overawed shock, and painfully wonder why so much of it leaves them feeling empty, evasive and inarticulate. In her lines, I often hear the serpent whisper, 'Come, if only you had the courage, you too could have my rightness, audacity and ease of inspiration.' But most of us will turn back. These poems are playing Russian roulette with six cartridges in the cylinder ...

Relatively early in the history of Plath publishing, the collection for which Plath is most famous, *Ariel*, establishes the connection between Plath's poems and her death.

The excerpts and Foreword in the first edition of *Ariel* frame Plath's own writing, and suggest that the poems themselves made their author's death inevitable. Before the reader can even begin to read Plath's own words, this idea is repeated again and again. The other extracts inside the book's front cover appear to take their cue from Lowell. Robert Penn Warren is quoted, describing the poems as 'a keen, cold gust of reality', while George Steiner writes, 'These poems take tremendous risks ... They are a bitter triumph, proof of the capacity of poetry to give to reality the greater permanence of the imagined. She could not return from them.' Alvarez is also quoted. While he does not lose his appreciation of Plath's technique, the intervention of her death adds a new note to his account of her poetry, which, for him, becomes confessional, real and deadly. 'In a curious way, the poems read as though they were written posthumously', he muses. 'It needed not only great intelligence and insight to handle the material; it also took a kind of bravery. Poetry of this order is a murderous art.'[11] Only the most independent-minded of readers could read the *Ariel* poems without being affected by the unanimous conclusion of the voices cited within its dust jacket.

The lines for future Plath criticism are established here, and the language is strong. The poems killed her ('she could not return from them'; 'murderous art'; 'written posthumously'). The poems are literal and true; they are of her own life (two reviewers use the word 'reality'). Writing the poems was a 'risk' or act of 'bravery', a gamble that Plath lost like 'Russian roulette' (though the 'six cartridges' of Lowell's figurative language spoil his gambling metaphor, allowing no chance of winning). In Lowell's Foreword, these points are pushed further. Mixing metaphors of beasts and machines, he returns to the notion that Plath is somehow not human at all. 'Everything in these poems is personal, confessional, felt, but the manner of feeling is controlled hallucination, the autobiography of a fever. ... this *Ariel* is the author's horse. Dangerous, more powerful than man, machinelike from hard training, she herself is a little like a racehorse, galloping relentlessly with risked, outstretched neck, death hurdle after death hurdle topped.'[12] I want to show in this book that not everything in Plath's poems is 'personal, confessional, felt'. Rather, I want to reveal these poems as often being about subjects much larger than one woman's autobiography. Whether that subject is environmentalism or national identity, or another writer's novel or poem, Plath's writing is very much about the things of this world. While I do not want to dwell on Plath's life and death, it seems important to look sceptically at Lowell's influential view of her as an animal or superhuman death machine that produces bullets of words before inflicting them on herself.

There are not many works of fiction whose front covers carry illustrations of their authors. Throughout the 1990s, Faber and Faber's often reprinted paperback edition of *The Bell Jar* placed a large, airbrushed illustration of Plath on its front cover, and a smaller illustration of her on its back. Both images are based on well-known photos of Plath, and depict her at moments in her life during which she was close to her heroine's age. The front cover picture of Plath in profile and pearls is based on a shot of her taken during her summer as guest editor for *Mademoiselle*.[13] The back cover shows her standing in front of her mother's house, her suitcase beside her, in the spring of 1954, just before returning to Smith College after her breakdown and suicide attempt.[14]

Faber's popular posthumous edition is a far cry from the cover design of the first English edition of *The Bell Jar*, published by Heinemann in early 1963. The front cover of this first edition presents a photographic, shadowy image of a girl at a desk. She rests her chin on her hands. A clear glass bell jar (which resembles a cake cover) encloses the desk, chair, and girl. In purple letters are the author's 'name', Victoria Lucas, and the title. The back cover simply lists other recent Heinemann Fiction, while the inside of the back cover is blank. Inside the front of the dust jacket, potential readers are given a summary of 'a remarkable first novel by a young American woman ... which uses detail and imagery to evoke a concrete, recognisable world and never to obscure it, and ... treats the subject of break-down with unusual directness and understanding'.[15] Again, such language may present contemporary readers with a feeling of the uncanny. Plath, here, is simply 'a young American woman', not a legend or a myth, not yet dead. Her famous novel is described in objective, impersonal terms, as a believable, 'concrete' and 'recognisable' *work of fiction*, rather than as an autobiography.

Like the first edition itself, press cuttings from the time of *The Bell Jar*'s debut appearance offer us a glimpse of what seems now to be a long-vanished world. *Time & Tide* published a short piece entitled 'Quotes from Books',[16] which appeared on 17 January 1963, three weeks before Plath died. 'Quotes from Books' provides eight brief excerpts from recently published novels. The qualifying characteristic for each excerpt is that it be funny, and *The Bell Jar*, that novel which has since earned a popular reputation for grimness and humourlessness, is included (it is the passage where Esther mistakenly and rather morti-fyingly consumes the water and cherry blossoms from the finger bowl[17]). This is another of those brief and rare instances before it was widely known that Plath was Victoria Lucas, and that she was dead. Here, *The Bell Jar* was not regarded as a depressing autobiography about a death wish. At this point in time, again a moment of innocence, reviewers and readers looked at the book without presumptions, and found laughter.

The use of Plath's own image to sell her books is not reserved for her prose. Even the front cover of Faber's English edition of her *Collected Poems* depicts Plath herself, though the picture is smaller in scale and, as a pencil sketch, somehow more restrained than the al-most lurid colour images that sprawl across *The Bell Jar*'s cover. This sketch, cropped just below the breast, is based on a photo of Plath typing 'At home, the summer of *The Bell Jar*, 1953'.[18] In the case of both *The Bell Jar* and the poems, the blunt message, a strange form of a health warning, can only be: this is Sylvia Plath's own story, do not read as fiction. The reader is not simply purchasing a novel or a book of poems; they are invited to buy an autobiography.

It is less surprising that the cover of Faber's *Letters Home* uses an actual photograph of Plath, sitting and typing.[19] (It is in fact the same photo on which Faber bases the cover sketch of the *Collected Poems*.) Relatively speaking, the relationship between Plath the 'real person' and

Plath the narrator of her letters is not so contestable as the relationship between Plath the 'real person' and her other types of texts and literary personae. This is not to say that Plath's letters are not carefully structured and 'fictionalised', or that they were not designed to have specific effects on the person to whom they were written. It is not to say that she did not sometimes use her letters to tell stories, or even occasionally write them with multiple, future readers and posterity in mind.

The status of *Johnny Panic and the Bible of Dreams and Other Prose Writings*, a posthumously published collection of some of Plath's stories, journalism and journal fragments, is also indeterminate. As in the case of the letters, Plath's personal relation to the journalism and journal fragments – the sense that they are 'about' or directly from her – is less, or, more precisely, differently complicated than it is in relation to the stories. Yet the collection does consist *largely* of stories. That is to say, stories are what the majority of the book is made of. Given this, Faber's airbrushed front cover illustration, again based on an actual photo of Plath, suggests once more to the reader that Plath's fiction is somehow always 'about' her. *Johnny Panic* gives the reader another well-known image. Plath smiles up from beach sand, her hair bleached, during the 'platinum summer'[20] of 1954.[21] Few critics or readers would dispute the idea that interpretation is affected by foreknowledge. Of course, readers cannot 'un-know' what they know, but the packaging of Plath's work ensures that they are predisposed to 'know' as much as possible about the connection between her life and her writing before they even begin to read.

Since the first American edition of *The Bell Jar* appeared in 1971, this has been the strategy for marketing Plath's work in America. An early newspaper advertisement quoted from Robert Scholes's review of the book. Beneath a photo of Plath herself, the reader is told that 'THE BELL JAR is a novel about the events of Sylvia Plath's 20th year, about how she tried to die, and how they stuck her together with glue'.[22] In one sentence, the reader is offered not just a biographical account of Plath's novel, but also of her poems (by using a variant of 'Daddy's' line, 'And they stuck me together with glue').[23] American cover designs for Plath's writing have not been any subtler than their British counterparts in perpetuating the message that Plath's life is the subject matter of her art. The back cover of the first American edition of *The Bell Jar* reproduces a photograph of 'Sylvia Plath as she appeared in the August 1953 issue of *Mademoiselle*'.[24] Above the photo we are presented with an excerpt from the novel where Esther is 'holding a paper rose and facing the magazine photographer'.[25] Like subsequent American issues of the novel, this first American edition of *The Bell Jar* also includes 'A Biographical Note' by Lois Ames. Presumably this is just in case the reader somehow missed the message that *The Bell Jar* 'reveals so much about the sources of Sylvia Plath's own tragedy',[26] or the fact that 'The central themes of Sylvia Plath's early life are the basis for *The Bell Jar*'.[27]

The blurb on the back of Bantam's paperback edition of *The Bell Jar* rightly (and uniquely) acknowledges that the book is 'more than a confessional novel, it is a comic but painful statement of what happens to a woman's aspirations in a society that refuses to take them seriously'. Yet the effect of such a useful description is diminished by the fact that the comment comes only after the reader is told that the book is 'An autobiographical account of Sylvia Plath's own mental breakdown and suicide attempt'.[28] In 1996, twenty-five years after its publication in America, HarperCollins released a Twenty-Fifth Anniversary Edition of the novel. The back cover of this edition, which reproduces less typical, more critically careful comments from reviewers,[29] contrasts with the more familiar line of its inside dust jacket. '*The Bell Jar*', we are told, 'is a largely autobiographical work about Plath's own summer of 1953'[30]

Like the Anniversary Edition's cover, the Foreword inside, by Frances McCullough, is unusual. McCullough tells the entertaining story of the oddities and impediments to *The Bell Jar*'s publishing history in America, and acknowledges the book's very infrequently credited 'hilarity'. Despite such acuteness, she writes that 'Sylvia Plath herself was just two years older than the fictional hero, Holden Caulfield'.[31] This point about relative age is true of Plath's college heroine, Esther Greenwood. It is *not* true of Plath herself, who was in her late twenties when she wrote the novel, and thirty when it was published in Britain. Again, the reader is led to believe that Plath and her fictional character are one, and entirely exchangeable. The effect of Faber's own special edition of the novel, also released in 1996, is similar. Though restrained and dignified in its simple grey parchment paper, the cover quotes a confident declaration by Joyce Carol Oates: 'It is proper to say that Sylvia Plath represents for us a tragic figure involved in a tragic action, and that her tragedy is offered to us as a near-perfect work of art in her books'.[32] Before the reader even begins to read, they are informed that what they hold in their hands is Plath's own story – '"*her* tragedy"'.

Because of their continuing influence, such assumptions of exchangeability between fiction and real life, and the continuing effects of Plath packaging, are worth pointing out. Scholars and reviewers are not immune to this suggestion of equivalence between Plath and her characters. Nor are supposedly less 'expert' readers of Plath – from school children, to higher education students, to the general reader. Readers are likely to start with *The Bell Jar* or some of the poems, then move on to *The Journals of Sylvia Plath* or *Letters Home* because they want to discover more about Plath, and her work. They want more of her writing. Many of them want answers. Why did she kill herself? What was she like? What did the writing *mean*? Where did it all come from? As genres that are akin to autobiography, the *Journals* and *Letters Home* are the most obvious source, or next step, for the reader who wants to learn more about Plath from Plath herself. At first glance, they may be assumed to have the authority of Plath's own voice.

Yet these texts possess no such authority. Jacqueline Rose has done important work on the state of the Plath archives, and written interestingly about the omissions in *Letters Home* and in the 1982 edition of the *Journals*. She has examined the criteria for selecting what does actually end up in these published editions, and suggests that what is left out of them distorts the impression made by what is left in. For instance, the edited letters depict 'Plath as someone whose misery simply feeds off itself' because Plath's references to the physical illnesses that intensify her distress are excluded. Rose also considers the effects of the editorial commentary that interrupts and imposes its own meanings upon Plath's words.[33] She demonstrates that Plath's texts exist in no pure form.

The cover of the 1982 American edition of the *Journals* is another of those queer forms of instruction booklets that tells the reader how Plath's novel and poems might safely be read. It begins with an unsubstantiated value judgement about the significance of the *Journals* themselves: her 'diary … is in fact her best prose'. Moreover, the *Journals* reveal Plath's 'deep psychic crack that left her open to frequent depression, anxiety, and panic – as she described in *The Bell Jar*'.[34] The place of the *Journals* in reading the poems is also melodramatically asserted: 'What is electrifying in these pages is Plath's voice itself: the brilliant, clear voice of the late poems, heard so hauntingly in this logbook of a terrifying journey in which she was the only traveler'.[35] The message seldom varies: Plath's poems can be reduced to a ceaselessly repeated personal monologue about her own frightening and lonely experiences.

The cover of Karen Kukil's meticulously edited edition of the *Journals*, published early in 2000, indulges in no such propaganda. Exceptionally in the history of Plath publishing, and helpfully, its dust jacket tells us matter-of-factly what the book contains, and leaves the reader free to make his or her own judgements. Nonetheless, not all reviewers have followed the example of the book itself. While Jacqueline Rose, Erica Wagner and Tim Kendall have written careful, thought-provoking reviews,[36] others have greeted the 2000 edition in the terms with which the 1982 edition was received. Michael Sheldon sees the new *Journals* as 'evidence of' Plath's 'hopelessly deranged thinking'. For him they are 'a thousand pages of Plath's self-incriminating testimony', 'her own suicide note'.[37] For Allison Pearson the new *Journals* 'read like the longest suicide note ever written', and reveal Plath as a 'tortured specimen preserved in her bell jar … forever young, forever anguished, forever betrayed by her man' and trapped within her 'cast-iron solipsism'.[38] What such reviews miss is the fact that Plath used her *Journals* as a writer's notebook where she tried out various tones and experimented with ways of injecting her writing with different emotions. As journals so often are for writers, Plath's were a place where she could lock onto the page material that she would use later on. Much of the writing in her *Journals* is carefully crafted; there is too large a gap between her 'real' experience and the mediation of writing for us to use the *Journals* as simple documentary evidence of her mental state or emotions. To do so is to diminish the value of an important resource to scholars; it is to overlook the pleasures that Plath's *Journals* offer to readers.

Given the relentlessness of the message of Plath packaging, it is not surprising that student essays on Plath endlessly engage in a quest for documenting her biography by using her writing as evidence, or, reciprocally, explaining her poetry by citing the evidence of her life. Frequently in essays, students will go so far as to refer to the narrators of poems as 'Plath'. It is understandable that students should come to believe that such practice is acceptable, or even desirable. If that is what book covers, reviewers and literary critics do, is it not what is expected of students too? Take for example Jacqueline Rose, who, even while making an important point in a distinguished book, can still slip into dubious substitutions of 'Plath' for her narrators. Rose writes, 'As Plath puts it in "Blackberrying" … "they must love me".'[39] Rose's syntax makes the narrator Plath herself ('me'). Rose makes Plath herself express something ('As Plath puts it'). The something that Rose gives us is not from a journal or a letter, but from a poem that is spoken by a fictional persona. The weight of such material, sanctioned by experts, makes it very difficult to convince students that they might try to be attentive to the novel or story or poem in front of them, or consider its place in history and culture rather than how 'real' it is. Readers are not sufficiently impressed by the fact that they have no direct or dependable access to the writer's life or mind. Any biographical relationship between life and work cannot be known or proved.

Where is Sylvia Plath?

It is instructive to open up and peer into an instance of Plath biography, in order to observe the insistent flaw of such knowledge. To do so reveals how very discordant the different accounts of one supposed incident in Plath's life can be. Here is Plath's own tale of an outing with her newborn daughter:

> I had an immensely moving experience and attended the arrival of the Easter weekend marchers from the atomic bomb plant at Aldermason [sic] to Trafalgar Square in London. Ted and Dido had left at noon ... I left later with the baby to meet a poet-friend of Ted's, Peter Redgrove, and go to Trafalgar Square with him. ... we carried the sleeping baby easily between us, installed the cot on the lawn of the National Gallery ... Our corner was uncrowded, a sort of nursery, mothers giving babies bottles on blankets ...
>   ... I found myself weeping to see the tan, dusty marchers ... I felt proud that the baby's first real adventure should be as a protest against the insanity of world-annihilation.[40]

Anne Stevenson's description of the event bears little relation to Plath's own:

> It seems that Sylvia had telephoned Peter Redgrove and invited him to go with her. Recovering from childbirth and more than usually vulnerable, she may have conceived that Ted, in going to the march with Dido, had given her just cause for 'revenge.' His 'punishment' had its desired effect: when Ted returned with Dido to the flat, he had no notion of where his wife and baby were. ... [Redgrove] and Ted ... went out for a beer and talked about general matters. It would have been out of character for Ted to complain about his marriage.[41]

Linda W. Wagner-Martin also writes of the excursion. 'Sylvia grew more and more tired. She tried to do everything she ordinarily would – such as taking Frieda to a 'Ban-the-Bomb' march and rally when the child was only a few weeks old – but she was not up to her usual routines'.[42] Finally, here is Paul Alexander's rendition: 'Normally, the Hugheses would employ the Babyminder Service ... but on Sunday the 17th they took Frieda on her first outing, a ban-the-bomb march'.[43]

To characterise these accounts crudely, Plath's is that of a political and emotional woman, Stevenson's is that of a prosecutor of Plath and defender of Hughes, Wagner-Martin's is that of a feminist in sympathy with a tired new mother, Alexander's is relatively neutral in tone. The contradictions of fact and blatantly opposing moral inflections of these four stories illustrate how impossible it is to assert with any certainty the 'truth' about any event in Plath's life. My choice of the ban-the-bomb story could have been arbitrary, for there are countless opposing versions of numerous incidents in Plath's life. Plath's, Stevenson's and Alexander's renderings do not even agree about *who* attended the march with Plath and Frieda. Alexander states that Hughes went with his wife and baby. Plath's and Stevenson's accounts assert it was Redgrove, which does seem more credible (to her credit, Stevenson writes tentatively here, using the phrase 'It seems'). All that can be said, with relative certainty, is that Plath attended the Aldermaston march and took Frieda. If any conclusions can be drawn from this 'fact', it is not that Plath was a saint struggling to keep her life meaningful while nursing a new baby, or that she was a vindictive, pathologically jealous wife who made life impossible for her husband. If the relevance of this event is to be assessed, it seems safest, and most valuable, to assert that her attendance at the march was evidence that Plath did exhibit interest in larger world events in general. The 'fact' of Plath's attendance of the march demonstrates that she was concerned about the effects of nuclear weapons and fallout on human life and health, a worry that we will see had a great impact on her writing.

In spite of the problems of biographical knowledge, it would be absurd to say that there is nothing of 'Plath' in her fiction or poetry. The point is that what there is of her is less obvious, and provable, than many readers allow. Plath is gone, and cannot tell us herself. Those who knew her and still live, like all human beings, forget or misremember. They may be guided by an understandable wish to tell a story that they think makes them look good. They may remain silent for the sake of peace and privacy. They may want revenge, or vindication, or justification, or to brag,[44] or to give the 'true' account. They may regard themselves as Plath's defenders or opponents, and yet feel certain of their own objectivity. Their intentions may be good, bad, or, more likely, a fluctuating combination of the two, but whatever they are, the quality of the intentions does not increase the reliability of a witness. There are few people who would not be able to think of a story in which they were involved, and which they altered depending upon whether the audience was their mother or lover or best friend. A variation of tone, or the omission of certain facts without necessarily lying, might ensure their own role in the events was seen as they wished it to look.

The narrator of A. S. Byatt's novel *Possession: A Romance* tells us that 'There are things which happen and leave no discernible trace'.[45] This statement comes towards the end of Byatt's book, where something occurs that would mean a great deal to one of the characters, but this character is never allowed to know of it. Analogously, Plath inevitably thought and did things to which there were no witnesses, or which were witnessed but never spoken of, or whose physical records were discarded or lost. There are events and ideas and emotions that influenced her writing, and we simply cannot know them, however much literary biographies or the book covers which are designed to entice buyers would wish to deny this. Although Byatt is a writer of subtlety and imagination, and can write of 'things which … leave no discernible trace', even she can fail to recognise that these words apply to Plath also. In her otherwise illuminating review of *Letters Home*, Byatt nonetheless concludes that Plath's last poems 'are a deliberate exploration of the nature of death and the poet's enduring relationship with it. They made it real.'[46] If you believe that things can happen and leave no trace, then I think you must also believe that visible traces – sometimes in the form of words – cannot be trusted to represent an absolute version of a 'real' thing that happened, be that thing a thought or a deed.

It is not in the service of a conspiracy theory that I cite book cover after book cover of unselfconscious propaganda for the notion that Plath and her fictional personae are interchangeable. Nor do I wish to deny that there are elements of Plath's life in her work, though I have little confidence in my own or anybody else's ability – let alone authority – to determine what they may be. Of course, in ways that resemble the circumstances of *The Bell Jar*, Sylvia Plath *did* have a breakdown and *did* attempt to kill herself. Yes, Plath, like every daughter who ever lived, did harbour angers towards, as well as love for, her mother. Likewise, the speakers of poems such as 'The Disquieting Muses' and 'Medusa' feel strong ambivalence about their mothers. Yet these coincidences of Plath's own plots and emotions with the plots and emotions of her literary creations are not *all there is* to be said of the work.

That is the real purpose of this book: to look at Plath in different ways; to uncover what has always existed in her writing, yet has been insufficiently seen. What we *can* know of Plath are the historical and cultural events in which she lived. There is much unkindness, not to mention little value and reliability, in using poetry and fiction as evidence for Plath's supposed anger towards her husband or parents or female rivals; or, at the opposite extreme, as proof of her presumed victimhood. To treat Plath's writing in this way is to belittle her work, for the implication of such an exercise is that Sylvia Plath was too unimaginative to make anything up, or too self-obsessed to consider anything of larger historical or cultural importance. It would be more valuable (and methodologically sound) to offer close readings of neglected texts, or examine Plath's response to environmental issues and the instabilities of language and national identity that result from living in two different countries, or evaluate the presence of other writers' texts within Plath's own.

And yet it would be absurd to deny that Plath's story is a fascinating one, compelling as any drama with brilliant, glamorous characters. Tragedy, a thrilling plot, and conflict are present in this story, as they are in the most exciting of novels. Readers pay a high price for this story, nonetheless. Many do not notice that they are being cheated, for the fascination with the personal too often interferes with any serious attentiveness to the writing, thereby limiting the ways of responding to and appreciating it. As Martin Amis puts it, 'It's much easier to grasp a personality than a body of work'. Amis is right and wrong here. Right to point out our tendency to concentrate on a writer's life instead of their work – and that this is an easier option. Wrong in his implication that personality can be grasped at all. Germaine Greer rightly observes that the 'more someone is biographed, the less he or she is read'.[47] This can certainly be said of Plath's work, though Greer might have added the clause, 'or the more he or she is *mis*read'. One of the oddest circumstances about studying Plath is that, in spite of the volumes of studies to be found on library shelves, so very little detailed argument is actually made about her *writing*.

Take for instance 'A Secret', which Plath wrote on 10 October 1962. Few critics look at this poem at all. If they do mention 'A Secret', it is only in passing, as part of a list of 'Plath's most devastating reappraisals of Hughes',[48] or to point out that it was one of the poems Plath chose for *Ariel* but Hughes omitted.[49] Other critics have avoided the issue by dismissing 'A Secret' as a piece of 'cryptic fury',[50] as if the poem's very nature prevents us from understanding it. But can't we say more? Admittedly, 'A Secret' is difficult. Riddle poems are supposed to be. One way to solve a riddle is to pick it apart. If we look at the specific objects around which 'A Secret' builds its meanings, and at its relationship to other pieces of Plath's writing, the poem begins to make more sense. We can read it as a story about writing and about gossip, about what writing can do and how it can injure. The speaker receives a letter, which is 'blue and huge, a traffic policeman'. In other words, it makes you stop, as letters do, wondering what they contain before you open them. The letter may be blue because it is written on lightweight airmail paper and put in the corresponding blue airmail envelope. When the speaker declares, 'I have one eye, you have two. / The secret is stamped on you, / Faint undulant watermark', the image is literal and symbolic. Because she has only 'one eye' her view is limited and skewed; she is unable to see everything, like writing itself. The 'one eye' also calls to mind the nib of a pen rimming its eyeball-like point. The 'watermark' shows a picture of a man with 'two' eyes (who, like the 'traffic policeman', holds up his hand). The African animals who 'stare from a square, stiff frill'[51] are depicted on the stamp.

'A Secret' was written the day before 'The Applicant', which gives us more clues about the sort of poem it is, and how we might read it. Both poems are highly compressed, but give us numerous speakers. Plath experiments with the range of dramatic voices a poem can contain. These layers of voices are what make the poems so demanding, but they are also one of the keys to unlocking their stories. 'A Secret' gives us the main narrator who receives the letter, as well as a sort of chattering Greek chorus whose words appear in speech marks. Linda Wagner-Martin includes 'A Secret' and 'The Applicant' in a list of poems that Plath read for the BBC 'with an intense and sure speed and inflection that suggested ample practice'.[52] If we take Plath's lead when reading 'A Secret' aloud, it becomes clear that we must use a variety of tones, as if reading the different parts of a play. The narrator talks to her letter as if it were a person; the speech marks contain what she says to the letter, which doubles as her mimicry of the sorts of things gossips say to and about someone who has had bad news or been involved in a scandal. The poem's slangy idiom describes gossip as a knife that can 'lever the dirt'. ' "It won't hurt" ', the speaker reassures the letter before opening it with a knife.'"It won't hurt"' is also what she herself is falsely promised before reading the letter's contents. The end rhymes of 'dirt' and 'hurt' establish the link between words and the damage they can do.

Writing becomes tangled with the domestic in the poem. The letter contains news of an 'illegitimate baby' that must be hidden away – one of the 'secrets' to which the poem's title refers. This 'baby' may be an ill-conceived poem, or the letter itself, which, though kept in a drawer (where many of us stow our treasures and secrets), will not be forgotten. The speaker tries to resist the unasked-for advice she is given about the writing or baby. This advice resembles the bossy interference and old wives' tales of mothers and grandmothers who tell new wives or mothers how to cook, keep house, and deal with their newborn infants.'"Stab a few cloves in an apple"' to hide its smell and disguise its presence, they tell her.'"Do away with it"', they demand, in spite of the speaker's pleas on its behalf. The gossip, the baby, the news in the letter, writing itself – these erupt as if a 'stopper' has been removed or a 'stampede' has been unleashed. This recalls the animal stamps, and suggests that the letter has spawned others; more stamps have been used to spread the news. When the speaker refers to 'The knife in your back' she evokes both the slit-open envelope, and the pain inflicted by those who have gossiped about you, letting 'out' the 'secret' and leaving you '"weak"'.[53] As the gossips vacillate in their advice and argue about meaning from one line to the next, the poem warns its reader that information is seldom reliable or first hand, interpretation never stable.

'A Secret' suggests that other people's lives and words should be regarded with caution and treated with care. Biographers would do well to read it, for biography, in the end, can only ever be gossip. A handful of scholars, Jacqueline Rose and Janet Malcolm among them, have explored the problems posed by biography as a genre, and argued that the facts of any life can never be known. Nonetheless, the uptake of these points by publishers, the general public, and even academics, has been low. Scholarly books about Plath have been no less manipulative about what they tell the reader before they are opened than editions of Plath's own work. Like Plath's own letters and journals, scholarly books and literary biographies are where those with an interest in Plath might 'go' when they wish to know more. Yet demarcations between biography and literary criticism are blurred, especially when the subject is Sylvia Plath.

Jacqueline Rose's *The Haunting of Sylvia Plath* begins by making the important point that 'accounts of the life ... have to base themselves on a spurious claim to knowledge, they have to arbitrate between competing and often incompatible versions of what took place'.[54] Though Rose manages to avoid biographical criticism, her book nonetheless uses yet another photographic image of Plath herself[55] on its front cover.[56] To be fair to Rose, she is likely to have had nothing to do with the cover design of her book, which was probably a product of her publisher's design department. Nonetheless, the packaging of *The Haunting of Sylvia Plath* undermines Rose's argument before it even begins. The fact that Rose's back cover reproduces Henry Fuseli's *The Nightmare*, a painting of a dead-looking woman's uncomfortably bent and supine body, compounds this sabotage (the monster that squats upon the woman's stomach in the Fuseli is not shown, but is obscured by a leaf). The back cover reproduces fragments of Plath's own hand-written draft of 'Daddy'. Rose means for her title to suggest the ways that 'Plath haunts our culture'.[57] Nonetheless, the effect of the title, en-meshed as it is with the cover's other images, is to raise an expectation in readers that they are about to be given an argument which links Plath's life, death and writing. The first visual impression of Rose's book can only be that Plath was 'haunted', tormented into a 'nightmare' like the woman in Fuseli's painting, and driven to spit out 'Daddy' before killing herself.

Rose's book is not an isolated case of literary criticism making use of Plath's image while at the same time reinforcing stereotypical ideas about her. The cover of Janice Markey's *A Journey into the Red Eye* uses a photo of Plath relaxing back into a couch, taken in Boston during the spring of 1959.[58] While Steven Gould Axelrod's book does not use Plath's image on its cover, it does place a photo of her inside the text. Publishers and marketing teams who use Plath's picture in this manner are curiously unimaginative about finding different images of her, and fresh ways to use them. Like the back cover of the American first edition of *The Bell Jar*, Axelrod quotes from the passage where Esther describes her distress while having her photo taken with a paper rose, and his book then reproduces the photograph of Plath herself holding the paper rose for *Mademoiselle*.[59] The echoes between the novel and Plath's life are so strongly established that the effect is an assumption of utter equivalence between these fictional and actual events. The illus-tration on the cover of Harold Bloom's collection of essays on Plath – and this is his own description – shows 'The poet Sylvia Plath against the background of her own deathly vision of "Lady Lazarus"'.[60]

As it is with journals and letters, the use of photographic images on biographies is a different matter from their use on literature or literary criticism. Anne Stevenson probably had little say in it, but the cover of

Bitter Fame uses the same photograph as Janice Markey's critical book. However flawed or inaccurate they may be, biographies are in the business of being 'about' a person's life. Photographic images only make explicit their very reason for existing. This is not the case, however, for literary criticism. At least it *should* not be the case. Nonetheless, as far as Plath is concerned, many critics assume that life is fair game in their readings of her writing. Such a critical methodology would not be so troubling if it were preceded by some effort to rationalise the use of biographical evidence in literary reading, or theorise the relationship – and gaps – between life and art.

Many might wonder what drives readers to Plath in the first place. School and higher education syllabuses certainly influence the sales of her books around the world. However, many readers turn to Plath without 'having to'. Culture, in the widest sense of the word, does much to publicise Plath's life, and draw readers to her work.

It is not difficult to find Sylvia Plath. Pick up the irresistibly titled *Great American Bathroom Book*, trawl through its two-page summaries of books and writers' lives, and there she is. It is a familiar story, and one that is assumed by most – quite wrongly – to be unquestionably true. The story is not what I wish to dwell on in this book, but it seems best to get it over with quickly. As reprised in the *Bathroom Book*, the story goes something like this.

She was born in Boston, in 1933. Her professor father died when she was eight, an event which, so the story goes, was to obsess her for the rest of her life, shape her poetry, and culminate in 'Daddy', which she used to express her 'bitterness and anger at her father's death'. Hostile and sycophantic biographers alike agree that precocity, ambition and self-destructiveness were all present from the beginning. The *Bathroom Book* is ridiculous but not unique in asserting that these tendencies were in evidence when Plath was an infant, because 'she crawled toward the ocean, unafraid'.[61] Anne Stevenson searches through Plath's childhood letters for early signs of dysfunction, and finds in them 'a prudery that intimates that happiness for Sylvia may have been a hard-won valuable among her "rowdy" peers in Winthrop'.[62] (Who can read this and not blush at the thought of their own childhood letters being submitted to such scrutiny?) Smith College brought success, but also a severe depression that resulted in an infamous suicide attempt with pills in her mother's basement. The *Bathroom Book* anthologises 'Lady Lazarus', and tells us that 'Plath exclaims, "I have done it again. One year in every ten I manage it."

Apparently referring to her previous suicide attempt, these lines became ironically prophetic'.[63]

It is not difficult to tease out the primary assumptions that drive the
Great American Bathroom Book. Less expectedly, these same assumptions
are also fundamental to a good deal of the literary criticism and biography
of Sylvia Plath. They go like this. Speakers of poems can be assumed to
be Plath herself, instead of literary characters ('Plath exclaims').[64] The
facts of Plath's life are what the poetry is about ('her previous suicide
attempt'). In turn, the poetry causes the life, or rather, the death
('ironically prophetic'). Literary criticism and biography are not separate
enterprises. The premise is that to explain the life, readers can look at the
work. Reciprocally, to explain the work, they can turn to the life.

If we return to the 'story', we find ourselves forced swiftly to the
end. Plath falls in love with Ted Hughes, they have two children, their
marriage breaks down, and she dies.

As far as the story is concerned, what is reliably true or entirely
knowable in the above three paragraphs can be reduced to nine words:
'She was born ... they have two children ... she dies'.

Those who prefer high culture to bathroom books can look for
Sylvia Plath in a concert hall. Using Plath as their inspiration, Aribert
Reimann, Ned Rorem and Ran Shulamit have all written musical
scores using the words of her poems as the lyrics.[65] It is worth describing at least one of these in detail. Shulamit takes Plath's poem
'Apprehensions', written on 28 May 1962, and composes in four sections. Each of Shulamit's sections represents a stanza. There is a silent
pause between each section, as in the pause between songs on a record.
Shulamit's comments on 'Apprehensions' are interesting:

> What immediately struck me upon reading it was what I
> perceived of as the musical suggestiveness of the poem's
> central idea and formal plan: in four stanzas, the colors
> white, gray, red and black are used as a metaphor for the
> metamorphosis of a state of mind . . . the poem's form
> hinted at the possibility of great contrasts between move-
> ments held together and propelled forward by one central
> idea. The overall shape of a gradual ascent to a horrific
> climax culminating in a steep fall.[66]

Shulamit uses clarinet, piano and soprano. His work is a mixture of the
ambitious, the thoughtful and the absurd. Though a different genre
altogether, his piece echoes what is best, and worst, in Plath criticism.

The music's opening notes are, predictably, funeral dirge-like. The first three minutes of the piece are spent trying to spit out the poem's first three lines. It takes seven minutes to churn out the entire first stanza. The soprano is a stutterer unable to spit out the words. Then, cured briefly and suddenly, she obsessively repeats a line, a few words or even just a syllable. For listeners who know Plath's work, the effect is a heightened awareness of a trick that Plath does not use in 'Apprehensions', but does often play elsewhere in her poetry. By this I mean the broken record, 'tongue stuck in my jaw' effect famously used in 'Daddy' ('Ich, ich, ich, ich), 'The Applicant' ('Will you marry it, marry it, marry it'), and 'The Disquieting Muses' ('I learned, I learned, I learned elsewhere'). [67] Frequently such effects are used in the music where they do not appear in the poem, or they are exaggerated. 'There is a white wall – white wall' screeches the voice again and again, off key, stretching out the words in a mad melodrama that complies with the most prevalent of stereotypes that see Plath as crazed and hysterical. The second stanza begins with a voice that sounds like the bitter shriek of a witch. The poem's question, 'Is there no way out of the mind?', is asked only once, but for Shulamit it becomes an obsessive chant. The implication is, yet again, that this was Plath's only subject. The chant is relieved only by the shrill scream of clarinet, followed by a bomb of piano, rising towards a terrible clashing cacophony which finally exhausts itself, leaving the peace and quiet of a soft song.

It is only fair to acknowledge that, in spite of occasional predictability, *Apprehensions* also challenges existing readings of Plath. Lines are oddly but suggestively interwoven and juxtaposed. Especially surprising is Shulamit's last 'stanza'. Given what precedes it, we might expect still more hysteria. Instead, the piano notes are gentle. The voice is calm. The poem's last line, 'They move in a hurry', is sighed out slowly, forcing the listener to rethink the poem's meaning, and the state of Plath's speaker. In the end, the music leaves us with a voice that battles for control, in contrast with any reading of the poem – and Plath herself – as paranoid and depressive. The music even carries a physical register of languid pleasure, and it is a pleasure in things and existence that is truly present in the poem, but usually overlooked. Linda Wagner-Martin, for instance, believes that 'Apprehensions' tells a story of 'despair and loss'. While 'desolation',[68] to use Wagner-Martin's word, may indeed be part of the poem's story, it is not all of it. However isolated the speaker of 'Apprehensions' may be, he or she enjoys the extraordinary beauty of a sky that 'Angels swim in ... and the stars'.[69] Even if these wonderful sights are cloaked in 'indifference' to the speaker, their visual existence is a sort of present. Perception itself, the poem makes clear, is a gift even in the midst of apprehensions. And apprehension does not only mean to feel anxious. Apprehension is also about grasping meaning, about appreciating and understanding. In Plath's poem, the speaker is engaged in all of these activities at once.

The Plath Archives

Any idea that Plath's writing can be regarded as mere cries of personal pain can only be shaken by a visit to Smith College's Rare Book Room, where the handwritten drafts of sixty-seven of Plath's last poems are held. The Rare Book Room catalogues these poems as the *Ariel* poems (though not all of them appeared in *Ariel*). To achieve these sixty-seven poems, Plath generated enough paper to fill seven box files, each three inches thick and filled to the brim. There are dozens of revisions for each poem. Stanzas are crossed out, again and again, until she gets there. Plath calculates and chooses. She selects and deletes. A line is written over and over, with countless insertions, cancellations, and restorations – often of a single word or phrase – until Plath pushes the poem into what she wants it to be. The evidence of detailed planning and careful craftsmanship – the very opposite of any uncontrolled emotional outpouring of rage and despair – is incontrovertible. To say that the writing is merely biographical, when confronted with this tangle and weight of work and effort, with this proof of discipline, can only be regarded by anyone who has seen the physical bulk of these papers as absurd. Many of the successive drafts of these poems are written on the back of early typescripts of *The Bell Jar* or other manuscripts by Plath or Hughes. We will discover throughout this book the importance of the relationship between what is happening on both sides of Plath's manuscript pages. The impression of dauntless hard work and scrupulously considered composition is impossible to escape. One is repeatedly confronted with the same scene in different versions, or the same page typed over and over again, tangled with handwritten cross-outs and additions.

The archives allow us to correct small, but very significant, corruptions of some of the most important poems of this century. Until my visit to Smith College's Rare Book Room, the third line of Plath's 1962 poem 'Lyonnesse' had always perplexed me. According to Arthurian legend, Lyonnesse was a country that adjoined Cornwall until it sank into the sea and was lost. Plath's poem is about forgetfulness. The poem talks about a man whose memory has closed over. This man is chided for his lack of memory:

> No use whistling for Lyonnesse!
> Sea-cold, sea-cold it certainly is.
> Take a look at the white, high berg *on* his forehead –[70]

This is one of those poems of Plath's where identity circulates, and the reader's own position, like that of the narrator and the man with the forehead, cannot be pinpointed. We might read the first two lines, and the narrator's second person direct address, as a speech to the amnesiac man, or to someone else, perhaps even to the reader. The voice is at once scolding and conspiratorial. The narrative perspective snaps into a shift in the third line. Here, either more insistently speaking to the reader, or shifting attention away from the man, the narrator makes the man into a sort of spectacle who is talked about in the third person. The reader is warned as if they were another potential victim of the forgetful man. The reader is also appealed to like a doctor, as if for a second, professional opinion of that 'berg'.

The image of this berg in that third line is of someone growing a giant boil on his forehead. As a result, I found it difficult to conceptualise the poem, and see from the outset, as the poem means you to, that the man is likened to the sea that has swallowed Lyonnesse, as well as the God who forgot about the land and allowed it to slip away. Plath's handwritten drafts and typescripts resolve the difficulty. They clear up a transcription error that has been perpetuated through various published editions of the poem. The line should read 'berg *of* his forehead' (my italics), as Plath's own papers make clear.[71] The image is thus of a forehead as big as an iceberg, and not of a forehead growing an iceberg. Try saying both renditions of the line aloud. You will see that as far as rhythm is concerned, the f of the correct word 'of' moves the line more swiftly, as opposed to the slightly too long pause inflicted by the n in 'on' in the corrupted version. I am not implying that the mistake is the result of a conspiracy. Rather, the slip of a human finger on a keyboard during some now untraceable moment of Plath publishing history – a slip of one letter – is most likely what caused the sense and sound of the line to go askew. Most readers of the poem possess the misprinted version. The error has been duplicated through four books: the English and American editions of the *Collected Poems*, and both editions of *Winter Trees*.[72]

For what we can learn about Plath's poems, her writing process, and the dates of composition, these drafts are very exciting. The successive versions of 'Amnesiac' reveal Plath's original intent that 'Lyonnesse' and 'Amnesiac' should be one long poem, all under the title of 'Amnesiac'. What was finally to become 'Lyonnesse' was part 1, while what was to become 'Amnesiac' was part 2. While the *Collected Poems*, and Plath's own hand, date both poems as 21 October 1962, Plath probably did not decide to pull the poems apart until early the following month. This is in response to a letter of 7 November 1962, from Howard Moss of *The New Yorker*, in which he tells Plath, 'I'm sorry we decided against these poems. We like the second section of AMNESIAC very much, but cannot see any relation between it and the first section … But would you think over the possibility of printing the second section alone under that title?'[73] Ever anxious to publish in *The New Yorker*, Plath must have thought very quickly, and answered yes. It is only in the penultimate typescript (still typed as parts 1 and 2 under the one title of 'Amnesiac', and dated in Plath's black pen, 21 October 1962) that Plath used red ink to cross out what was to become 'Lyonnesse'.[74] In the same red ink, near section 2 of this typescript, she wrote, 'New Yorker'. The final typescript of 'Amnesiac', the only one without the 'Lyonnesse' stanzas, is actually the proof for *The New Yorker*, which the editor has dated 'Dec. 3 1962'.[75]

If we return to the question of transcription errors, we find that 'Lyonnesse' is not the only one of Plath's poems to have been seriously corrupted by such a slip. Plath's handwritten drafts and typescripts of 'Elm' make it absolutely clear that the first line of 'Elm's' last stanza should read, 'Its snaky acids hiss'.[76] So does the first publication of the poem in *The New Yorker* on 3 August 1963.[77] The first English editions of *Ariel* and the *Collected Poems* publish the line incorrectly, as 'Your snaky acids kiss'.[78] Subsequent reprints of these English editions correct the mistake, so that the 'acids hiss' as Plath meant them to. American editions of Plath's work, however, have never recognised the error, and so have never corrected it. The 'kiss' persists in first and reprinted American editions of the *Collected Poems* and *Ariel*,[79] as well as in Diane Wood Middlebrook's 1998 selection of Plath's work for Everyman's Pocket Library.[80] For its effects in sound and sense, the mistake is actually an interesting one. I like the idea of acids kissing instead of hissing, of something caustic and dangerous doing something gentle and tender. Plath might have liked the effect too, had she thought of it. Plath's handwriting can be hard to decipher. It would have been easy to confuse the letters h and k, and then reproduce the error through edition after edition. A similar error occurs in 'Amnesiac', where the American editions of *Ariel* and the *Collected Poems*, and Middlebrook's 1998 selection, give us the line 'Four babies and a cooker'. The English editions, on the other hand, give us 'Four babies and a cocker'. Again, Plath's drafts and typescripts settle the question of which letter the poet has shaped. These leave no doubt that Plath's intended word is 'cocker'.[81] Strangely, there is a sort of 'rightness' about the mistake. Like the correct word, it is in keeping with the poem's rhetoric of domesticity.

The exigencies of publishing – probably exacerbated by the time and money needed to travel to and work in archives – mean that editors and publishers of subsequent editions rarely go to Plath's original sources, and simply trust whichever of the numerous previous published versions is closest to hand. What certainly is needed is a new edition of the *Collected Poems*, where every poem is transcribed freshly, and checked and double-checked, to ensure that readers have versions that they can rely on. The transcription errors in 'Lyonnesse', 'Elm' and 'Amnesiac' are not isolated incidents. Karen Kukil, Associate Curator of Rare Books at Smith College and editor of the 2000 edition of Plath's *Journals*, pointed out to me that in the American edition of *Winter Trees* 'Purdah' differs from the English edition. Again the difference is of one letter. Are we talking about 'air that all day *flies* / Its crystals / A million ignorants'?[82] Or is it air that '*plies*' its crystals?[83] Unlike the case of 'on' or 'of' with 'Lyonnesse', the reader is not so likely to be brought up short by the confusion of meaning. Though the sense differs dramatically, without recourse to Plath's drafts, a case might be made for both 'flies' and 'plies'. Nonetheless, Plath's recording of 'Purdah' in late October of 1962, and her successive drafts of the poem, resolve the matter. At every stage of Plath's handwritten drafts and typescripts it is clear that her intended word is 'plies'.[84] This is also how Plath reads 'Purdah' in a recording she made for Peter Orr of the BBC on 30 October 1962[85] which is a treasure of a resource for Plath scholars. Nonetheless, the slip-up in transcription is more common than the correct transcription. Only readers of the American edition of *Winter Trees* would have the poem Plath intended. The misprint echoes through the English and American editions of the *Collected Poems*, and the English edition of *Winter Trees*.[86]

A similar one-letter corruption has passed through the published versions of 'Nick and the Candlestick', and is significant in terms of both the visual image and the sound. In her 30 October recording for the BBC, Plath reads 'Waxy stalac*mites* / Drip and thicken, tears / / The earthen womb / Exudes from its dead boredom'.[87] In every one of the ten handwritten drafts and typescripts of 'Nick and the Candle-stick', Plath writes 'stalacmites'.[88] Stalacmites is her chosen word. Yet the English and the American editions of *Ariel*, and both editions of the *Collected Poems*, print the word 'stalactites'.[89]

In this case, the mistake may not be a simple copying error, but could be the legacy of some well-meaning copy-editor or typist who, quite wrongly, thought they were correcting Plath's little mistake. To be certain of the difference between stalactites and stalacmites many people look the words up or use tricks (for example, must hang on *tight*ly ... pointing down ... stala*ctite*). Plath herself certainly knew the difference, or at least took the trouble to learn it. She would have considered carefully the dissimilarity in consonance between the m and the t, as well as the distinct technical meanings of the two words. She highlighted their definitions in her own well-worn and much under-lined dictionary:

> **stalactite** ... <u>oozing out in drops, dropping</u>. ... A deposit of calcium carbonate resembling <u>an icicle,</u> hanging <u>from the roof or sides of a cavern.</u>
> **stalacmite** ... <u>*stalagmos* a dropping, dripping</u>. ... A deposit of calcium carbonate like an inverted stalactite, formed on the floor of a cave by the drip <u>of calcareous water</u>. [90]

My underlining exactly duplicates Plath's own. Plath underlined the entry for stalacmite in her dictionary, but left the entry for stalactite un-touched. Perhaps she meant to record the choice she made when she wrote 'Nick and the Candlestick'.

Another of the treasures of the Plath archives are the numerous, beautiful lines and stanzas that Plath discarded, though in many cases discarded uncertainly, restoring, deleting, restoring, and deleting again. There is a whole question of whether a poem was finished or not, and of whether it has a 'final' form. In 'Medusa', for instance, Plath repeat-edly types, but then crosses through, the lines

> That martyr's smile!
> That loony pivot!
> That stellar jelly-head!
> And a million little suckers loving me![91]

The lines do not appear in the last draft of the poem, which Plath com-pleted on 16 October 1962.[92] Plath nonetheless restores the cancelled lines when she reads 'Medusa' for the BBC fourteen days later.

Plath similarly strikes out lines from her written drafts of 'Lady Lazarus' on 23 October 1962, but then resurrects them for the same BBC recording for which she read 'Medusa'.[93] After the line 'Do I terrify?——' in 'Lady Lazarus', Plath includes the additional stanza

> Yes Yes Herr Professor
> It is I
> Can you deny

She lengthens the line 'I may be skin and bone' to 'I may be skin and bone, I may be Japanese'. These extra lines had been present in the early drafts of the poem. They remained part of 'Lady Lazarus' until an advanced stage of its composition on that same day, when Plath crossed them out, reinstated them, then omitted them once more.[94] It was only seven days later that Plath reinserted them for her recording.

The manuscript of 'Stopped Dead' also contains arresting lines that Plath wrestled with cutting. Successive drafts unveil another litany of deletions and restorations. These follow the line 'Where do you stash your life?':[95]

> In your breast, in your vest, in your haunch, in your paunch –
> That snail-furl of breath?
> That start of the heart?
> You see, I see a sort of a twig
> That might just hold me, but not you, you're too big.[96]

There is excitement and drive here. The short phrases, with their pace, metre and fast, close internal rhyme, are compelling. The result is memorable writing. The reader is rushed along, stopped for a question, rushed breathlessly forward again, and stopped for another question until at last we reach the change of movement in the longer final two lines and their direct, talky insult to the person addressed by the speaker. Again, though Plath deletes these lines from the final version of the poem on 19 October 1962, she restores them when she records 'Stopped Dead' for the BBC eleven days later.[97] This is one of many moments where the finality of a given poem is rendered uncertain.

What version is 'right', we might ask, when Plath removes lines from a final typescript, restores them when she reads later for a recording, and then removes them again in the final typescript of *Ariel*? We cannot easily resolve the matter by concluding that the *Ariel* typescript should have the final say on the matter because it contained the latest-known versions of these poems.[98] The extra lines that Plath restores for the BBC reading do not appear in the *Ariel* typescript. Do we, or should we, prioritise later versions over earlier ones, or written evidence over oral? How, if you've read these cancelled or unpublished lines, can you forget them? Even if *Ariel*'s typescript was indeed the latest version Plath ever produced, we cannot discount her vacillation, or conclude that she did not have, or would not have had, further thoughts on the matter had she lived. As Ted Hughes has said, 'She was forever shuffling the poems in her typescripts – looking for different connections, better sequences. She knew there were always new possibilities, all fluid.'[99] The *Ariel* typescript reflects Plath's continued aversion to 'finality'. On its title-page Plath types three titles – *A Birthday Present, The Rabbit Catcher,* and *Ariel* – before crossing out two of the options and allowing *Ariel* to remain. She then inserts a new, clean, exclusively *Ariel* version of the title-page and files it in front of its multi-titled draft.[100]

Oscillation is again the case with 'Fever 103°'. From the first hand-written draft of the poem until its fourth typewritten copy, 'Fever 103°' contains the lines

> O auto-da-fé!
> The purple men, gold crusted, thick with spleen
>
> Sit with their hooks and crooks and stoke the light.[101]

Plath dated the drafts of 'Fever 103°' 20 October 1962. By the final typescript, she had decidedly removed the lines from the poem. When she read 'Fever 103°' for the BBC ten days later, she restored the lines that had been so present until fairly late in the poem's composition.[102] We could speculate that Plath was attached to the lines, but also doubtful about them, as she was in the cases of the other poems in which she vacillates between deleting and retaining, finally changing her mind aloud, but not on paper. It would appear that Plath thought carefully about the meaning of *auto-da-fé*, and wanted the sense in the poem, for she underlined the definition in her own dictionary. *Auto-da-fé* is the 'ceremony accompanying the pronouncement of judgement by the Inquisition, followed by the execution by the secular authorities; hence, the execution, esp. the burning, of a heretic'.[103] *Auto-da-fé* – and the Inquisition that it conjures – is one of numerous specific cultural and historic references in a poem that also evokes Cerberus, Isadora Duncan, Hiroshima, and Paradise.

One of the assumptions about Plath, and especially about her late poems, is that they are an anguished, uncontrolled cry for help; utterly personal. As Anne Stevenson puts it, 'Sylvia reported in her poems on the weather of her inner universe and delineated its two poles: "stasis" and rage'.[104] One glance at the drafts of these poems, and the hard work that they evidence, makes any such claim laughable. 'Ariel' itself is an example of this labour, again, through beautiful lines and words, many ultimately discarded, just to achieve two words. Before she was able to write 'I unpeel'[105] for the first time, Plath needed to write and cross through

> Hands, heart, dead men
> Dead men
> Hands, hearts, peel off –
> Old
> Dead hands, dead stringencies![106]

The sheer care and labour expended, sometimes to reach just one line or find the right word, are the very opposite of uncontrolled extremity or a preoccupation with any 'inner universe', however distressed Plath may indeed have been while writing.

In his Introduction to the *Collected Poems* Ted Hughes explains that he

> resisted the temptation to reproduce the drafts of these last poems in variorum completeness. These drafts are arguably an important part of Sylvia Plath's complete works. Some of the handwritten pages are aswarm with startling, beautiful phrases and lines, crowding all over the place, many of them in no way less remarkable than the ones she eventually picked out to make her final poem. But printing them all would have made a huge volume.[107]

Hughes is right about the remarkable nature of the lines and words that lie in the archives, unpublished. Two such wonderful lines, from 'Mirror', do not make it into the final poem. In them, the eponymous speaker imagines itself with legs, walking from its room and into the world so that it can show others their reflections: 'The trees and the stones would know where they stood. / The trees would not dream of redness, nor the stones of transparency'.[108] At the top of the first page of Plath's manuscripts for 'Burning the Letters', we find the teasingly warning, sexually knowing lines

What sweat nectar attracts them?
They zing. They are bits of jet.
Watch it. You are in a cat's cradle, my love, my love. My pet[109]

These lines are full of energy and excitement. They are beautiful, though Plath crossed them out and abandoned them. Perhaps the lines are relics from another poem (Plath drew a line beneath them before writing the first line of 'Burning the Letters'). Or perhaps they are a false start to the compellingly stressed and rhymed beginning of 'Burning the Letters': 'I made a fire, I was tired'.[110] ('I was tired' is, for me, stronger than the less active 'being tired'[111] that Plath chose for the final version of the poem.) We might wonder whether the 'sweat' nectar was intentional on Plath's part. It is certainly what she wrote on the draft, though her hand may not have obeyed her brain. Our instinct is to say 'sweet', but the unexpected sweat is interesting, linking the fluids of the flowers with those of human beings, and rupturing the customary cliché of sugar, giving us salt and sour instead.

Once seen, it is impossible to discount these unpublished materials, or regard them as anything less than an integral part of what is actually published. One analogy might be to regard the published poems as the tip of the iceberg visible above the water, and the unpublished drafts as the invisible part below. Unseen, but no less vital: without the bottom the top might float away, unanchored – or might never have been sufficiently substantial to exist at all. These discarded or alternate versions of lines allow us a more complete picture of Plath's intentions as a writer, and help us to understand her work more fully. They also give us pleasure in themselves. Ideally, any new editions of Plath's work would find a way of providing her cuts and variants, perhaps in footnotes, or in a lighter, italicised font. Thereby the reader would have access to the published version of a poem or piece of prose, as well as its ghosts; the lines Plath found difficult to excise, or did abandon, but are nonetheless worth reading.

Admittedly, such a project would not be simple. Hughes was right to observe that it would be a huge undertaking to publish everything – a comment that anybody who has seen the mass of paper that comprises the manuscripts for the *Ariel* poems would understand. Fitting just these, let alone *all* of Plath's manuscripts, into any sort of volume would be a monumental project. Volumes, rather than a mere book, would be necessary. In the end, they would be expensive to produce and buy. The expense, coupled with the very specialist interest, would probably disqualify this as a project for the mass market. Very advanced photographic technology would need to be used to preserve the layers of Plath's scrawls and cross-outs, so allowing the reader to decipher what lies beneath them (as we can with the originals). A facsimile of Plath's manuscripts should be arranged so that the reader could see exactly what lies on the reverse side of her paper (for instance, a poem by Hughes, or a typescript page from *The Bell Jar*). Such an enterprise would heavily multiply the amount of paper needed to produce Plath's manuscripts.

Dearly Beloved

I have made it clear that I do not want to speculate on the events of Plath's life by extrapolating from her writing, or vice versa. Yet I do not want to pretend that looking at the material in the archives at Smith College and Indiana University is not an intensely moving and engaging experience. David Machin, Plath's editor at Heinemann (who published the first edition of *The Bell Jar*) writes to Plath on 12 February 1963, 'Did something go wrong about our lunch date yesterday or did I put down the wrong day?'[112] What went wrong is now one of the most unforgettable and debated events of literary history. Plath did not turn up for lunch because she was dead. She missed what should have been an exciting meeting with the editor of her first novel. It is difficult to know what to feel in the face of this dramatic irony; this knowing with hindsight what Machin could not know as he waited in that restaurant or pub or café, or the next day, as he wrote to Plath.

I am reluctant to become a hagiographer, but I want to record that I was startled by my sense that to work with Plath's manuscripts and papers was to experience a strong sense of her physical presence, and of my own contact with material residues that she left behind. Those who work in the archives trail their hands over letters covered in Plath's fingerprints, open envelopes that she licked before smoothing them shut on her DNA. These materials seem far removed from the copies of her words onto clean white pages that we find in libraries and shops. The original draft of a poem is blotted with ink that leaves blue-black specks sparkling on the skin of those who handle it. The edge of a paper or corner of a letter is smudged dull red as dried blood or green as mould with something unidentifiable that Plath smeared or spilled.

Frequently in the Plath archives I came upon the unexpected. They hold numerous drawings, paintings, collages, scrapbooks, and other pieces of Plath's art, made from the time she was a small child until just before her death. To reproduce these, and comment on them, would fill a very welcome, and very large, book. The Lilly Library, for instance, possesses 118 paper dolls, accompanied by a wardrobe of exclusive Plath gowns that she designed and cut herself. Exquisitely made, these clothes are in the style of Hollywood glamour; Plath modelled the dolls on female film stars. We are cued to this Hollywood world of the late 1940s and 1950s by *Movies*,[113] a paper doll magazine that Plath made for her little mannequins. The Lilly Library also holds twenty-five homemade cards that Plath carefully crafted for her family. In one of them, made by Plath for her mother in 1952, a beautiful girl lounges on an upholstered and scrolled chaise longue. The chaise longue is pink with red hearts, and the girl looks wan and dramatic, perhaps prefiguring the last image of Plath's 1956 short story, 'The Wishing Box'. She holds a rose in her hand, which trails, exhausted, onto the floor. Her other hand falls to her head. 'I SHALL FALL INTO A DECLINE – IF YOU WON'T BE MY VALENTINE!'[114] (The exclamation mark is dotted with a heart instead of a full stop.)

Some may think that these materials demonstrate the high degree of effort, imagination and artistic competence that Plath was prepared to devote to delighting the people close to her. Others might 'diagnose' Plath through them, seeing them as evidence that she was excessive in her desire to please. Still others might argue that such excess is what produces exceptional work. Yet there are less problematic, more productive ways of looking at these materials. We might evaluate them in artistic terms (you can see the influence of Picasso in this painting) or find ways in which they connect with other aspects of Plath's work (that drawing gives us the visual image in that poem). Or we could read them in terms of the cultural comments they make (she was being ironic about an aesthetic that asks women to look like dolls).

In a folder of Plath's correspondence, there is a thick homemade envelope illustrated with flowers. On it is written 'for mother ~ welcome to Court Green ~ from Sivvy & Ted'.[115] Inside the envelope, still obeying the creases Plath must have folded into it and fitting exactly in its paper case, is a blue Liberty scarf that Plath presented to her mother. Unsure of what it was at first, I shook the scarf out and watched it balloon softly until it fell over my own bare arms. Fearing I'd accidentally broken one of the library's rules, I folded the scarf back up. Hoping that nobody was watching me, I was careful to duplicate the lines Plath had made in it.

Sifting through one of the containers in the Lilly Library, I came upon a narrow, coffin-shaped box. A strand of long, dark blonde hair lay across the top of it. As it was the colour and length of my own, I picked the hair up, brushed it away, and opened the container. My neck was bent so that my hair spilled into the box and brushed its contents. Quickly, I straightened my neck and pushed my hair behind my ears, then reached into the box, unthinking, to finger a long plait of Plath's hair. With hindsight, I wonder if I'd trespassed against another of the library's rules, though I still don't recall a sign requesting that library users refrain from caressing Plath's hair. The hair was still soft and silky. It was not dead hair, brittle and juiceless. Or rather, it did not feel like the hair of a dead person, or how I'd always imagined the hair of a dead person would feel – if I'd ever imagined such a thing at all. It felt like the sort of hair you find attached to a head with blood still pulsing through its arteries and veins. Accidentally, I might have tossed away a precious archival resource, though I've no way of knowing whether that stray hair I'd flicked from the top of the still-unopened box was my own or hers. What I do know is that I contaminated the rest of her hair by sprinkling it with invisible bits of my own body, specks of skin, oil from my fingertips, as others must have done before. It is impossible to work in the archives and not leave an invisible physical imprint on the materials there.

Without visiting the archives, it would be impossible to comprehend just how prolific Plath's output was. There is a considerable amount of fiction and poetry, all written in a lifetime that ended at thirty, plus Plath's regular correspondence with numerous people. When you see letters that you previously knew only in excerpt (between the covers of a book and sandwiched with editorial commentary), the physical sense of their writer and her labour is striking. Most of Plath's letters are written on light blue, featherweight airmail paper. Most of them are typed. Frequently, Plath types to the edge of the page, even circling round and round the perimeter of the paper, creating a sort of type-written frame so as not to waste a millimetre. (Plath's mother commented that her daughter could type eighty words per minute, and that Plath once declared, 'the typewriter is an extension of my body'.[116]) It may be that Plath wants to get the full value of postage and paper, shunning financial waste, and perhaps even ecological waste too. The reader of Plath's published letters does not just miss the physical appearance of Plath's paper, with its blots and crowded type. One of the other things they lose is the presence of Aurelia Plath, whose annotations upon her daughter's correspondence are worthy of study in their own right.[117]

Excepting impersonal correspondence, the gesture of writing upon somebody's letter to you, of putting your own mark on it, may seem odd – even taboo; it is certainly not something that many people do to the communications sent to them by their friends or family. There is a letter that Plath wrote on 6 February 1961, in which she tells her mother: 'I lost the little baby this morning and feel really terrible about it ... I am as sorry about disappointing you as anything else'.[118] This letter is published in *Letters Home*, but in the original, the second sentence is underlined in red ink. Alongside it, in the margin, written in the same red ink, are two words and a date: '2/14/63 My Sylvia'.[119] The handwriting is unmistakably Plath's mother's. (For anyone who examines Plath's letters, this handwriting soon becomes familiar.) The date, 14 February 1963, is two years after Plath wrote the letter, and three days after her death. Mrs Plath's annotation provides another of those skin-bristling archive moments. Just three days after her daughter's death, Mrs Plath must have been sitting in her home in a despair of grief and love, rereading her daughter's letters and annotating them even as she searched for an echo of her child's voice. (Mrs Plath did not fly to England with her son and daughter-in-law for the funeral.) The annotations suggest a curious mixture of uncontrolled emotional desperation (I must somehow make contact with my child) and calculation (I will write on these papers, and date my markings, to tell my own side of things and ensure the impression for posterity that I want to leave).

In his study of epistolary writing, *The Rape of Clarissa*, Terry Eagleton reminds us that letters can be 'waylaid, forged, stolen, lost, copied, cited, censored, parodied, misread, rewritten, submitted to mocking commentary, woven into other texts which alter their meaning, exploited for ends unforeseen by their authors'.[120] What Eagleton describes has been true of Plath's writing, and continues to be so. In this very book, I copy, comment upon, weave Plath's texts into my own, and use them in ways Plath could never have predicted. Due to the practical demands of publishing a selection of letters, and Aurelia Plath's dual role as editor and mother, *Letters Home* necessarily excerpts, selects, misinterprets (what mother could perfectly interpret her child's letters?) and attempts to manipulate and control the reader's interpretation through its commentary. Aurelia Plath's writing *upon* Plath's letters is perhaps the most immediate example of a commentary that weaves Plath's text into another and uses her letters in a way she could not have foreseen. As Eagleton says of Samuel Richardson's *Clarissa*, and we might say of Plath's own correspondence, 'As one letter spawns another

... the impulse to protect and control writing grows accordingly sharper'. Eagleton observes also the 'troubling gap ... between "experience" and "expression"',[121] and this may help us to gain insight into why Aurelia Plath reaches for those letters when her daughter is dead. Perhaps Mrs Plath immerses herself in her child's 'expression', in words that fictionalise 'experience', to find a story that is bearable. In this case, the 'gap' between experience and expression might not have been 'troubling', but comforting: a refuge.

Whatever the mixture of spontaneity and calculation that prompts Aurelia Plath's annotations, Mrs Plath scrawls immediate answers to her daughter's queries, as if impelled to help and answer as fast as she can, and also, presumably, as rough notes upon which she later bases her replies. We see this, for instance, when Plath writes to her mother in 1961 about the mortgage arrangements she and Hughes are making. Mrs Plath scribbles her own sums directly on the letter, calculating on her daughter's behalf, and then concludes, 'Still $ 1,680 short'.[122] On another letter, this one composed when Plath was pregnant with her first child at the beginning of 1960, Mrs Plath writes, 'Paint has lead! Poison! Keep away See that baby's crib has no lead paint!'[123] Such a warning may be recognisable to any of us with fondly overprotective mothers. Yet Mrs Plath's annotations, no less than Plath's own original letters, are subject to the capacity of writing to 'exceed and invert her precise meaning'.[124] Mrs Plath imparts what she thinks is factual information that her daughter and future grandchild urgently require. But other readers of this comment (Plath or Hughes, you or I) might interpret it in a way that would have surprised her. Doesn't Mrs Plath think Plath must have known about the dangers of lead paint, we might wonder? (Actually, Mrs Plath was unusually well informed for her time; the toxicity of lead paint was only beginning to be more widely acknowledged in the late 1950s and early 1960s.) Is this not excessively interfering, others might ask? Is the 'precise meaning' here that Mrs Plath has doubts about her daughter's fitness to mother a child? These questions are ungenerous, and I do not cite them because I think the answer to any of them is yes. Rather, I cite them to illustrate how quickly and easily our words spin out of our own control, and become subject to the meanings that other people make for us.

Mrs Plath annotated an envelope that Plath mailed to her in April, 1962: 'My last birthday letter from Sivvy –'.[125] Similarly affecting is Mrs Plath's typed note about an unpublished story that Plath wrote for a teacher at Smith in 1951, 'Mary Ventura':[126]

> I look upon this story as very symbolic of Sylvia's life. She
> <u>had</u> to pull the emergency switch that allowed her to escape
> from the train. As she dashed up the green hill, surrounded
> by beautiful countryside, she found the plump, kindly old
> lady (Grammy) sitting there, knitting, and smiling a
> welcome.[127]

In this carefully composed and sentimental note, Mrs Plath tries to
make sense of senseless death and writes her own story, imagining a
sort of heaven where her child is not really dead, but is active ('she
dashed'), happy and with her family.

What can we do in the face of all this emotion? Academic theories,
literary analysis – these threaten to wither in the face of Mrs Plath's
ceaseless annotations to herself to act on her daughter's behalf, during
Plath's life, and after it. These letters meant so very much to her, as she
tells us in her Introduction to *Letters Home*: 'I had the dream of one day
handing Sylvia the huge packet of letters. I felt she could make use of
them'.[128] When her daughter is irretrievably taken from her, they are
what she turns to in the immediate aftermath of her death: the closest
she can get to her child, and keeping her voice alive. This impulse
appears to be public as well as private: '<u>Sell</u> or donate <u>all</u> letters & have
public have access',[129] Mrs Plath writes on a photocopy of the letter in
which Plath tells her side of the story of her Christmas argument with
Olwyn Hughes. Poignant and real as the sentiments expressed in Mrs
Plath's annotations may be, there is something uncanny about writing
that is both deeply personal, but also intended for an audience of
strangers.

Beyond Her Own Skin

I've taken the title of this first chapter from Plath's fine and underrated
early poem 'The Thin People', which is preoccupied with context and
history. In this poem, originally titled 'The Moon was a Fat Woman
Once' and written in 1957, the narrator declares that 'the outline / Of
the world comes clear and fills with color'. For me Plath's poems do
exactly this, again and again giving us pieces of the world, plumping
them out and into three dimensions, and shooting the world through
with pigment. By taking Plath's writing away from the conventional
personal readings to which it is customarily subjected, we see that her

poems and fiction not only make our world vivid, but also that they are deeply, politically engaged with that world.

The 'things of this world'[130] matter deeply to Sylvia Plath and her writing, a fact that Plath herself stressed when she introduced a selection of her poems for BBC radio (this is quoted at length in the epigraph to this chapter). It seems fitting to take Plath's lead, and evaluate her writing for what she herself stated to be one of its most significant characteristics: involvement. Above all, Sylvia Plath's writing is sane – and I mean sane in at least two senses, neither of which in the least concerns Plath's own mental state. First, Plath's writing is sane in its argument and subject matter. Insistently, the writing concerns itself with real political and material issues, with 'definite situations', to reiterate once more from my epigraph. Second, the writing is sane in so far as it is controlled, methodical, and carefully wrought – a circumstance to which Plath's manuscripts in the archives testify. Both of these senses of sanity are the very opposite of the myth of Sylvia Plath as mad, depressed and pouring out her distress in an ink of blood.

'The Thin People' is itself a poem about history and culture; it is about the ways that the media of postwar capitalism dissociate us from the very occurrences they attempt to depict. The narrator speaks in the first person plural about how we hold the suffering of others at a distance by looking at past events through forms that strip them of their reality, and by regarding them as ancient history that can have nothing to do with us:

> ... we say:
> It was only in a movie, it was only
> In a war making evil headlines when we
>
> Were small.[131]

'The Thin People' dramatises the tendency of photographic, journalistic and cinematic representations to empty history of its three-dimensionality, diminishing its impact and our ability to believe it was ever real. At the same time, the poem suggests that these events haunt us nonetheless, so that images of dead bodies stacked in concentration camps ('How they prop each other up'[132]) cannot 'remain in dreams' or the 'contracted country of the head'.[133] When 'the outline / of the world comes clear and fills with color', the poem remarks upon the way that this terrible material stays with those who see it, and may also refer to the increasing popularity of technicolor film. Memorable (and now familiar) postwar photographs and newsreels of the liberation of concentration camps ('If the thin people simply stand in the forest'[134]) become elements of our collective psyche and history. We shall see that such visual images – from death camps to the aftermath of nuclear explosions – are part of the fabric of Plath's writing. In the late 1940s and through the 1950s, black and white still and cinematic images from the Holocaust were shockingly fresh. At the start of the twenty-first century, with the passage of relatively little time but huge leaps in photographic technology, such images have the look of ancient history. 'The Thin People' is one of Plath's many poems that force the reader to examine their distance from historical and cultural events, and the responsibilities and privileges, as well as poverty, of that distance.

Even at the age of sixteen Plath used her work to imagine worlds and lives far beyond her own. In 'Seek No More the Young', an unpublished poem written early in 1949, Plath writes of children playing in the park, not imagining the impending war and destruction. 'The steel-winged vultures came; the rifles whined'. This poem, remarkably adept for one so young, is about the darkness of war killing real children or leaving them orphaned; it is about the loss of innocence: 'The tortured panic of the world was there. / Ah! Seek no more the young with golden hair'.[135] Another unpublished manuscript, this time of a story, reveals Plath's political and world consciousness. 'Brief Encounter' was written in February 1952, according to Plath's handwritten note. It concerns a meeting on a train between two strangers: a young girl, and a veteran who has just returned from Korea on crutches, having left one of his legs behind. Given what has happened to the man, neither character can keep to the superficial banality of polite conversation. His physical and emotional scars leave him unable to pretend 'after the parades and the cheering, that nothing was the matter with the world at all',[136] a view that the inexperienced girl is brought to share.

'The Thin People' is a poem about the erecting of barriers, and how, in the end, such barriers are penetrable. Even if death camps are cordoned off into black and white photographs or cinematic representations, these images nonetheless move from the page or screen and into our collective and individual consciousness. Plath's writing is concerned with the relationship between human beings and this world that is around them, however painful that relationship, and powerful the temptation to deny it, may sometimes be. This is the other Sylvia Plath: one whose writing is much more than personal, who uses her poems and fiction to look at a world that extends far beyond her own skin, and invites us to look with her, beyond our own.

Notes

1. SMITH. Box: Plath – Broadcasts, Clipping, Financial. Folder: Broadcasts – 8 July 1961. ' "The Living Poet": Sylvia Plath'. Typescript. BBC Radio Broadcast. The Third Programme. Recorded 5 June 1961. Broadcast 8 July 1961. According to the typescript, the poems that Plath read were 'The Disquieting Muses', 'Sheep in the Mojave Desert', 'Suicide off Egg Rock', 'Spinster', 'Parliament Hill Fields', 'You're', 'Medallion' and 'The Stones'.
2. Lucas, Victoria. *The Bell Jar*. London: William Heinemann, 1963. First English edition.
3. Lucas, Victoria. *The Bell Jar*. London: Contemporary Fiction William Heinemann, 1964: back cover.
4. McCullough, 'Foreword to the Twenty–Fifth Anniversary Edition', 1996: x.
5. 'Under the Skin' (unsigned review), 1963: 52.
6. Lerner, 'New Novels', 1963: 54.
7. *The Colossus and Other Poems*, Knopf, 1962, first American edition, inside back cover.
8. *Ibid.*
9. *The Colossus and Other Poems*, Knopf, 1962, first American edition, inside front cover.
10. *Ariel*, Faber, 1965, first English edition, front cover.
11. *Ibid.*, inside front cover. Elsewhere – and quite strikingly – Alvarez has spoken of the material in the *Ariel* poems as 'poetic terrorism' which can 'blow up in your face' like the components of a bomb in the process of its manufacture. In the same interview, though, he speaks of these poems as 'highly disciplined and skilful' (Alvarez. Interviewed on *Voices & Visions: Sylvia Plath*. New York: Mystic Fire Video, 1988).
12. Lowell, 'Foreword' to *Ariel*, 1965: ix.
13. Copies of this photo are at LILLY, Plath MSS. II, Miscellaneous Photographs, Box 14, folder 7; and in Lameyer MSS.
14. The photo is reproduced in *Letters Home*, 121.
15. Lucas, Victoria. *The Bell Jar*. London: William Heinemann, 1963, first English edition, inside front cover.
16. SMITH. Box: Plath – Prose, Quotation. Folder: Quotation, *The Bell Jar – Time & Tide*.
17. *The Bell Jar*, 42.
18. The photo is reproduced in *The Journals of Sylvia Plath*, 1982: 180.
19. The photo is reproduced in *ibid*.
20. *Letters Home*, 143.
21. The photo is reproduced in *ibid.*, 139.
22. SMITH. Box: Plath – Adaptations, Advertisements, Artwork. Folder: Advertisements – Books.

23. *Collected Poems*, 224.
24. *The Bell Jar*, 1971, first American edition: photograph attributed inside the back cover.
25. *Ibid.,* back cover.
26. *Ibid.,* inside back cover.
27. Ames, 'Sylvia Plath: A Biographical Note', 1971: 279.
28. *The Bell Jar*, Bantam paperback edition, 1972: back cover.
29. These comments include a *New York Times* critic's dissension from received theory: '[This] is not a potboiler, nor a series of ungrateful caricatures; it is literature'. Plath, *The Bell Jar*, HarperCollins, 1996: back cover.
30. *The Bell Jar*, HarperCollins, 1996: inside front cover.
31. McCullough, 'Foreword to the Twenty-Fifth Anniversary Edition', 1996: xviii, xv.
32. Oates, *The Bell Jar*, Faber and Faber, 1996 edition: front cover. The Oates quotation is taken from her essay 'The Death Throes of Romanticism: The Poetry of Sylvia Plath', 1976: 113.
33. Rose, *The Haunting of Sylvia Plath*, 1991: 79, 65–113.
34. *The Journals of Sylvia Plath*, 1982: inside front cover.
35. *Ibid.*, inside back cover.
36. See Rose, 'So Many Lives, So Little Time', 2000: 11. See Wagner, 'Love That Passed All Understanding', 2000: 21. See Kendall, 'Showing Off to an Audience of One', 2000: 12.
37. Sheldon, 'The "Demon" that Killed Sylvia', 2000: 9.
38. Pearson, 'Trapped in Time: Sylvia Plath', 2000: A1, A2.
39. Rose, *The Haunting of Sylvia Plath*, 1991: 133.
40. *Letters Home*, 378 (letter to her mother dated 21 April 1960).
41. Stevenson, *Bitter Fame*, 1989: 192. See also Dido Merwin's account of the event in her Appendix to *Bitter Fame*: 327–8.
42. Wagner-Martin, *Sylvia Plath: A Biography*, 1987: 175.
43. Alexander, *Rough Magic*, 1991: 248.
44. The crudest form of the brag is exemplified by men who claim to have had sex with Plath, such as Peter Davison, who 'remembers that on almost every occasion, as they had on their first date, they ended up sleeping together' (Alexander, *Rough Magic*, 1991: 164). Plath, of course, is no longer here to tell her side of the story, or lack of it.
45. Byatt, *Possession*, 1990: 508.
46. Byatt, 'Sylvia Plath: *Letters Home*', 1976: 254.
47. Amis and Greer made these comments in an episode of *Bookmark* entitled *Lifers: The Rise & Rise of the Literary Biographer*. It was first screened on BBC 2 on 9 March 1996.
48. Van Dyne, *Revising Life*, 1993: 9.
49. Perloff, 'Sylvia Plath's *Collected Poems*', 1981: 294. Wagner, *Sylvia Plath: The Critical Heritage*, 1988: 7.

50. Stevenson, *Bitter Fame*, 1989: 264.
51. *Collected Poems*, 219.
52. Wagner-Martin, *Sylvia Plath*, 1987: 224.
53. *Collected Poems*, 220.
54. Rose, *The Haunting of Sylvia Plath*, 1991: xi.
55. This photo is of Plath at Cambridge, in 1957. A photo of Plath in the same pose, though with a slightly different expression on her face, is reproduced in Stevenson, *Bitter Fame*, 1989: 201.
56. It is only fair to acknowledge that not all scholarly books on Plath have cemented the link between her life and work through such blatant use of her image. The covers of Pat Macpherson's, Robyn Marsack's and Susan Bassnett's books are simply designed and entirely text based.
57. Rose, *The Haunting of Sylvia Plath*, 1991: 1.
58. The photo is reproduced in *The Journals of Sylvia Plath*, 1982: 185.
59. Axelrod, *Sylvia Plath: The Wound and the Cure of Words*, 1990: 10.
60. Bloom, *Sylvia Plath*, 1989: front cover and inside back cover.
61. Anderson (ed.), *The Great American Bathroom Book*, 1993: 283.
62. Stevenson, *Bitter Fame*, 1989: 8.
63. Anderson (ed.), *The Great American Bathroom Book*, 1993: 284.
64. Ted Hughes, writing at what some might assume to be the opposite cultural pole from *The Great American Bathroom Book*, similarly equates Plath's life and work. Quoting from her 1963 poem 'Kindness', he says of Plath's character, 'The notion of her forcing herself, in her "Japanese silks, desperate butterflies", deeper into some internal furnace, strengthens throughout these pages'. Hughes, 'Sylvia Plath and Her Journals', 1982: 182.
65. Reimann, *Six Poems by Sylvia Plath for Soprano and Piano*, 1987; Rorem, *Ariel: Five Poems of Sylvia Plath, for Soprano, Clarinet and Piano*, 1974; Shulamit, *Music of Ran Shulamit* [includes *Apprehensions, for Voice, Clarinet and Piano*], 1991.
66. Shulamit, *Music of Ran Shulamit*, 1991: 3–4 (CD cover/booklet).
67. *Collected Poems*, 223, 222, 75, and *passim*.
68. Wagner-Martin, *Sylvia Plath*, 1987: 205, 206.
69. *Collected Poems*, 195.
70. *Ibid.*, 232 (my italics).
71. SMITH. Box: Plath – Ariel Poems, Amnesiac – Berck-Plage. Folder: Ariel Poems, 'Amnesiac', Drafts 1–3, Typed Copies 1–4.
72. English *Collected Poems*, 232; American *Collected Poems* (ed. Ted Hughes. New York: Harper & Row, 1992), 233; English *Winter Trees*, 30; American *Winter Trees*, 31.
73. SMITH. Box: Plath – Letters (A–Z). Folder: Letters, *The New Yorker*, T.L.s. 7 Nov., 1962.
74. SMITH. Box: Plath – Ariel Poems, Amnesiac – Berck-Plage. Folder: Ariel Poems, 'Amnesiac', Typed Copy 4.

75. SMITH. Box: Plath – Ariel Poems, Amnesiac – Berck-Plage. Folder: Ariel Poems, 'Amnesiac', Typed Copy 5.

76. SMITH. Box: Plath – Ariel Poems, Daddy – Event. Folder: Ariel Poems, 'Elm', Draft 7c and Typed Copy 1.

77. 'Elm' was first published as 'The Elm Speaks' in *The New Yorker,* 3 Aug. 1963: 28.

78. First English edition, *Ariel*, 1965: 26. First English edition, *Collected Poems*, 1981: 193.

79. American *Collected Poems* (see n.72 above), 193; *Ariel*, 16.

80. Middlebrook, *Sylvia Plath*, 1998: 153.

81. SMITH. Box: Plath – Ariel Poems, Amnesiac – Berck-Plage. Folder: Ariel Poems, 'Amnesiac', Draft 1, p. 2; Draft 2, p. 2; Draft 3, p. 1; Typed Copy 1.

82. English edition, *Winter Trees*, 18 (my italics).

83. American edition, *Winter Trees*, 42 (my italics).

84. SMITH. Box: Plath – Ariel Poems, Nick and the Candlestick – Sheep in Fog. Folders: Ariel Poems, 'Purdah'.

85. Orr, *Plath Reads Plath*, 1975.

86. English *Collected Poems*, 243; American *Collected Poems* (see n. 72 above), 243; English *Winter Trees*, 18.

87. Orr, *Plath Reads Plath*, 1975 (my italics).

88. SMITH. Box: Plath – Ariel Poems, Nick and the Candlestick – Sheep in Fog. Folders: Ariel Poems, 'Nick and the Candlestick'.

89. English *Ariel*, 40; American *Ariel*, 33; English *Collected Poems*, 240; American *Collected Poems* (see n. 72 above), 240 (my italics).

90. SMITH. *Webster's New Collegiate Dictionary*. Springfield, Massachusetts: G. & C. Merriam Co., 1949: 824.

91. SMITH. Box: Plath – Ariel Poems, Lady Lazarus – Mystic. Folders: Ariel Poems, 'Medusa', Typed Copies 1–3 (Revised).

92. Had the lines been included, they would have followed the phrase 'Overexposed, like an X ray'. English *Collected Poems*, 225.

93. Orr, *Plath Reads Plath*, 1975.

94. SMITH. Box: Plath – Ariel Poems, Lady Lazarus – Mystic. Folders: Ariel Poems, 'Lady Lazarus', Typed Copy 2 (Revised); Typed Copy 3 (Revised).

95. English *Collected Poems*, 230.

96. SMITH. Box: Plath – Ariel Poems, Stings – Years. Folders: Ariel Poems, 'Stopped Dead', Drafts 1–2, Typed Copies 1–2, Typed Copies 3–4 (Revised).

97. Orr, *Plath Reads Plath*, 1975.

98. This latest version was Christmas of 1962 according to Ted Hughes (1980), 'Introduction' to the English *Collected Poems*, 14.

99. Hughes, 'The Art of Poetry LXXI', 1995: 79.

100. SMITH. Box: Plath – Ariel Poems – Typescript, Notes, Proofs. Folder: Ariel Poems, Final Typescript.

101. SMITH. Box: Plath – Ariel Poems, The Fearful – Kindness. Folder: Ariel Poems, 'Fever 103°', Typed Copy 3 (Revised). In the drafts of the poem, these lines precede the line 'The tinder cries'.
102. Orr, *Plath Reads Plath*, 1975.
103. SMITH. *Webster's New Collegiate Dictionary*. Springfield, Massachusetts: G. & C. Merriam Co., 1949: 60. The underlining is Plath's.
104. Stevenson, *Bitter Fame*, 1989: 262.
105. English *Collected Poems*, 239.
106. SMITH. Box: Plath – Ariel Poems, Amnesiac – Berck-Plage. Folder: Ariel Poems, 'Ariel', Draft 3.
107. Hughes (1980), 'Introduction' to the English *Collected Poems*, 17.
108. LILLY. 1961, Oct. 23. Plath MSS. 'Mirror'.
109. SMITH. Box: Plath – Ariel Poems. A Birthday Present – Cut. Folder: Ariel Poems, 'Burning the Letters', Draft 1, p. 1.
110. SMITH. Box: Plath – Ariel Poems. A Birthday Present – Cut. Folder: Ariel Poems, 'Burning the Letters', Draft 1, p. 3.
111. English *Collected Poems*, 204.
112. SMITH. Box: Plath – Letters (A–Z). Folder: Letters, William Heinemann Ltd., T.L.s., 12 Feb. 1963.
113. LILLY. Plath MSS. II, Miscellaneous Artwork. Box 14, folder 3.
114. LILLY. Plath MSS. II, Miscellaneous Artwork. Box 14, folder 1.
115. LILLY. Plath MSS. II, Correspondence, 1962, May–July, Box 6a. 'June 21 1962' is pencilled on the flowered case in Aurelia Plath's hand.
116. *Voices & Visions: Sylvia Plath*. New York: Mystic Fire Video, 1988.
117. The evolution of *Letters Home* is a story that can be read through Aurelia Plath's notes and papers in the Lilly Library. At one point, Mrs Plath planned to subtitle *Letters Home* with the words *A Testament of Love*, and organise the book around titles such as 'A New Life in the Old World', 'Return to the Promised Land', 'The Other Side of the Desk', and 'The Song of Frieda Rebecca'. LILLY. Plath MSS. II, Writings, *Letters Home* – Notes. Box 9, folder 11.
118. *Letters Home*, 408.
119. LILLY. Plath MSS. II, Correspondence, 1961, Jan.–May, Box 6. Sylvia Plath to Aurelia Plath. 6 Feb. 1961.
120. Eagleton, *The Rape of Clarissa*, 1982: 50.
121. *Ibid.*, 41.
122. LILLY. Plath MSS. II, Correspondence, 1961, June–Dec., Box 6a. Sylvia Hughes to Aurelia Plath. 7 Aug. 1961. Annotation not dated.
123. LILLY. Plath MSS. II, Correspondence, 1960, Jan.–Apr., Box 6. Sylvia Plath to Aurelia Plath. 24 Jan. 1960. Annotation not dated.
124. Eagleton, *The Rape of Clarissa*, 1982: 42.
125. LILLY. Plath MSS. II, Correspondence, 1962, Jan.–Apr., Box 6a. Sylvia Plath to Aurelia Plath. 25 April 1962. Annotation not dated.
126. LILLY. Plath MSS. II. Prose Fiction. Box 8, Folder 15: M–O.

127. LILLY. Plath MSS. II, Miscellaneous Miscellany. Box 15, folder 67. Mrs Plath's note is not dated.
128. *Letters Home*, 3.
129. LILLY. Plath MSS. II, Correspondence, 1961, Jan.–May, Box 6. Sylvia Plath to Aurelia Plath. 1 Jan. 1961. Annotation not dated.
130. SMITH. Box: Plath – Broadcasts, Clipping, Financial. Folder: Broadcasts – 8 July 1961. '"The Living Poet": Sylvia Plath'. Typescript. BBC Radio Broadcast. The Third Programme. Recorded 5 June 1961. Broadcast 8 July 1961.
131. English *Collected Poems*, 64.
132. *Ibid.*, 65.
133. *Ibid.*, 64.
134. *Ibid.*, 65.
135. LILLY. Plath MSS. II, Writings, Poetry – S. Box 8, folder 3.
136. LILLY. Plath MSS. II, Writings, Prose – fiction – A – B. Box 8, folder 10.

CHAPTER 2

STRADDLING THE ATLANTIC

Orr: Now you as a poet, and as a person too, straddle the
Atlantic, if I can put it that way. Being an American
yourself —

Plath: That's a rather awkward position but I'll accept it.
[laughs]

Orr: On which side does your weight fall, if I can pursue
the metaphor?[1]

Your Puddle-Jumping Daughter

Sylvia Plath moved from America to England late in 1955, when she
was twenty-two years old. Two years later, in the summer of 1957
and at the age of twenty-four, Plath returned to America with her husband, Ted Hughes. They spent two and a half years there, but soon after
Plath's twenty-seventh birthday they returned to England. Plath lived in
London and Devon until the age of thirty, when she died.

Given her residences in both countries, it is not surprising that
Plath's speaking voices hover at different points over the Atlantic. In her
recorded interviews and readings they trespass against all forms of
borders.[2] Similarly, her writing is a 'polyglot stew'[3] of American and
English vocabularies. Her accents and lexicon are difficult to reconcile
with her description of herself as straightforwardly American: 'Well I
think that as far as language goes I'm an American. I'm afraid I'm an
American. My accent's American. My way of talk is an American way
of talk. I'm an old fashioned American.'[4] Despite such a rare and disingenuous assertion, what makes Plath's work so compelling is that it
retains some material residue of a voice that moves *between* England and
America. Plath's multiple, unstable national identity was the gift of at

least two cultures and languages. These allegiances to different countries had a considerable impact upon Plath's work. Without this complicated national and linguistic identity, the vividness, energy and originality of Plath's writing would not have developed as fully as it did. If Plath had never lived in England, she would have been a very different writer, and probably not such a good one.

In spite of her association with two countries, Plath's midatlanticism is largely ignored by critics, who contest ownership of Plath and the 'facts' about her life and work by fighting over her nationality, making her one thing or the other, or disregarding the issue of nationality altogether. Plath's writing plays out a perpetual displacement, a midatlanticism that is neither American nor English. To show this, however, I will at times need to rely upon a binary opposition between Americanness and Englishness that Plath herself challenges. As the years spent living in England increased, the tensions in her work between Americanness and Englishness increasingly registered as a larger crisis about what might constitute European identity.

Plath's story 'Stone Boy with Dolphin' was written in 1957–8, and she saw it as the 'kernel chapter'[5] of *Falcon Yard*, the novel she began to plan in the summer of 1957.[6] (*Falcon Yard* was either abandoned unfinished, altered beyond recognition, or never published.) 'Stone Boy with Dolphin' chronicles its American heroine's impressions of Cambridge. It examines strains and differences between Englishness and Americanness, and evidences Plath's readiness to make national identity a key project. 'American versus British',[7] Plath said of 'Stone Boy with Dolphin' in her *Journals*, and the story does truly play upon familiar stereotypes:

> Miss Minchell presided, tight-lipped and grim, over the Arden breakfast table. She'd stopped speaking, it was rumored, when the American girls started wearing pajamas to breakfast under their bathrobes. All British girls in the college came down fully dressed and starched for their morning hot tea, kippers and white bread. The Americans at Arden were fortunate beyond thought, Miss Minchell sniffed pointedly, in having a toaster. Ample quarter pounds of butter were allotted each girl on Sunday morning to last through the week. Only gluttons bought extra butter ... and slathered it double-thick on toast while Miss Minchell dipped her dry toast with disapproval into her second cup of tea.[8]

Here, Americans are free and expressive to the point of vulgarity, materially overprivileged, greedily consumerist, and hedonistic. The English are uptight, repressed, ascetic. The satiric narrative voice is implicated in the viewpoint of the American heroine, Dody Ventura. It is a voice that is sympathetic to America, constructing a democratic free-spiritedness in resistance to oppressive rules. The simplicity of such an oppositional view, we will see, could not be sustained in Plath's later work, which increasingly addresses what Homi Bhabha has described as the postmodern 'contingency and ambivalence in the positioning of cultural and political identity'.[9]

Such contingency and ambivalence are apparent in the ease with which we can upset the values attributed to the contrast between niggardly Englishness and expansive Americanness. American generosity can become greed. Freedom of expression can sometimes be gained only at the expense of someone else, or even of the environment, as Plath made clear in her early unpublished poem 'I Am An American'. (The manuscript is not dated, but according to a list provided in the *Collected Poems*, it was written sometime before 1956.[10])

> We all know that certain truths are self-evident:
>   That we believe in liberty and justice for all
>   Like the great green lady with the bronze torch
>   Lifted beside the door marked 'Members Only.'
>   That we are all free to speak our piece from the ivory soap box
>   And to letter our liberal opinions
>   In white exhaust on the spacious skies[11]

Likewise, English meanness can be seen as 'green' thrift: recycling in sympathy with the world's limited materials. To shift the oppositions yet again, we might see 'English' values allying themselves with a disdainful 'aristocratic' view of American bourgeois consumption as *nouveau riche*.

Anne Stevenson's treatment of Plath in *Bitter Fame* typifies these shifts. Here, Plath is frequently viewed as an extravagant consumer, spurning the 'secondhand shops' and offers of furniture from friends that are a part of English life and surprising her acquaintances by wearing 'new outfits' despite her assertions of poverty.[12] This disapproval is replicated by Lucas Myers, himself American, in his Appendix to *Bitter Fame*. Contrasting the attitudes of Plath and Hughes to their work, he writes: 'Sylvia was determined that it should be read. Ted was determined that it should exist'.[13] The intimation here is that to seek an audience is an act of gross indecency; Plath's vulgar production of commodities is juxtaposed with Hughes's high-minded creation of art. On the surface, Stevenson's and Myers's comments seem to be about consumer goods. Neither of them admits (or perhaps recognises) that their discussions are implicitly about nationality. Writers deny, assert or ignore Plath's Englishness and Americanness in accordance with their own (often-unconscious) agendas.

We see this in the battle by which Plath's critics and family alike attempt to 'own' Plath by sharing or obscuring her nationality. To the Americans who knew her, it was important that Plath should preserve her Americanness. Yet Plath's speaking voice, like the language of her poetry and prose, was not hermetically sealed, and so became softened by English language and culture. Anthony Smith uses the term 'collective cultural identity' to describe a 'sense of continuity, shared memory and collective destiny'. This 'collective cultural identity' is 'embodied in distinctive myths, memories, symbols and values retained by a given cultural unit of population'.[14] We might say that Plath's own 'shared memory and collective destiny' were shaped by her midatlanticism. Donning her family-pleasing voice, Plath writes in a letter to an American relative: 'I am delighted you think I have an English accent, Dotty. Everybody over here thinks I come from the Deep *South*; they think my American accent is so broad'.[15]

This incident is instructive. It reveals the predicament Plath's midatlantic national identity became for her: of being neither sufficiently American nor properly English, of partaking in different 'collective cultural identities'. The term transatlantic is often used to describe a hybrid *accent*, or someone who is on one side or the other, depending on where she stands. Midatlantic is a more apt description of Plath's position: a refusal to choose between two places. Such a mindset is nicely represented when Plath closes a letter with the signature, 'Your puddle-jumping daughter',[16] or entitles a 1962 poem 'Crossing the Water' and makes it impossible to identify just what water is being crossed. Stan Smith has argued that the imagery of Plath's 1962 poem, 'The Swarm', sets up 'a conflict of powers and allegiances'.[17] The same could be said of the larger body of Plath's writing. Plath institutes a twofold rhetorical strategy for dealing with her own 'conflict of powers and allegiances', pointed out by Dotty in what is really a polite and hurt accusation that Plath has betrayed her roots by losing her accent. First, Plath reinforces the charade that the accusation is a compliment. Second, she claims that nobody can tell where she is from.

The Dotty incident and letter come towards the end of Plath's life, in December of 1962. Yet from the beginning of her residence in

Britain, Plath balanced carefully between retaining her Americanness and accommodating England. In one of the first letters written to her mother from England, on 25 September 1955, Plath says of the moment her ship docked in Cherbourg, 'I'd felt I'd come home'. She then adopts the language of picture postcards, writing of France in exactly the reassuring touristy way one would expect of a young American abroad for the first time: 'Such warmth and love of life. Such color and idiosyncrasy. Everything is very small and beautiful and individual. What a joy to be away from eight-lane highways and mass markets'.[18] Praise of Europe cannot be made without a critique of its antithesis – American commercialism and size. Plath uses the comparison to show her mother that they are getting their money's worth: Plath is having just the experience and responses that she ought.

But the point is made too well. Presumably realising that the critic-ism may be taken as a traitorous anti-Americanism that overshadows the commendation, Plath moves from the statement 'I'd felt I'd come home' to 'I do feel so cut off from home',[19] suggesting that, however wonderful, Europe can never really displace America. Four years later, when Plath returns to England with Ted Hughes, she repeats the earlier epistolary gesture of reassuring her mother almost as soon as she has landed. Just a few weeks after arriving in England, as if already missing what she has left behind, she writes in an unpublished letter of 24 Jan-uary 1960, 'Next Christmas you might think of a subscription to the LHJ for me, or the NY! I need a constant flow of Americana to enrich my blood!'[20] Although she has left America, Plath makes it explicit that America and all things American remain necessary and important to her.

Early in her writing career, Plath addresses the guilt and ambivalence of the traveller who has left her native ground, yet desires, but also fears, returning. In the 1956 poem 'Dream with Clam-Diggers', a woman dreams that she has returned to her 'early sea-town home',[21] and walks in her 'shabby travel garb' to the water. When she reaches the ocean, 'Clam-diggers' rise from 'the dark water at her offense'. It is not clear until the subsequent lines who has committed the 'offense', or who feels offended: the woman or the clam-diggers. Soon we learn that the woman is the guilty party, and that her crime was to leave in the first place. The clam-diggers are 'Grim as gargoyles from years spent squat-ting at the sea's border' and waiting patiently 'To trap this wayward girl' on her return. 'Now with stake and pitchfork they advance, flint eyes fixed on murder'.[22] Though darkly comic, the poem becomes a night-mare. The heroine's predicament, her guilt and fear that she will be staked like a witch and punished by death for leaving, is serious. The poem explores the initial sense of danger some feel when departing from a familiar landscape into a foreign one, the fear that that original landscape may be unable to accommodate them again, or worse yet, may become positively hostile upon their return. Also, the poem suggests the possibility – recognised first in the unconscious, through the speaker's dream – that home is a threat before we ever leave it. Indeed, that is why we must go.

Plath Our Compatriot

An acquaintance who saw Plath during that last, difficult month of her life writes of her 'bright smile and eager American expression',[23] attempting to dispel any apprehensions Plath's mother may have had. The premise here is that as long as Plath remains intrinsically American, she will be fine. To use Plath's own words, 'health' will not be 'a country far away'[24] if that country can be carried within Plath herself. Nor then will the 'health' of those who surround Plath be threatened. E. J. Hobsbawm invokes the health metaphor (as Plath does) to argue that

> The anguish and disorientation which finds expression in this hunger to belong, and hence in the 'politics of identity' – not necessarily national identity – is no more a moving force of history than the hunger for 'law and order' which is an equally understandable response to another aspect of social disorganization. Both are symptoms of sickness rather than diagnoses, let alone therapy.[25]

Plath herself has been fought over by those who wish to own a piece of her and hence themselves 'belong'. In an attempt to possess Sylvia Plath by partaking in her nationality, Jeni Couzyn gives *The Bloodaxe Book of Contemporary Women Poets* the subtitle *Eleven British Writers*. Although Plath is no 'pure Mayflower dropping, somebody *English*',[26] Couzyn provides no rationale for authorial selection, and no explanation of what might constitute national identity. This is noteworthy given Couzyn's own multi-national circumstances. She 'was born in South Africa ... became a Canadian citizen' and 'now lives in London'.[27] Claims that Plath is English or American reveal more about the claimant's own denial of the complexity of nationality than they do about Plath's.

Janet Malcolm's *The Silent Woman* questions 'the legitimacy of the biographical enterprise', arguing that biography reveals more about the biographer than her subject. Certainly critics and biographers confirm Malcolm's argument by the ways in which they gloss over Plath's own nationality. Indeed, Malcolm is rare in acknowledging the influence of Plath's 'Americanness', and the Americanness of those who write about Plath – herself and Anne Stevenson included.[28] Stan Smith is unique in counting Plath as one of those writers, like Ezra Pound or T. S. Eliot, who is 'the outsider, the American expatriot half-assimilated to the English tradition, who registers its strains most forcefully'.[29] Anne Stevenson, herself American-born and educated, colludes in *Bitter Fame* with Jane Baltzell's sense of

> Sylvia's bumptious insensitivity to the kind of behavior the British found ridiculous. Self-conscious about any appearance of naiveté or gushiness, Jane was embarrassed when Sylvia rode up to a bobby to ask in her twangy American accent for directions to 'somewhere really picturesque and collegiate' in which to eat.[30]

The cattiness of this attack on Plath may reflect a sort of displacement through which Baltzell and Stevenson attempt to offload their own anxieties about class and nationality. It is as if they want Plath to carry the weight of their own remembered, and then denied, experiences of uncertainty and awkwardness as young American women newly arrived in England. There is a value judgement in these references to belonging, and it is a judgement that Plath herself addresses (though with more ambivalence and complexity). The judgement is this: to belong is a good and comforting thing, an achievement of sorts, while to be excluded is painful and bad, and reflects poorly on the person who is not a part of things. Stevenson describes Dido Merwin as possessing 'an innate sense of belonging (something Sylvia never had)'.[31] The parentheses here do not play down the comment they contain, or mark it off as less important than the rest of the sentence. If we put aside the disconcerting presumption of 'knowing' what Plath thought or felt and then criticising her personally on that basis, what seems to be at stake in these remarks is the need of their authors to belong. Ironically, Plath's own work strips away any possibility of the 'innate sense of belonging' that Stevenson implicitly claims for herself and Merwin.

Baltzell's 'embarrassment' by Plath's so-called 'bumptious insensitivity' – a mortification with which Stevenson appears to sympathise –

does not simply stem from an unacknowledged anxiety about foreignness and a concomitant wish to belong. Class and femininity also play strong parts in occasioning their disapproval. Indecorousness, lack of restraint, forwardness, vulgarity, little reticence – these are what Stevenson and Baltzell describe in the incident where Plath asks the policeman to recommend that '"picturesque"' restaurant. Lucas Myers describes Plath as 'effusive', and admits frankly that she evoked his 'puritanical disapproval', reminding him of 'the demanding style of some American women of the period'.[32] In a poem about Plath entitled 'The Heroine', Peter Davison declares that she was

> the meanest spirit to claim a martyrdom
> since sainthood ended. What a cunning braggart
> she was, a frailty who pictured herself
> as a rider of skis, of waves, of men.[33]

Effusive but demanding. Mean but saintly. Cunning but frail. These oppositions are noteworthy because they concern paradoxical economies of femininity and material goods. What makes these men – and women – uncomfortable is a woman who seems innocent and unthreatening, giving or helpless one moment, but is boastful, manipulative, dominant, selfish or mean, the next.

Some of the oddest contradictions in *Bitter Fame* occur when questions of femininity coincide with those of nationality. English women, Stevenson suggests again and again, just don't behave that way; they don't think that way. Plath's bad example of American femininity is tacitly contrasted with the sophistication, avoidance of *gaucherie*, and indifference to consumer goods incarnated in English women such as Dido Merwin and Olwyn Hughes. Writing about Plath's 1961 short story 'Day of Success', Stevenson declares:

> One imagines that even in 1961 its catch-your-man-and-be-happy philosophy would have sounded naive. But Sylvia's attitude *was* naive; she really *did* imagine that any 'real' man would find it a drag to come home to diapers and cod-liver oil instead of the Japanese silks and French perfume of the story.[34]

Plath is convicted here of subscribing to outmoded fantasies of feminine behaviour (though even at the beginning of the twenty-first century, women's magazines are littered with short stories that purvey the 'catch-your-man-and-be-happy philosophy' Stevenson here dismisses). Stevenson also chides Plath for flouting the very feminine ideals that she criticises her for believing in elsewhere. 'While exiled in Devon', Stevenson writes, 'she had let her looks go: she was thin after her miserable summer and wore clothes that she had saved from before her pregnancies'.[35] The word slut, in its oldest sense, refers to a slovenly woman, and that is what Stevenson only just stops short of calling Plath here. What was Plath to do? Dress in Japanese silks and be mocked for it, or in old clothes, having 'let her looks go', and be condemned for that? These blatant inconsistencies reflect the irreconcilable expectations that Plath's culture had for women, and their persistence into our own time, of which Anne Stevenson is part. Stevenson's comments reveal little, if anything, about Sylvia Plath herself.

By contrast, Ted Hughes's 1995 remarks about Plath's Americanness are atypical of the ways she is customarily discussed. Underpinning them is a frankness about the fact that Plath's Americanness is a function of his own needs and perceptions. 'To me, of course', Hughes explains, 'she was not only herself: she was America and American literature in person'. He pushes the point further: 'When I met Sylvia, I also met her library, and the whole wave hit me. I began to devour everything American'.[36] More usually in commentary about Plath's nationality, Plath is either convicted of being American, as she is by Stevenson, or unconvincingly appropriated as English, as she is by Couzyn. Such assumptions of perfectly discrete categories of literature and nationality are criticised by Ronald Warwick. Warwick argues against the post colonialist enterprise which 'assumes that ... English literature can be divided into three parts: English, American and Post-colonial'.[37] Plath's writing is not one or another of these things, but all at once.

Janet Malcolm remarks that 'How the child, "plump and golden in America," became the woman, thin and white in Europe ... remains an enigma of literary history'.[38] She emphasises with some force the impact of Plath's nationality, and appears to acknowledge the fact that Englishness and Americanness are not separate, stable entities. Her use of scare quotes around George Steiner's phrase 'plump and golden in America' signals an awareness of its positioning within the available rhetorical styles through which we constitute our identities – national and otherwise. Benedict Anderson writes: 'Communities are to be distinguished, not by their falsity/genuineness, but by the style in which they are imagined'.[39] Plath's writing makes a similar argument, as we see in her use of what might be read and dismissed as stereotypes, but are also *styles* of speaking and imagining (for instance in those gushy epistolary comments about the quaintness of Cherbourg). Such comments are more productively seen as vocabularies and stances that align Plath's writing with variously 'English' or 'American' modes of expression and their attached cultural assumptions. In *The Bell Jar* American terms such as 'cotton candy'[40] and ' "I would like a bite to eat" '[41] coexist with very English usage, for instance, 'party-frocks',[42] ' "You ought to read French and German" '[43] or 'I just had to go to the toilet'.[44] In her 1963 account of her American education, the journalistic 'America! America!', Plath signals her adult residence in England with the phrase 'bins of dustmen',[45] foregoing what would be the American equivalent (to translate crudely, 'trashcans of garbage men').

Ambivalence characterises Plath's feelings about both of the two countries in which she lived. This is in keeping with her status of not belonging, and with her neither entirely American nor purely English accent. She oscillates between Anglophilia and Anglophobia. Perhaps if Plath had not been so young when she first arrived in England, she would not have been so easily imprinted with its culture and accent, or so quick to adopt her voice and language to a new country. In the autumn of 1955, having just arrived in Cambridge, 'the most beautiful spot in the world', Plath writes to her mother as if she is fully immersed in the idealised pastoral fantasy of a green and pleasant land. It is a land where 'large black rooks (ravens) fly over quaint red-tiled rooftops with their chimney pots'.[46] Plath speaks 'English', here translating 'rooks' into a subordinated American that rests within the parentheses. Moreover, the translation is wrong; a raven is not equivalent to a rook, though both are part of the crow family. Rooks are not found in North America, though ravens are.[47] Rather touchingly, the first three poems of the *Collected Poems*,[48] written early in 1956, all use the word rook. It is as if Plath delights in wielding what she thinks of as her newly English vocabulary – a new toy. Like most speakers of a new language who visit a foreign country for the first time, she does not quite get it right.[49] Nonetheless, Plath dots the poems of 1956 and 1957 with a usage that she assumes her mother does not know,[50] and even puts a rook in the title of a poem.[51] In turn, when Plath describes English birds from the point of view of an American outsider narrating a piece of travel journalism, she speaks 'American' and uses the word raven. Ravens are not abundant in Great Britain.[52] In 'Leaves from a Cambridge Notebook' Plath refers to 'those ubiquitous large black ravens ... muttering perhaps ... "Nevermore" '.[53] Given the context and subject matter of 'Leaves from a Cambridge Notebook', it is fitting that Plath invokes

Edgar Allan Poe, who so loved to play at being English. As a counter-point to Plath's games with rooks and ravens, Ted Hughes reasserts a usage that is *equally* American and English, and uses it correctly, four-teen years later, in *Crow*.

Plath's awe of England lasts for about a day. Not long after she arrives, what at first enchants her, what she tries hard to make her own, becomes irritating. She refers for instance to Cambridge University's 'grotesque Victorian dons'.[54] A piece of Plath's journalism from 1956, 'Poppy Day At Cambridge', is written from the perspective of someone who is firmly, gladly foreign. The narrator is as struck by the strange English custom of marking the anniversary of Armistice Day with a 'poppy for the buttonhole' as she is by their unappetising food. She sarcastically describes the 'hedonistic delight of … cold pork pie, stewed prunes, and custard sauce',[55] paying homage to the sorry dinner served to the female scholars in *A Room of One's Own*. The visual strangeness and foreignness of the poppy day custom, and of English history and culture, were to resurface in a poem that Plath wrote six years later, 'Poppies in October', composed on 27 October 1962. The speaker observes 'the woman in the ambulance / Whose red heart blooms through her coat so astoundingly'.[56]

In her 1956 poem[57] 'Landowners', Plath regards with a different eye the unfamiliarity that she depicted one year earlier as 'quaint' in that letter to her mother about 'red-tiled rooftops with their chimney pots'.[58] Something more jaded, yet still American in perspective, displaces the simplistic American tourist view of Englishness: a 'leaden perspective / Of identical gray brick houses' with 'orange roof-tiles' and 'chimney pots'. The row of English terraced houses is a 'Corridor of inane repli-cas' depleted of imaginative and physical space. However, in the poem's last two lines, the speaker reaches yet another conclusion. Because it refuses the extremes of gushing enchantment or cynical recoil, it is a more mature, complex conclusion at that. The speaker comes to the realisation that to live 'on one-land tract', or be rooted in any one place, is a sort of death. To be alive is to reject any such allegiance and em-brace 'wayfarings'.[59]

If 'Landowners' is to be believed, the wayfarer can have no one national identity, allegiance, or notion of acceptable architecture. None-theless, England does not improve over time for the narrator of 'Home Thoughts from London', an unpublished poem that Plath probably wrote late in 1960. Again the English cityscape, this time of London instead of Cambridge, is found wanting. Each of the poem's eight stanzas offers an image of a London in which everything is weak and watered down and flavourless. Chestnuts 'taste mild as oatmeal'. The 'parachute silks' of clouds 'sag'. The weather itself is found wanting, in comparison to the weather on the east coast of America: 'No rampant hurricanes named after women / Have shaken our pulses up. The weather's tender // And weepy as an ageing maiden aunt'. The speaker feels 'smothered by a fuzzed gentility'. She concludes, in stark contrast to the ending of the earlier 'Landowners', that 'we're strangers here'.[60]

From the start, Plath's love affair with England was necessarily complicated and ambivalent. On 7 November 1955, only a month and a half after arriving there, she describes herself and an American friend as 'enthusiastic, demonstrative, and perhaps trusting and credulous to the point of naïveté. A strong contrast to the Englishmen, who have a kind of brittle, formal rigidity and, many of them, a calculated sophisticate pose'.[61] A year and a half later, in a section omitted from a 15 March 1957 letter published in *Letters Home*, Plath's epistolary reverence for England has evaporated further:

> How I despise the dead ideas, the dead blood, the dead dead aristocratic inbreds. England is dying so fast it is unbeliev-able: but I gather, from reading Blake & D. H. Lawrence, the deadness has been growing for a long time. Everything is frozen, stratified. The 'social security' system is a laugh: doctors are striking to get off it & charging $3 for any visit now – even a nosedrop prescription. & tales of operations & mistakes are gory & numerous.[62]

Writing in a similar vein three months later, Plath describes Cambridge as a 'mean, mealy-mouthed literary world'.[63]

Likewise Plath's feelings about America vacillate. Late in 1959, she says of England in her journals: 'I could write a novel there. ... Without this commercial American superego. My tempo is British'.[64] In an unpublished letter of 22 July 1961 to her brother and his wife, Plath writes: 'Our American way of life is efficient, comfortable, but makes us soft, dependent upon mechanics, quite inflexible in our mode of living – most of us'.[65] A few years earlier, in 1956, she expressed a yearning for the luxuries that are the products of the commercialism she was later to shun verbally, if not in her everyday life. She writes: '(I'll be so happy to have an American kitchen ... with orange juice and egg beater and all my lovely supplies for light cookies and cakes!)'[66] Plath uses 'style' here to set up a rhetorical identification with her narratee/ mother through a celebratory praise of American domestic appliances.

The confiding parentheses heighten the effect, suggesting that Plath and her mother are involved in a shared conspiracy that must privately rest between the two of them. Plath had reassured her mother only a few months earlier with the words, 'I am happier every day to be an American! For all the golden "atmosphere" of England, there is an oppressive ugliness about even the upper-middle-class homes, an ancient, threadbare dirtiness which at first shocked me'.[67] While Plath is critical of American commercialism, she is not satisfied with what some might regard as its opposite: English shabbiness. She moves between dissociation and identification with Americanness. Her sense of herself as less foreign than a tourist suggests that she assumes a sort of hierarchy of alienation (and is also an instance when Plath herself asserts, or rhetorically manufactures, her own status as belonging). Later in 1956, speaking as a we who constructs other Americans as different, Plath is confident that she and Hughes can provide her visiting brother with 'the atmosphere as we know it, not as the tourists find it'.[68]

Jacqueline Rose asserts that 'Only at one point, in 1956, does America appear unequivocally positive for Plath, ... as the land that is big enough for Hughes ... and an escape from the horror of Suez'.[69] If, for a moment, we want to play the crude game of judging things as 'positive' or 'negative', we can find many 'positive' references to America, often (and usually rather amusingly) made at the expense of England. In an unpublished 1956 letter to her mother, Plath writes:

> Here, the people have such an absurd inertia. They go around dying with flu and just plodding on and on. Perhaps the most shocking indication of their neglect is evident in their teeth. Almost every single British boy I know has his whole appearance ruined by the absence of several important front teeth; it is horrible, they evidently just let them rot in the mouth, and don't seem to mind the gaps, like Emily Hahn said. I feel like a total martyr. I am sick of ... constantly shivering & biking in siberian[70] winds.[71]

Plath returns to the horror of British teeth in another unpublished 1956 letter, this time to her brother. She writes: '... it's simply scandalous neglect, which is all over England: they let things decay, and then grudgingly try to repair or get rid of them. How I miss our American hygiene, preventative and wise'.[72]

The excerpted letters for the early months of 1960 in *Letters Home* do not come close to conveying the seriousness (and inadvertent humour) of Plath's interest in and admiration for American appliances and domestic arrangements. Letter after letter in the Lilly Library testifies to Plath's immersion in schemes for papering, painting and furnishing her London flat in preparation for the birth of her first baby. Plath dedicates herself to filling her home with American-style appliances, a big bed, and bathroom tiles.[73] In a typed letter to her mother, Plath uses ink to sketch a floor plan of her new apartment.[74] Tremendously excited and wanting to share her plans, she sends her mother a wallpaper specimen, carefully labelling it in blue ink, 'Bedroom paper' (the paper is white, and covered in roses and buds of red and pink, as well as mossy green leaves).[75] Ever careful to get the fullest value of stationery and postage, Plath types a two-page letter to her mother, brother and Sappho the cat on the back of samples of her 'waterproof and very cheerful' kitchen paper.[76] (The kitchen paper is printed with old-fashioned bicycles, carriages, carts, passenger balloons, early automobiles, lamp-posts and table lamps.) The recurring note in the passages that do not appear in *Letters Home* is of Plath's despair that she will not 'be able to get the American size'[77] refrigerator, and then her excitement when she does. In a letter of 2 February 1960, Plath writes: 'My pride and joy arrives Thursday: a beautiful refrigerator ... Most of the fridges here are diminutive ... a freezer just big enough for icecubes. Women here need a sales talk to buy one – most of them just use "cold-cupboards", the coldest windowsill or closet!'[78]

We have seen that Plath often writes about America, and especially about American medicine and consumer goods, in a way that is 'unequivocally positive' (just as we have seen her severely criticise America). It is worth asking, then, why a critic of Jacqueline Rose's subtlety would assert that Plath wholly approves of America 'only at one point'. For one thing, Rose can admit Plath's Americanness only in the context of a seemingly more important project of criticising other political evils. By alluding to Plath's repudiation of Britain's colonialist involvement in Suez, and linking this to Plath's consequent (if fleeting) desire to embrace America, Rose constructs Plath as right-thinking. Rose's omission of Plath's 'positive' published 1956 reference to American kitchen appliances might be explained by a need to read Plath as 'serious', to see her political commitment as absolute. It is clear from Rose's book that she worked carefully in the Plath archives, and was likely to have seen the unpublished examples of Plath's 'positive' comments about American dentistry and refrigerators that I quoted above. It may be that Plath's approbation of America concentrates on matters that seem trivial to Rose, matters not sufficiently serious and political and therefore not worthy of notice. Yet to Plath, refrigerators and wallpaper were of great importance. Domestic arrangements took up a great deal of space in her writing, as they did in her life. It may also be that in each of the unpublished 'positive' passages, Plath's admiration for America is tied up with a momentary contempt for England that Rose does not wish to recognise. Rose herself is English, and one wonders whether the unconscious forces of the patriotism that none of us can ever entirely escape are working upon her. Moreover, Rose appears to value Plath and her work; perhaps she does not want to be excluded from 'Plath' through a difference of nationality, needing what she admires to be what she herself is. Plath is either self or not self. She is 'one of us' for her American family and friends, just as she is for the multi-national Jeni Couzyn and English Jacqueline Rose. Or she is 'one of them', as she is for Anne Stevenson.

Where Are We?

There is a moment in *The Bell Jar* that mirrors the indeterminacy of midatlanticism. Esther explains to her soon-to-be ex-boyfriend: ' "… I could never settle down in either the country *or* the city. … If neurotic is wanting two mutually exclusive things at one and the same time, then I'm neurotic as hell. I'll be flying back and forth between one mutually exclusive thing and another for the rest of my days." '[79] Nicole Ward Jouve had 'no youth in England', and no 'adulthood in France'.[80] Plath's position is similarly rootless. Emigration and expatriation disrupted her 'collective cultural identity'.[81] This is very like what Stan Smith describes as T. S. Eliot's self-conscious 'deracination'. Smith quotes a letter from Eliot to Sir Herbert Read:

> Some day I want to write an essay about the point of view of an American who wasn't an American, because he was born in the South and went to school in New England as a small boy with a nigger drawl, but who wasn't a southerner in the South because his people were northerners in a border state and looked down on all southerners and Virginians, and who so was never anything anywhere and who therefore felt himself to be more a Frenchman than an American and more an Englishman than a Frenchman and yet felt that the USA up to a hundred years ago was a family extension.[82]

While Plath is technically American, there are temporal and cultural gaps in her experience of her native country that are filled by her adult life in England, a life that she cannot be expected to have experienced untouched. Yet it must be said that there is an arrogance and assumption of privilege in the ability to 'puddle-jump'. As Aijaz Ahmad observes, 'the entire logic of the kind of cultural "hybridity" that Bhabha celebrates presumes the intermingling of Europe and non-Europe in a context already determined by advanced capital, in the aftermath of colonialism'.[83]

'Cultural hybridity' is central to *The Bell Jar*, which questions any notion that there can ever be a perfectly enclosed place. In Plath's writing, geographical location can never be severed from cultural identity. In an evocation of inauthenticity that could almost be an echo of T. S. Eliot's letter, Esther describes a movie she has seen:

> It starred a nice blonde girl who looked like June Allyson but was really somebody else, and a sexy black-haired girl who looked like Elizabeth Taylor but was also somebody else ... Everybody in a technicolour movie seems to feel obliged to wear a lurid new costume in each new scene ... with a lot of very green trees or very yellow wheat or very blue ocean rolling away for miles.[84]

Plath is part of a continuum of writers who see American culture as a patchwork quilt composed of the derivative and the imitative, of the never pure. Esther says of her grandfather: 'He taught me how to eat avocados by melting grape jelly and French dressing together in a saucepan and filling the cup of the pear with the garnet sauce. I felt homesick for that sauce'.[85] This food is a literalised melting pot. The American grape jelly combines with the French dressing to fill the English-termed 'pear' for which Esther is homesick.

'Daddy', that most anthologised of poems, is preoccupied with cultural hybridity. The poem has been read as Plath's man-hating vengeance against her father and Ted Hughes.[86] Plath's right to appropriate the experiences of Holocaust victims as literary material has been questioned.[87] Recognising the complex nature of Plath's own national identity, Peter Orr makes one of the most astute critiques of the poem in his October 1962 interview with her. A 'real American', he remarks, 'could not have written with the same feeling and grasp with which you have written ... because it doesn't mean so much, these names do not I think mean so much on the other side of the Atlantic, do they?'[88]

'Daddy' explores the status of any national identity as contingent and multiple. One of the ways it does this is to invoke the Jews, who have been historically associated with wandering and homelessness, and have been persecuted for an ethnicity that threatens the supposed purity of others. Early drafts of the poem make even more explicit the narrator's fear of her own race and religion, and sense that she may be punished for her diluteness. The abandoned line, 'I am brown eyed & scared of you'[89] followed Daddy's 'Aryan eye bright blue' in Plath's first draft of the poem. This is the miscibility – signalled by the discarded brown eyes – that the speaker later embraces. Initially the speaker '... never could tell where you / Put your foot, your root'. To unstick her tongue and regain her voice, the speaker tells us, 'I began to talk like a Jew', and declares, 'I may be a bit of a Jew'.[90] In the face of no sure nationality, the sense that she possesses no native tongue, the speaker's strategy is to adopt different voices that are not entirely, if they are at all, her own. In a moment of seemingly wilful deracination, the speaker pulls up roots to assert her autonomy.

Daddy himself is in the end a 'bastard', of uncertain identity and parentage. He is not simply German. He is also the American continent itself, and the geography in the poem is important. Daddy's American-spelled 'gray toe' is 'Big as a Frisco seal': an image of the hugeness of Daddy himself, coloured and shaped like the animal in one of Plath's visual similes, and of his swollen toe. Through his association with San Francisco, and his likening to its seals, Daddy stretches from the north coast of California where his toe bathes in the Pacific, to the easternmost tip of Cape Cod or 'Nauset', where his head lies 'in the Freakish Atlantic'.[91] Given the poem's irony about the cross-breeding of identity, it is difficult to resist seeing this picture of Daddy's gray largeness, capped by that head in the Atlantic, as an image also of the Statue of Liberty, that great symbol of America as a melting pot. The poem systematically destroys any pretence that ethnicity can ever be uncomplicated or verifiable. The tourist-brochure line, 'The snows of the Tyrol, the clear beer of Vienna', is unravelled by the line that follows it: the revelation that the snow and beer 'Are not very pure or true'.[92] In 'Daddy', language and nationality, like Daddy himself, can only be an assemblage of disparate parts, of associations and substitutions that never quite add up to a whole; 'Daddy' is a working out of linguistic and national metonymy.

What makes 'Daddy' such a compelling piece of writing is its disconcerting sexiness; its discomfiting juxtaposition of a serious political project with the language and rhythms of the nursery rhyme. If we were to make these disturbing and exciting tensions literal, we might visualise the speaker as a woman dressed in stiletto heels and a baby-doll nightgown, who speaks with passion and intelligence about sex and politics, even as she engages in sexual and political acts. Such a package is taboo, and I think helps to explain the extreme reactions of recoil or adoration for the poem, neither camp pausing to analyse how the poem works, or what it is trying to say. Uncomfortably (especially for feminist readers who want to find a Sylvia Plath who is always politically correct), the poem's very grown-up irony about sexual politics is mixed with cradle talk. This mix-up is nicely signalled by the proliferation of 'oo' sounds that rhyme in the poem (do, shoe, Achoo, you, blue, Ach du, two, gobbledygoo, through, who, glue). It is a sound that is both babyish, and associated with erotic excitement. The poem begins with its repetitive infant babble of 'You do not do, you do not do / Any more, black shoe',[93] simultaneously calling up James Joyce and Mother Goose, the beginnings of *A Portrait of the Artist as a Young Man* and 'The Old Woman Who Lived in a Shoe'.

The line 'Every woman adores a Fascist'[94] is not endorsed by the poem, as many readers have assumed. Rather, it mocks such a stance, inviting the reader to take issue with a stereotypical comment of the sort a rapist might utter (justifying his action along the lines of 'She asked for it'). If we recall the association between Daddy and the female Statue of Liberty, Daddy's gender, his masculinity and patriarchal authority, is rendered unstable. Remember that Daddy is repeatedly likened to a vampire in the poem: 'If I've killed one man, I've killed two—— / The vampire who said he was you / And drank my blood for a year'.[95] Vampires make their victims what they themselves are. Hence, like gender and nationality, the roles of aggressor and quarry become mercurial in the poem; the speaker is not just drained of blood, is not just killed or bitten, but commits these acts herself. Every character in 'Daddy' is a vampire, and thus filled with other people's blood, so that no identity is left untainted. Every character is 'other', part of someone else in ways that cannot be reliably measured, or even entirely known.

It is this otherness, and the fear of finding it in one's self, that Plath turns to again and again. She repeatedly concerns herself with that tendency to construct somebody else as alien, as outside and foreign, even in, or especially in, the so-called melting pot of America. In *The Bell Jar* Esther is horrified by the brutal treatment of the Rosenbergs, and especially by the way they are regarded as marginal, as 'such people'.[96] As Pat Macpherson argues, Plath's heroine sees that 'The Rosenbergs were scapegoated as spies, Communists, traitors in our midst, with their Jewishness and Ethel Rosenberg's strong womanhood seen as part of the Alien nature of this Enemy Within'.[97] Yet Esther is capable of scapegoating other identities. Humiliated and powerless in the mental hospital, she abuses the one person whom she recognises as less powerful than herself: she commands a black kitchen worker as if he were a servant, and then kicks him, mimicking the doctor's attitude towards Mrs Tomolillo. We meet Mrs Tomolillo earlier in the text, when she undergoes an appalling medicalised childbirth during which she is treated like an animal by the largely male medical staff. The kitchen worker caricature resembles a character from one of the technicolor films Esther so dislikes (yet watches): '"Oh Miz, oh Miz ... You shouldn't of done that, you shouldn't, you reely shouldn't"'.[98] Mary Ellmann rightly says of *The Bell Jar*, 'The American Girl is the topic. Her growing up suburban, with saddle shoes and "fifteen years of straight A's"'.[99] If the American Girl is *The Bell Jar*'s topic, exposing her as a dangerous fiction is at the top of its agenda. Plath uses the novel to acknowledge the cultural heterogeneity of an America that, despite its myth of itself as a 'melting pot', represses and debases this very diversity.

Plath's 1963 story 'Snow Blitz', like *The Bell Jar*, is not complicit with preconceived ideas about culture and nationality, but rather refuses to allow the reader to naturalise them, or take them for granted. 'Snow Blitz' rests somewhere between fiction and journalism. The narrator is an amused and bewildered American woman struggling to survive a cold London winter. For the most part, she regards the English as another species. From the first sentence it is clear that she is an alien, and that the implied reader, like her, is non-English: 'In London, the day after Christmas (Boxing Day) – it began to snow: my first snow in England'.[100] The implied reader is constructed as unknowing and American, in need of a definition of the very English term Boxing Day. The narrator herself speaks 'American'. The English that she translates and subordinates to the parentheses is a second language. Even illness is seen as foreign, and therefore must be defined, so that 'flu is 'that British alternation of fever and chills for which my doctor offered no relief or cure'.[101] The story's humour turns on the narrator's stereotypical assumption that the English are backward in their use of technology, that they can no more cope with viruses than frozen pipes. The narrative voice sustains itself through a conviction of its own difference. She survives by emphasising her distance from these events, and a consequent illusion that her foreignness renders her immune to the situation. Contradictorily, she survives also by taking on and gently mocking a readily available English persona of brisk blitz-courage:

'Dress up warm, lots of tea and bravery'. The English strategy does not displace, but must coexist with, the narrator's Americanness, which resurfaces in the story's concluding sentences, playing on a very American colloquialism: 'I brew waterless tea … If the gas, too, is not kaput'.[102]

Plath's 1962 story 'Mothers' also destabilises stereotypes. (The story may offer us another glimpse of Esther Greenwood, years after the events of *The Bell Jar*.) The American heroine living in a Devon village cannot 'get used to people opening the door and calling in without ringing first'.[103] Esther shuns a behaviour one would presume to be familiar and 'American' by virtue of its informality, expressing a self-reserved and thereby 'English' thirst for privacy. Yet this difference can as easily be between city and village ways as between English and American habits. Or it may simply be indicative of the way people behaved in Britain in the 1950s and 1960s. The story focuses on Esther's inability to read the codes of village life. Esther wonders: 'If Mrs Nolan, an Englishwoman by her looks and accent, and a pub-keeper's wife as well, felt herself a stranger in Devon after six years, what hope had Esther, an American, of infiltrating that rooted society ever at all?'[104] Notably, Plath inserts 'an American', by hand, in one of the final typescripts of 'Mothers',[105] thereby indicating the importance of her heroine's nationality and foreignness to the story. Despite the masquerade of accent, Mrs Nolan remains non-U, not English. It transpires that Mrs Nolan is ostracised from the Mothers' Union on the grounds that she is divorced. Despite her 'looks and accent', Mrs Nolan's foreignness contributes to her alienation, and reinforces Esther's own. The possible Irishness of Mrs Nolan's name does not signify for Esther. Nor does the implication of her working-class status as a pub-keeper's wife, which Esther regards as an attribute. Whatever its cause, the social cruelty shown towards Mrs Nolan causes Esther to reject the Mothers' Union and embrace her own difference from parochial Englishness (an ending that is in keeping with the patness that too often creeps into the story).

'Mothers' speaks about, and from, a position of national, local and social difference. Another set of tensions may also be at work in the story. The women's magazine genre with which Plath is trying to comply is at odds with the more serious political, linguistic, and aesthetic preoccupations that nonetheless erupt in it. Plath herself says of a different (but similarly strained) piece of her writing, the 1959 poem 'Watercolor of Grantchester Meadows': '"Wrote a Grantchester poem of pure description … a fury of frustration. Some inhibition keeping me from writing what I really feel"'.[106] Such inhibition may stem from a discomfort with unfamiliar material and language, whether English landscape or the social intricacies of English village life. In the poem, the delicacy of a conventional watercolour is subverted; the landscape is punctured by a vision that refuses to accept it as the clichéd English chocolate box, or 'country on a nursery plate' that foreigners are supposed to see. Here, only those who don't belong can see the landscape's darker subtext, the predators and prey hiding in the seemingly benign meadows. Those who do belong are 'unaware'.[107]

The 1960 poem 'Leaving Early' dramatises alienation and debunks the idea that anyone can naturally belong anywhere. To make her case that the poem is about lesbianism, Janice Markey attempts to fix the genders of the poem's speaker, and her or his sexual partner, as female,[108] while Jacqueline Rose unquestioningly assumes the speaker is male.[109] However, there is nothing in the poem to tell us categorically whether the narrator is a man or a woman. To stabilise the genders of Plath's speakers is to mask Plath's important project of questioning sexual identity. Moreover, to do this is to neglect the coincidence of unspecified gender with ambiguous nationality. The poem's last three lines do not merely enact the speaker's disorientation (he or she has woken up in an unfamiliar place after a sexual encounter with a stranger). They also depict the confusion of an American in England:[110]

> ... Lady, what am I doing
> With a lung full of dust and a tongue of wood,
> Knee-deep in the cold and swamped by flowers?[111]

Through its mocking allusion to the English upper classes, the word 'Lady' aligns the speaker's sexual partner with Englishness. The numerous references in the poem to English things that seem strange also emphasise the speaker's status as alien, and associate the sexual partner with a derivative 'Englishness' that is constructed by cheap objects. For instance, there is the cold that anticipates 'Snow Blitz'; there are the flowers for which England is famous but which here are disparaged as decaying and too numerous; there are the 'Coronation goblets' and the 'toby jug'.

Most pressingly, the speaker's feeling of what Freud described as '"unheimlich" ... the opposite of what is familiar', is experienced through language itself, through an inability to communicate in the Lady's speech. This unfamiliarity resembles what Freud called the 'uncanny'. To experience the uncanny can also be to face 'the "double" ... the uncanny harbinger of death'.[112] This sense of the uncanny as a death warning provides a way of understanding the speaker's attention to the dead roses, and her/his annoyed comment that 'Now I'm stared at / By chrysanthemums ... // In the mirror their doubles back them up'.[113] The hopeless deadness of the cut flowers strikes the speaker dumb; hence the 'tongue of wood' that signifies death as well as speechlessness. The flowers are reminders that age and mortality are inevitable. Any attempt to hold them off through a depressing sexual encounter is hopeless.

'New Year on Dartmoor' (1962) also plays with the instability of national and linguistic identities. The poem can be read as the speaker's address to a young child. It describes the painful process of coming into language, of being drawn into a symbolic order that is not your own. The poem can also be read as a galling self-address through which the speaker plays out her own alienation from what seems to be her own language, but proves to be foreign. At the very least the speaker's position is one of identification with the child's isolation. Her perception of a 'glinting', 'clinking' 'falsetto' evokes not just the snowy scene and the glass-like crunch of frost beneath feet, but also characterises an American's first impression of an English accent. Like the 'slippiness' and 'slant' of the hill she tries to climb, these physical images work as social and linguistic codes. They provide an illusion of familiarity, but then shift in ways that maintain the speaker's or child's position as outside. This is a position mimicked by the physical separation of the words 'Only you' from the sentence which they begin and are thus not *entirely* part of. It is a sentence that plays out the aloneness imposed by incomprehension. The words that the narrator and narratee do 'know' are both American speech and baby talk: a metonymic 'elephant', 'wheel', and 'shoe' that are not merely physical means of transport, but also modes of communication.

In this poem the relation between American speech and English is, to use a crude analogy, like that of baby talk to the Queen's English (or what Kristeva described as the pre-Oedipal semiotic to the grammatically and culturally ordered symbolic[114]). In the poem, familiar words are inscribed within the established order of language: here, English. But they occupy a marginalised position. It is a position of oppression as well as potential subversion: the position of the American in England. Convention would assume America to be powerful and England oppressed, but Plath reverses the hierarchy. By doing so, she highlights the contingency of these positions, their shifts through different historical, political and cultural moments. It is an emphasis supported by the sense of England as first, as original.

Plath does not choose to set this poem of disorientation (disorientation that the reader is forced to share) in Bath or Stratford. Such cities are better known and typically 'English' to non-English readers than Dartmoor. Foreign as these tourist circuit towns are, Plath increases the sense of defamiliarisation by choosing an unexpected piece of England. Like Anthony Smith, Plath recognises that 'historical events and monuments of the homeland can be "naturalized"', or made so familiar you barely notice them. Discussing Stonehenge, Smith argues that 'so much part of the "British" (Briton) landscape did it become, that it became difficult to imagine that it was not natural and inherent in the British ethnic character, as much part of its original nature as the Wessex plains and hills around'.[115] Plath will not allow the speaker, or reader, of 'New Year on Dartmoor' to take landscape, nationality or language for granted. The poem concludes with the speaker's identification of herself with a larger body of outsiders, or tourists, who have 'come to look'. This opposes the still untainted child addressed by the speaker, who is 'too new' to wish for the world to be trapped within a 'glass hat'.[116] Such a world is imitated instead of experienced; commodified into one of those water-filled glass balls that you shake until snow floats over a miniature church or town.

Despite a title that seemingly directs the reader to a geographical location, and to France, 'Stars Over the Dordogne' (1961) also refuses to let the reader naturalise landscape. The poem strips the reader of any bearings, rendering ambiguous the place from which the speaker speaks, and the question of where her home is. Calmly, the speaker identifies with the stars that drop from the sky and land in places they have not chosen and do not know. Her home is as much a state of mind as a place. This is indicated by the odd syntax which begins the second of the poem's five octaves, or eight-line stanzas: 'Where I am at home'. At first the night sky at which the speaker gazes appears to be constructed by its differences from the night sky of her home: 'The Big Dipper is my only familiar. / I miss Orion and Cassiopeia's Chair'.[117] Initially, the reader is misled into an assumption that it is geographical difference which renders Orion and Cassiopeia's Chair invisible. However, these winter constellations can be seen at the same time of the year everywhere in the northern hemisphere.

The speaker admits that there may be other explanations for their absence. The stars may be 'present' but 'their disguise so bright' she misses them 'by looking too hard'. 'Perhaps it is the season that is not right', she thinks. Perhaps 'the sky here is no different, / And it is my eyes that have been sharpening themselves?'[118] The Big Dipper is the American name for what the English call The Plough. While it is a visual constant, something always accessible whether home or away, in the United States, England or the Dordogne, in this poem it is the only reliable signal of difference. Again, this difference is one of language. As in 'New Year on Dartmoor', this difference of language could be seen as one of American English versus English English. The speaker tells us: 'Such a luxury of stars would embarrass me. / The few I am used to are plain and durable'.[119] Again, Plath makes us rethink differences of national identity. The seemingly American speaker recoils against supposedly American excess, instead identifying with English sparseness.

What masquerades as being the same is, in subtle and slippery ways, different. While 'Stars Over the Dordogne' focuses on the situation of the American as alien, it positions any British reader unacquainted with the term Big Dipper as outside, and any American who uses such a vocabulary as inside. For reader and speaker alike, in and out are unstable entities that depend on not just where you are from, but where you are at any given moment. 'Stars Over the Dordogne' is in line with Philip Schlesinger's point that 'the making of identities is an active process that involves inclusion and exclusion. To be "us", we need those who are "not us". ... collective identities have a spatial referent'.[120] By destabilising the 'spatial referent' through the poem's confusing geographical landscape, Plath reveals just how fluid ' "us" ' and ' "not us" ' can be. The histories of France, England and America increase this destabilisation, for Plath opens the poem out into a larger European and world landscape. We can create an Anglo-American alliance that separates the two English-speaking countries from France. Or we can leave England isolated, and pair France with America (given the links between the American Revolution and French republicanism, and France's support for America during the War of Independence). Who is us? Who is not us?

'Blackberrying' and 'Finisterre' are emblematic of the movements between spatial referent, perspective and identity. Plath wrote the poems one after the other, six days apart, in September of 1961. So often in Plath's work, it is difficult to see the poems as separate entities, and more fitting to see them as parts of a larger whole. Ted Hughes pointed to the connections between Plath's poems, the way one spills into another. He intimated a way of reading that does not view the poems as discrete at all. Introducing Plath's poems for a BBC radio programme in 1971, Hughes described 'Insomniac' as 'an egg from "The Colossus" and "Ariel" is just cracking out of it'. 'A step or two further', he added, 'and "The Insomniac" becomes "The Surgeon at 2 a.m." '[121] Hughes noted that 'Blackberrying' and 'Finisterre' have 'the same outlook' – the Atlantic – 'Blackberrying' from an English 'cliff cove' and

'Finisterre' from the 'westernmost tip of Brittany'.[122] Robyn Marsack has argued that in 'Blackberrying' the line 'These hills are too green and sweet to have tasted salt'[123] captures the way 'foreigners … are struck by the way lush pastureland lies along the sea in Britain'.[124] The speaker of 'Finisterre' is told that the shells sold to tourists 'do not come from the Bay of the Dead down there, / But from another place, tropical and blue, / We have never been to'.[125] In 'Finisterre', what is sold as indigenous proves not to be native. In 'Blackberrying', what is actually authentic looks as if it does not belong. The effect of taking the two poems together is to compound such confusion and alienation.

'Stars Over the Dordogne' concludes with the speaker 'drink[ing] the small night chill like news of home'.[126] This is a far cry from the concluding lines of Plath's 1956 poem 'Monologue at 3 a.m.', in which the homesick speaker attempts to come to terms with her sense of herself as 'wrenched from / my one kingdom'.[127] Home is not a place for which the narrator of 'Stars Over the Dordogne' is nostalgic, but, rather, something that she associates with a chill.[128] It is a paradox similar to the last two lines of Plath's 1961 poem 'Tulips', where the speaker who lies in a hospital bed explains: 'The water I taste is warm and salt, like the sea, / And comes from a country far away as health'.[129] Of course warm salty water is not health-giving when consumed, but, unlike the position of the speaker in 'Stars Over the Dordogne', the narrator of 'Tulips' perceives the distant place with fondness. This paradox might be explained by the water's evocation, through its warmth and salinity, of both tears and amniotic fluid. The country far away is, in one sense, the mother herself; it is salubrious and longed for as well as pernicious and to be kept at a distance.

Alienation and Belonging in the Bee Poems

Plath's famous series of 'bee poems', written late in 1962, dramatises the position of the foreigner in England and grafts this tension between belonging and not belonging onto a battle concerning gender. Though she later changed her mind, the drafts of these poems show that Plath experimented with calling the series 'The Bee Keeper's Daybook'.[130] With this title, Plath signalled the domestic, everyday preoccupations of a speaker who notes her thoughts and activities in a feminine diary or journal of daily transactions. While the original title had disappeared by the end of composition, its ironic and (given the poems that follow it) ambivalent connotation of a Victorian lady's record of her daily tasks remains.

In the first of these poems, 'The Bee Meeting', written on 3 October, the speaker comments: 'In my sleeveless summery dress I have no protection, / And they are all gloved and covered, why did nobody tell me?'[131] This difference of dress is no simple impracticality that makes the speaker vulnerable to the stings of the bees. It signifies her breach of village decorum, her transgression against social codes that she has not quite learned, revealing her as not just different, but also as somehow indecent, too sexually available. The speaker is numbly horrified by the attempt of the English village women, headed by the sinisterly named 'secretary of bees', to make her 'one of them' by dressing her in the bee-keeping garb. The I/they opposition that she maintains until the poem's end marks her difference.

The poem's lines are long. There are numerous beats per line, and the lines vary in their metrical patterns. With one exception, the lines defy any impulse on the reader's part to systematise their form. The deviation of measure occurs in the line 'They will not smell my fear, my fear, my fear'.[132] This is the only line in the poem composed entirely of monosyllables. It is also the only line in the poem of perfect, orderly iambic pentameter. The formal differences between this line and the rest of the poem set the line apart, and invite the reader to pay special attention to it. The line expresses a wish or a prayer. It also expresses denial. Additionally, the line is a sort of talisman on the speaker's part. The reasoning goes, if I say it enough times, if I brainwash myself, I will make it true. Nonetheless, the speaker recognises, in the end, that the villagers have made some mark upon her: 'Whose is that long white box in the grove, what have they accomplished, why am I cold'.[133] The speaker's omission of question marks after these interrogatives transforms inquisitiveness into incontrovertibility, and the deadening statements leave an impression that she has been brainwashed. 'Cold' suggests a lack of emotional responsiveness. It also reflects the speaker's penetrability, for the clothes are not sufficient barriers to the outside. She is cold in spite of them, which symbolises her vulnerability to being assimilated by the villagers. The white box is both a prison for the bees, and a house (or coffin) for her in the centre of village life that will strip away her individuality.

Susan R. Van Dyne alludes to the 'considerable cross-fertilization'[134] of the bee poems in her excellent essay introducing Smith College's facsimile of the manuscripts for 'Stings'. Only the day after writing 'The Bee Meeting', Plath wrote 'The Arrival of the Bee Box'. Here, the box full of bees becomes Pandora's box and Bluebeard's chamber, a place of knowledge, danger and entrapment whose inhabitants, like the village women, the speaker both identifies with and repudiates. As if rethinking the penultimate line of 'The Bee Meeting', 'The Arrival of the Bee Box' concludes with a transient optimism and sense of possibility: 'The box is only temporary'.[135] The line – and the idea it expresses – is important. This importance is signalled by its break with the poem's own form, as well as the form of the four other bee poems. All five bee poems are written in five-line stanzas. The last line of 'The Arrival of the Bee Box' is the only line in any of the poems that appears in isolation, the only moment in the series where the five-line stanza form ruptures. Emphasis is the effect of this departure from form, which stresses the hopefulness of the statement that 'The box is only temporary'.

'Stings' was written three days after 'The Bee Meeting', on 6 October. Like its predecessors, 'Stings' considers the interplay between difference and assimilation. In the first stanza the speaker admits to some degree of belonging, signalled by her use of the first person plural:

> Our cheesecloth gauntlets neat and sweet,
> The throats of our wrists brave lilies.
> He and I
>
> Have a thousand clean cells between us

It is noteworthy that the only villager with whom the speaker identifies is male, and even this is not sustainable. She soon abandons the first person plural 'our' and returns to the opposition between the third person plural and first person singular. The disconnection is heightened by the break between the stanzas and their subject matter of separation. The speaker explicitly dissociates herself from the village women:

> I stand in a column
>
> Of winged, unmiraculous women,
> Honey-drudgers.
> I am no drudge
> Though for years I have eaten dust
> And dried plates with my dense hair.

It becomes increasingly clear in the bee poems that what the speaker both resists and desires is not just English village life, but the particular brand of femininity she must wear to gain access to it:

> Will they hate me,
> These women who only scurry,
> Whose news is the open cheery, the open clover?

Despite her assertions of disjunction, some of her 'strangeness', or foreignness, has been lost — 'evaporate[d]' from her 'dangerous skin'[136] — and the poem questions whether femininity and domesticity are culturally or biologically constructed, whether the dense hair is caused by or made for drying plates.

By the penultimate bee poem, 'The Swarm', the reader is forced into sharing the speaker's disorientation, and the battle between belonging and exclusion inhabits a larger European stage. 'The Swarm' may be difficult, or it may just be confused. We can only speculate as to why Ted Hughes omitted it from the English edition of *Ariel*. Perhaps he too had reservations about its coherence. The speaker tells us, 'Somebody is shooting at something in our town', and asks, 'Who are they shooting at?' The more American word town has displaced village, and the speaker begins by asserting her membership of it. But we do not know where this town is, who is hunted or hunting, or just where the speaker fits in relation to these parties. Shooting, or hunting, is part of the fabric of English country life (as emphasised by the 'pack-dog'[137] mentioned later in the poem). The bees' activities are likened to Napoleon's exile at Elba and his last battle at Waterloo. Identities circulate in the poem, which refuses any resolution of the speaker's relation to the battle she describes. The narrator variously identifies herself with Napoleon, or in resistance to him. Napoleon himself is at times the swarm of bees, and at other times the beekeeper who manages them. In 'The Swarm', the bee box is more explicitly a place of death, 'a new mausoleum' that evokes Napoleon's tomb. It is a tomb that the speaker feels she has miraculously escaped. '"They would have killed *me*"',[138] she remarks in a mixture of terror and amazed relief.

The final poem of the bee sequence is 'Wintering', written on 9 October. The poem revisits the earlier references to houses and boxes. This time a cellar represents the dangerous and forbidden, Bluebeard's chamber and Pandora's box. 'Wintering' situates itself firmly back in an English village, where the bees are fed 'Tate and Lyle' sugar (a very English brand name). Janice Markey reads 'Wintering' as a 'feminist' poem in which 'only the females survive', and argues that the poem concludes with them 'in ascendancy'. Markey's stress on what she describes as a 'woman imagining life in a world without men'[139] neglects the poem's anxieties about the consequences of separatism, and ignores its scepticism towards those who would wish for it. The speaker refers to 'The blunt, clumsy stumblers, the boors'. Syntactically, it is unclear whether this phrase describes the absent men or the female bees. The bee, or woman, is 'a bulb in the cold and too dumb to think'.[140] Once more we are faced with an important ambiguity: is she too stupid to think or unable to do so because thinking cannot take place without speaking?

In the poem's penultimate line, the narrator asks, 'What will they taste of, the Christmas roses?', and then remarks in the concluding line, 'The bees are flying. They taste the spring'. Having 'got rid of the men' the bees may 'taste the spring', but whether they will find pleasure in it or reproduce to 'enter another year'[141] remains questionable. The first draft of the poem explicitly signposts these large question marks over the bees' future. Here, the uncertainty about what the Christmas roses will 'taste of' is followed by the narrator's attempts to imagine precisely what this flavour may be. 'Snow water?' she offers. 'Corpses? ... / Impossible spring?' The narrator then finishes with a plea, a cry as if for the impossible: 'O God, let them taste of spring'.[142] It is in the first typed copy of 'Wintering' that the poem's final stanzas begin to take the shape we recognise in the published version.[143] The successive drafts of the poem allow those who see them to witness Plath's decision to dispense with certainty and direct reference. Instead, we watch as she progressively renders the grammatical structures ambiguous, while retaining from the first draft the refusal to advocate any simple celebration of separatism. Women cannot dispense with men, the poem implies in every draft, however difficult and dangerous or even hurtful such relationships can be.

Taken as a whole, as I think they must be, the bee poems express unease with the tendency of the English to assimilate foreigners, the ambivalence of foreigners about being assimilated, and the impulse for women to regulate those who do not belong. As the final poem in the series makes clear, the bee poems play out the tensions and attractions between separatism and assimilation.

The Foreigner Within

Plath's 1962 poem 'Cut' systematically destroys any illusion that there can be any separate or genuine American identity or place. Like the bee poems, 'Cut' reveals the blurred edges between friend and foe, between native and alien. Alicia Ostriker strikingly argues that Plath's voice is 'distinctly American' because it 'represent[s] life without falsification'. Playing on 'Lady Lazarus', Ostriker believes Plath 'do[es] it, technically, so it feels real'. For Ostriker, the 'brusque, business like, and bitchy' quality of the speech of the *Ariel* poems marks them as an 'American language'.[144] She cites 'Cut' as an example. Ostriker makes a rare intervention in Plath criticism by identifying the American vernacular that seeps into Plath's work. However, she is on dubious ground in her implication that to be American is somehow to be authentic. She ends up with a view of Plath that is culturally and nationally absolutist because it neglects the fact that these local idioms are not protected, that they are frequently interrupted, displaced by or forced to coexist with other languages. While Ostriker's argument is an important one, it elides not just Plath's perception of herself as hybrid, but also the thematic and linguistic cross-breeding of her poems.

We can witness this cross-breeding if we digress for a moment to the 1962 poem, 'The Tour'. 'Cut' was written on 24 October; 'The Tour' was written the following day. My point is that during the time Plath was writing those supposedly 'distinctly American' *Ariel* poems, we find her deliberately parodying an overdetermined *English* voice. 'The Tour' is composed of eight six-line sestets, each sestet with three pairs of perfect end rhymes that vary in sequence. It begins: 'O maiden aunt, you have come to call. / Do step into the hall!'[145] Towards the poem's end, the speaker tells her visitor:

> Toddle on home, before the weather's worse.
> Toddle on home, and don't trip on the nurse! –
>
> She may be bald, she may have no eyes,
> But auntie, she's awfully nice.
> She's pink, she's a born midwife –
> She can bring the dead to life
> With her wiggly fingers and for a very small fee.[146]

The humour and satire rest not just in the exaggerated English voice and the Gothic parody, but also in the mocking of the stereotype by which the stoical English find a virtue in anything and everything. Plath wrote 'The Tour' five days before saying to Peter Orr in an interview, 'I feel that gentility has a stranglehold. The neatness, the wonderful tidiness which is so evident everywhere in England is perhaps more dangerous than it would appear on the surface'.[147] It is just such gentility that Plath mimics in 'The Tour', and ruptures at the poem's end by breaking the strict formal rules that have governed the poem until its last line. This is set apart from the previous stanzas, a messy, stray line: 'Toddle on home to tea'.[148] It does not fit with 'neatness' or 'wonderful tidiness' into the careful order of the sestets that precede it, however perfectly it rhymes with, and puns, the line that goes before, 'Well I *hope* you've enjoyed it, auntie!'

The comic stoicism of 'Cut' appears to bleed into 'The Tour' when Plath writes it only a day later, though in 'Cut' the stoicism is more American in character. 'Cut' dramatises the transatlantic flux between Englishness and Americanness, though Anne Stevenson dismisses it as 'a playful poem' which 'commemorates a real event'.[149] The speaker gazes at her thumb, the top of which she has sliced off while cutting an onion. In 'America! America!' Plath expresses her conviction that Americans are educated 'Invisibly', breathing in 'a world of history that more or less began and ended with the Boston Tea Party – Pilgrims and Indians being, like the eohippus, prehistoric'.[150] In an early draft of 'Cut', Plath began the third stanza with the line 'Little white man', but crossed this out, substituting 'Little Pilgrim'.[151] Both versions pick up on the vocabulary through which American schoolchildren are taught about cowboys and Indians, and about the settling of America and the American Revolution; it is a vocabulary of pilgrims and Indians and scalping and turkeys. Speaking as if to an injured child, the speaker of 'Cut' describes and addresses the cut thumb, telling it that 'soldiers run' from the break in its skin. Moreover, these soldiers are 'Redcoats', and the speaker asks 'Whose side'[152] they are on. Certainly this poetic language makes the reader see the sliced and bleeding thumb differently, or perhaps evokes the vagina leaking menstrual fluid. The physical split of the skin flap also comes to represent an incorporeal division of identity itself. In the poem's first four stanzas, the thumb is separated into pieces, but described through images that are wholly American. Many Americans pour hydrogen peroxide over a wound to clean and disinfect it. The reference to 'pink fizz' suggests the visual impression of diluted blood, almost carbonated in appearance, which results from this therapy. Despite such a very American treatment of the injury, Americanness itself cannot be sustained. What emerges from inside the American shell

in the fifth quatrain is alien: the Redcoats who were America's opponents during the Revolutionary War. The outside layer of familiar
American history contains the British enemy within, and the speaker is
not sure who is who, or where their allegiances lie ('Whose side …?').

Psychoanalysts often speak of the 'other' as that which we blame for
our own alienation, our own lack of belonging; rather than confront our
own strangeness, it is less painful and threatening to call somebody or
something else 'other'. The catch is that what we like to think of as
other is already inside us. Kristeva has argued that the abject is that
which is 'opposed to I', and therefore threatens this sense of self.
Abjection is strongest when the self, or 'subject, weary of fruitless
attempts to identify with something on the outside, finds the impossible
within; when it finds that the impossible constitutes its very *being*'.[153]
This seems a good description of what happens to the speaker of 'Cut',
when she discovers that the Redcoats aren't coming but have been
there all along, inside her very self (or finger, as it were). What better
image of something that should be inside, instead of outside, than the
'turkey wattle' fabric of the bird's neck? With the 'turkey wattle', Plath
gives us a visual image of something that looks like brains or intestines.
But the poem does not comply perfectly with Kristeva's notion of
abjection, which has it that abjection is 'directed against a threat that
seems to emanate from an exorbitant outside or inside … It lies there,
quite close, but it cannot be assimilated'.[154] For a brief instant, the
speaker of 'Cut' does absorb what is different from her. She can be said
to take pleasure in it through the mesmerising effect of the injury, and
the hybridity the wound comes to signify. Yet this position is not
maintained for long.

'Cut' shifts dramatically from the language of the nursery and the
speaker's seeming excitement at the mixture of English and American
identities, to an unease and violence which explore the impact of a
larger world. The poem catapults us from the speaker's loving fascination to her assertion of illness. The thumb ceases to represent distant
historical events. In contrast to the thumb's present bleeding state, these
events have been drained of their material reality by time, and by the
infantalised rhetoric of the schoolroom. Current history crowds out the
past; the now-bandaged thumb, wrapped in gauze, takes on a number of
national identities that have threatened America from without and
within during the twentieth century. There is the Japanese 'Kamikaze
man', or suicide bomber who attacked the United States during the
Second World War and proved with deadly clarity that American borders were penetrable. Yet threat does not issue only from outside United

States borders, for the Kamikaze man is also addressed as a saboteur, as one who causes material or political damage from within. The blemish on his 'Gauze Ku Klux Klan / Babushka'[155] represents the dangers and destruction that come from inside the heartland of America itself, from a group which has appointed itself to police cultural and racial whole-someness, and to obliterate all infringements against that nonexistent entity: pure American nationality. The Russian reference to 'Babushka', or little grandmother, is to those dolls within a doll that provide another image of the transgression of borders. (Visually, the Babushka duplicates the finger puppet thumb swathed in its bandage, which resembles the shawl that a Babushka wraps around its head and neck.) Like the thumb, the Babushka hides something unexpected within.

Kristeva argues that what causes abjection is

> what disturbs identity, system, order. What does not respect borders, positions, rules. The in-between, the ambiguous, the composite. The traitor, the liar ... Any crime, because it draws attention to the fragility of the law, is abject, but premeditated crime, cunning murder, hypocritical outrage ... heighten the display of such fragility.[156]

This account could double as a description of what disturbs the speaker of 'Cut'. The cut itself challenges the borders between inside and out-side, self and not self. The blood that issues from the thumb evokes menstrual blood. Menstrual blood, Kristeva argues, 'stands for the danger issuing from within the identity ... it threatens ... the identity of each sex in the face of sexual difference'.[157] The threats to identity that are played out in 'Cut', then, are not just to nationality and health, but also to sexual identity, as we see with increasing clarity by the poem's end. The thumb becomes a circus performer who jumps or performs tricks, and is, ultimately, of unresolved gender and nationality. It is both female, the 'Dirty girl' who, as Susan Van Dyne observes, symbolises 'her cul-ture's revulsion at female blood, sexuality and domesticity',[158] and male, a 'veteran' who finalises the poem's images of recent world war partici-pants. This dual, unresolvable gender was important to Plath. Successive drafts of the poem show that she repeatedly crossed out and reinstated her choice of words for the last line. Plath vacillated between 'Dirty' or 'pearly' 'girl', and 'Dirty' or 'Pale' 'Amputee'.[159] By discarding the Amp-utee and its probably male connotations, by choosing an image that is female to accompany the male veteran, Plath opted for mixed, indeter-minate gender. Male or female, the thumb is castrated, a 'stump' whose transgressions have left it, like the speaker, and, ultimately, like Sylvia Plath's reader, unsure of the borders not just of skin and gender, but also of country.

Notes

1. Orr, *Plath Reads Plath*, 1975: transcription from recording, mine.
2. Elizabeth Hardwick has also taken note of Plath's speaking voice, though she regards its sound as primarily English: 'these bitter poems were "beautifully" read, projected in full-throated, plump, diction-perfect, Englishy, mesmerising cadences … Poor recessive Massachusetts had been erased' (Hardwick, 'On Sylvia Plath', 1985: 115).
3. *Johnny Panic* ('America! America!'), 34.
4. Orr, *Plath Reads Plath*, 1975: transcription from recording, mine.
5. *The Journals of Sylvia Plath*, 1982: 185. *The Journals of Sylvia Plath*, 2000: 312.
6. *The Journals of Sylvia Plath*, 1982: 162. *The Journals of Sylvia Plath*, 2000: 285.
7. *The Journals of Sylvia Plath*, 1982: 185. *The Journals of Sylvia Plath*, 2000: 313.
8. *Johnny Panic*, 300–1.
9. Bhabha, 'Postcolonial Authority and Postmodern Guilt', 1992: 59.
10. *Collected Poems*, 'Uncollected Juvenilia', 339, 340.
11. LILLY. Plath MSS. II, Writings, Poetry – G–I, Box 7a, folder 12, 'I Am An American'.
12. Stevenson, *Bitter Fame*, 1989: 181, 274, 284.
13. Lucas Myers, in Appendix I to Stevenson, *Bitter Fame*, 1989: 314.
14. Anthony D. Smith, *National Identity*, 1991: 25, 29.
15. *Letters Home*, 486.
16. *Ibid.*, 165.
17. Stan Smith, *Inviolable Voice*, 1982: 216.
18. *Letters Home*, 182.
19. *Ibid.*, 183.
20. LILLY. Plath MSS. II, Correspondence, 1960, Jan.–Apr., Box 6. 24 Jan. 1960. (The acronyms are for the *Ladies Home Journal* and *The New Yorker*.)
21. *Collected Poems*, 43.
22. *Ibid.*, 44.
23. *Letters Home*, 496.
24. *Collected Poems* ('Tulips'), 162.
25. Hobsbawm, *Nations and Nationalism Since 1780*, 1990: 177.
26. *Johnny Panic* ('America! America!'), 34.

27. Couzyn, *The Bloodaxe Book of Contemporary Women Poets*, 1985: 214.
28. Malcolm, *The Silent Woman*, 1994: 10, 16.
29. Stan Smith, *Inviolable Voice*, 1982: 224.
30. Stevenson, *Bitter Fame*, 1989: 64
31. *Ibid.*, 193
32. Lucas Myers, in Appendix I to Stevenson, *Bitter Fame*, 1989: 313, 318.
33. Davison, in Ackerman, *About Sylvia*, 1996: pages not numbered.
34. Stevenson, *Bitter Fame*, 1989: 205.
35. *Ibid.*, 273.
36. Hughes, 'The Art of Poetry LXXI', 1995: 77, 85.
37. Warwick, 'A Common Wealth', 1995: 27.
38. Malcolm, *The Silent Woman*, 1994: 66.
39. Benedict Anderson, *Imagined Communities*, 1991: 6.
40. *The Bell Jar*, 5.
41. *Ibid.*, 53.
42. *Ibid.*, 23.
43. *Ibid.*, 35.
44. *Ibid.*, 45.
45. *Johnny Panic*, 35.
46. *Letters Home*, 183.
47. Heinzel *et al.*, *The Birds of Britain and Europe*, 1972, 1974: 308–11. Bull and Farrand, *The Audubon Society Field Guide to North American Birds*, 1977, 1993.
48. 'Conversation Among the Ruins', 'Winter Landscape, With Rooks', and 'Pursuit'.
49. Of the three words (crow, raven and rook), the only one that Plath marks in her copy of *Webster's Dictionary* is raven, where she underlines the word itself, and its adjectival definition 'Of the glossy black color of the raven'. She leaves the rest of its definition untouched. SMITH. *Webster's New Collegiate Dictionary*. Springfield, Massachusetts: G. & C. Merriam Co., 1949: 703. The unmarked entry for rook makes it clear that the bird is strictly European (735), while that for crow describes the bird as both American and European (199). The entry for raven tells us to 'See crow', but makes no mention of rook.
50. 'Prospect', 'The Queen's Complaint', 'The Snowman on the Moor', 'On the Difficulty of Conjuring Up a Dryad'.
51. 'Black Rook in Rainy Weather'.
52. Cady, *The Complete Book of British Birds*, 1992: 254–5.
53. LILLY. Plath MSS. II, Writings, Prose – Non-Fiction – A–R, Box 9, folder 1, 'Leaves from a Cambridge Notebook': 1.
54. *Letters Home*, 214.
55. LILLY. Plath MSS. II, Writings, Prose – Non-Fiction – A–R, Box 9, folder 1, 'Poppy Day At Cambridge': 1, 9.
56. *Collected Poems*, 240.

57. Nancy D. Hargrove, in her excellent technical analysis of Plath's early poems, and painstaking study of their chronology, argues that 'Landowners' was written in 1958 and therefore should not have been placed in the 1956 section of the *Collected Poems* (Hargrove, *The Journey Toward Ariel*, 1994: 16, 176). Hargrove bases her argument on a journal entry for 3 July 1958, in which Plath writes, 'I've already written a good short poem on the groundhog and on landowners'. While I greatly admire Hargrove's work (which is not talked about as much as it deserves), I'm not convinced that she is right in this particular instance. Plath could have been talking about an entirely different poem, or if she was talking about 'Landowners', she could have picked the poem up again to revise, or simply have been thinking about it as something she wrote much earlier. 'Landowners' feels part of other 1956 poems that were substantively concerned with the strangeness of English landscape (for instance, 'November Graveyard' and 'Black Rook in Rainy Weather'). *The Journals of Sylvia Plath,* 1982: 244. *The Journals of Sylvia Plath*, 2000: 399.
58. *Letters Home*, 183.
59. *Collected Poems*, 53.
60. LILLY. Plath MSS. 1961, Sept. 'Wuthering Heights'. 'Wuthering Heights' (1961) was written on the back of 'Home Thoughts From London', which is not dated, but I would guess Plath wrote in the autumn of 1960.
61. *Letters Home*, 194.
62. LILLY. Plath MSS. II, Correspondence, 1957, Mar., Box 6. 15 March 1957. The punctuation is Plath's.
63. *Letters Home*, 317.
64. *The Journals of Sylvia Plath*, 1982: 325. *The Journals of Sylvia Plath*, 2000: 521.
65. LILLY. Plath MSS. II, Correspondence, 1961, June–Dec., Box 6a. 22 July 1961.
66. *Letters Home*, 269.
67. *Ibid.*, 231.
68. *Ibid.*, 268.
69. Rose, *The Haunting of Sylvia Plath*, 1991: 197–8.
70. Plath herself omits the capital letter.
71. LILLY. Plath MSS. II, Correspondence, 1956, Jan.–Feb., Box 6. 24 Feb. 1956.
72. LILLY. Plath MSS. II, Correspondence, 1956, June–July, Box 6. 30 July 1956.
73. LILLY. Plath MSS. II, Correspondence, 1960, Jan.–Apr., Box 6.
74. LILLY. Plath MSS. II, Correspondence, 1960, Jan.–Apr., Box 6. 24 Jan. 1960.
75. The bedroom wallpaper sample is not dated, but it probably accompanied Plath's letter to her mother of 24 Jan., 2 Feb., or 7 Feb. 1960 (all three letters mention wallpaper). They are in: LILLY. Plath MSS. II, Correspondence, 1960, Jan.–Apr., Box 6.

76. LILLY. Plath MSS. II, Correspondence, 1960, Jan.–Apr., Box 6. 2 Feb. 1960.
77. LILLY. Plath MSS. II, Correspondence, 1960, Jan.–Apr., Box 6. 27 Jan. 1960.
78. LILLY. Plath MSS. II, Correspondence, 1960, Jan.–Apr., Box 6. 2 Feb. 1960.
79. *The Bell Jar*, 98.
80. Jouve, *White Woman Speaks with Forked Tongue*, 1991: 19.
81. Anthony D. Smith, *National Identity*, 1991: 25.
82. Stan Smith, *Inviolable Voice*, 1982: 80.
83. Ahmad, 'The Politics of Literary Postcoloniality', 1995: 17.
84. *The Bell Jar*, 43.
85. *Ibid.*, 29.
86. Stevenson, *Bitter Fame*, 1989: 268.
87. Rose, *The Haunting of Sylvia Plath*, 1991; Heaney, 'The Indefatigable Hoof-taps', 1988; Steiner, 'Dying is an Art', 1970.
88. Orr, *Plath Reads Plath*, 1975: transcription from recording, mine.
89. SMITH. Box: Plath – Ariel Poems, Daddy – Event. Folder: Ariel Poems, 'Daddy', Draft 1.
90. *Collected Poems*, 223.
91. *Ibid.*, 222.
92. *Ibid.*, 223.
93. *Ibid.*, 222.
94. *Ibid.*, 223.
95. *Ibid.*, 224.
96. *The Bell Jar*, 105.
97. Macpherson, *Reflecting on The Bell Jar*, 1991: 2.
98. *The Bell Jar*, 193.
99. Ellmann, '*The Bell Jar*: An American Girlhood', 1970. 222.
100. *Johnny Panic*, 125.
101. *Ibid.*, 132.
102. *Ibid.*, 133.
103. *Ibid.*, 106.
104. *Ibid.*, 108.
105. SMITH. Box: Plath – Prose, Quotation. Folder: Prose Works, 'Mothers', Typescript Original [copy 1].
106. *Collected Poems*, 288.
107. *Ibid.*, 112.
108. Markey, *A Journey into the Red Eye*, 1993: 20–1.
109. Rose, *The Haunting of Sylvia Plath*, 1991: 134.
110. Plath's comments to her mother about 'Leaving Early' might be described as systematic omission (or oversimplification). She prosaically summarised the poem as 'a monologue from the point of view of a man about the flowers in the lady's room upstairs (where he isn't working any more – her visitors are something she wants to keep secret…)' (*Letters Home*, 397).

111. *Collected Poems*, 146.
112. Freud, 'The "Uncanny"', 1919: 341, 357.
113. *Collected Poems*, 146.
114. Kristeva, *Revolution in Poetic Language*, 1984: 86–9. Using Kristeva's terms, another way to describe this relationship between America and England would be of the unconscious genotext to the syntactic phenotext. Kristeva writes: 'Designating the genotext in a text requires pointing out the transfers of drive energy that can be detected in phonematic devices ... such as rhyme ... and melodic devices (such as intonation or rhythm)'.
115. Anthony D. Smith, *National Identity* 1991: 66.
116. *Collected Poems*, 176.
117. *Ibid.*, 165.
118. *Ibid.*
119. *Ibid.*, 166.
120. Schlesinger, 'Europeanness: A New Cultural Battlefield?', 1992: 321.
121. LILLY. Sylvia Plath. *Crossing the Water*. With Commentary by Ted Hughes. London: British Broadcasting Corporation, 1971. BBC Radio Script. First broadcast 5 July 1971. Produced by Douglas Cleverdon.
122. *Collected Poems*, 291.
123. *Ibid.*, 169.
124. Marsack, *Sylvia Plath*, 1992: 7.
125. *Collected Poems*, 170.
126. *Ibid.*, 166.
127. *Ibid.*, 40.
128. Plath may have wished to counteract the possibility of her mother reading the poem in this way when she told her in a 1962 letter, 'The "News from home" is, of course, your letters, which I look forward to above all'. *Letters Home*, 452.
129. *Collected Poems*, 162.
130. SMITH. Box: Plath – Ariel Poems, Amnesiac – Berck-Plage. Folder: Ariel Poems – drafts, 'The Arrival of the Bee Box', Typed Copy 1 (Revised). Folder: Ariel Poems – drafts, 'The Bee Meeting', Draft 2. These drafts also show that Plath considered calling the series 'Bees' and 'The Beekeeper'.
131. *Collected Poems*, 211.
132. *Ibid.*
133. *Ibid.*, 212.
134. Van Dyne, '"More Terrible Than She Ever Was"', 1982: 3.
135. *Collected Poems*, 213.
136. *Ibid.*, 214.
137. *Ibid.*, 216.
138. *Ibid.*, 217.
139. Markey, *A Journey into the Red Eye*, 1993: 169, 19, 11.

140. *Collected Poems*, 219.
141. *Ibid.*
142. SMITH. Box: Plath – Ariel Poems, Stings – Years. Folder: Ariel Poems – Drafts, 'Wintering', Draft 1.
143. SMITH. Box: Plath – Ariel Poems, Stings – Years. Folder: Ariel Poems – Drafts, 'Wintering', Typed Copy 1.
144. Ostriker, 'The Americanization of Sylvia', 1984: 99, 100, 101, 103.
145. *Collected Poems*, 237.
146. *Ibid.*, 238.
147. Orr, *Plath Reads Plath*, 1975: transcription from recording, mine.
148. *Collected Poems*, 238.
149. Stevenson, *Bitter Fame*, 1989: 271.
150. *Johnny Panic*, 35.
151. SMITH. Box: Plath – Ariel Poems, A Birthday Present – Cut. Folder: Ariel Poems – Drafts, 'Cut', Draft 1.
152. *Collected Poems*, 235.
153. Kristeva, *Powers of Horror*, 1982: 1.
154. *Ibid.*, 5.
155. *Collected Poems*, 235–6.
156. Kristeva, *Powers of Horror*, 1982: 4.
157. *Ibid.*, 71.
158. Van Dyne, *Revising Life*, 1993: 148.
159. SMITH. Box: Plath – Ariel Poems, A Birthday Present – Cut. Folders: Ariel Poems – Drafts, 'Cut', Drafts 1 and 2. Folder: Ariel Poems, 'Cut', Typed Copy 1 (Revised).

CHAPTER 3

PLATH'S ENVIRONMENTALISM

Background

Silent Spring

If there is a previously unremarked concern with national identity in Plath's work, there is equally an attentiveness to environmental pollution. Indeed, there is a recurrent exploration of the ways that substances are exchanged between human beings and the environment, just as there is an examination of the interaction of languages and nationalities. Plath's environmentalism, like her midatlanticism, is concerned with the penetrability of borders and the relationship of any human being to the larger world. Whether she is talking about language, country, or the environment, Plath jolts the reader out of the luxury of the tourist's position – a position of being able to wander freely and without consequence, but also without the privilege of being part of things. Plath's writing insists upon involvement. Although Plath has been a powerful figure to generations of readers, she has so far not been identified as an environmentalist. Another way of bypassing the usual confessional readings of Plath's work is to place her as a writer who is concerned with such important public issues.

Gretchen T. Legler has described ecofeminist literary criticism as the 'analysis of the cultural construction of nature, which also includes an analysis of language, desire, knowledge, and power'.[1] Legler's account could double as an outline of what Plath gives us in her poems and prose. Much of Plath's writing hinges on exchanges within a global ecosystem that includes the climate, the soil, the air, animal life and the individual human body. Such a configuration is made more powerful by Plath's complex view of men's and women's shared places in this system, and contradicts the still prevalent view of Plath as self-obsessed. Plath's writing depicts the permeation and poisoning of the human body by toxic chemicals and pollutants; these *material* interpenetrations mirror the ideas of *cultural* movement and permeability that are also important in Plath's work. To understand this, we need to situate Plath's writing in the cultural and historical framework of environmental and ecofeminist concerns that began to emerge in the 1950s and early 1960s.

This emergent environmentalism was most famously expressed in Rachel Carson's *Silent Spring* (1962). Carson's exposé of the effects of pesticides on the environment was important in informing a wider public, of both scientists and non-specialists, that agricultural and industrial chemicals were having deadly and unforeseen consequences for animals, plants and human beings. *Silent Spring* is typically referred to as the 'classic environmental book of our times'.[2] It is now received cultural currency that the book 'sparked off the beginnings of the North's environmental movement'.[3] The book has had material influence on government policies, altering methods of pest control, and changing the types of chemicals used.[4]

Plath was clearly interested in Carson as a writer. There is evidence that she knew of Carson and her work as early as 1952.[5] In a letter to her mother written on 5 July 1958, Plath specifically acknowledges Carson's influence:

> I am reading ... the delightful book *The Sea Around Us*, by Rachel Carson. Ted's reading her *Under the Sea Wind*, which he says is also fine. Do read these if you haven't already; they are poetically written and magnificently informative. I am going back to the ocean as my poetic heritage and hope to revisit all the places I remember in Winthrop with Ted this summer.[6]

Plath did utilise her 'poetic heritage', at the same time expressing concern about the impact of technology on the ecosystem. Within days of this letter she wrote 'Green Rock, Winthrop Bay'. In it, the speaker regrets the changes wrought on the seaside since she last visited it. She laments the 'Barge-tar clotted at the tide-line'[7] and is saddened by how 'The cries of scavenging gulls sound thin / In the traffic of planes'.[8] The speaker also remarks upon the contamination of the air by metal machinery: 'Gulls circle gray under shadow of a steelier flight'.[9] She worries about the effects of capitalist consumerism upon the environment, rejecting the 'lame excuses'[10] by which people try to justify such destruction, and states that 'Loss cancels profit'.[11]

Silent Spring was published as a book in the United States in late September of 1962, and in Britain in 1963. Before publication in book form, however, roughly one-third of the material was serialised in three issues of *The New Yorker*, in June of 1962. Plath died early in 1963. My arguments about Plath's work do not depend on establishing with any certainty that she read the serialised version. Although Plath's environ-mental interests, and the specific images and references in her writing, made me suspect that she had read it, I could never find any allusion to *Silent Spring* in her published letters and journals, or in the Plath archives.[12] On the other hand, there is a good deal of circumstantial evidence that Plath had read *Silent Spring*. Her mother gave her a sub-scription to *The New Yorker* at the end of 1960,[13] and Plath refers to reading her weekly edition of the magazine in early February of 1961[14] (in one of the numerous references to it in her letters and journals[15]). More to the point, *The New Yorker* published many of Plath's poems in a period roughly coincident with the excerpts from *Silent Spring*.[16] Less probably, but still possibly, Plath could have got hold of the American edition of the book, posted or brought to her from America by a friend. Late in the writing of this book, I put myself out of this specula-tive misery by writing to Ted Hughes and asking him. He confirmed that she had indeed read *Silent Spring*,[17] though he was a bit uncertain about the dates.

Plath would almost certainly have been aware of the loud and very public controversy that followed *Silent Spring*'s first appearance in the summer of 1962. Ted Hughes has written of this period, 'To most of the world, Rachel Carson's *Silent Spring* came as an absolute shock'.[18] Frank Graham quotes a headline from the *New York Times* on 22 July 1962: '*SILENT SPRING* IS NOW NOISY SUMMER'.[19] In the years pre-ceding *Silent Spring*, a number of popular magazines and newspapers observed the dangerous effects of pesticides. Paul Brooks cites Carson's acknowledgement that *Silent Spring* was indebted to a letter published in the Boston *Herald* in January of 1958. In it, Olga Huckins observes the unintended mass murder of birds caught in the crossfire of aerial-sprayed DDT for mosquito control.[20] Frank Graham refers to 'an article strongly critical of current pesticide use' published in *Reader's Digest* in June of 1959, in which Robert S. Strother 'mentioned many of the alarming incidents which had prompted Rachel Carson'. (Plath could have read Huckins's letter and Strother's article, as she was living in Northampton and Boston, respectively, at the time they were published.) In the autumn of 1961 'a controversy about pesticide damage ... erupted ... on the editorial pages of the *New York Times*'.[21] These popular articles, like the more scientific and specialised bibliography Carson provides in the book version of *Silent Spring*, show that Carson was far from alone in recognising the dangers of chemicals and nuclear fallout. Rather, she was the first to articulate in a readily accessible and much-read publication the mounting concerns of many of her contemporaries.

The 'silent spring' of Carson's title is a 'spring without voices',[22] where the contamination of soil, air and water by chemicals has killed fish, birds and plants, resulting in an eerily quiet world of depleted wildlife. *Silent Spring* is a very literary book, both in its frame of reference and in Carson's style. In one of the three epigraphs to the book version of *Silent Spring*, Carson quotes from Keats's 'La Belle Dame sans Merci', 'The sedge has wither'd from the lake, And no birds sing'. With this epigraph, Carson makes it clear that, as Julian Huxley puts it, 'we are losing half the subject-matter of English poetry'.[23] Carson does this while making her most memorable point: that life is being damaged irretrievably by pesticides. Thereby Carson unites scientific argument with the literary.

Plath was among the first of a series of writers to deploy *Silent Spring*'s themes in prose and poetry, so challenging the arbitrary boundaries between 'literary' and 'scientific' writing. For example, A. S. Byatt's 1996 novel *Babel Tower* is set in the mid-1960s, and explicitly identifies the publication of Carson's book as an important historical moment. Byatt draws on Carson's information and figurative language, and on her use of Keats. Byatt's characters note the declining bird population, 'haunted by … lifeless lakes where no birds sing'. They worry over the effects of the very pesticides Carson describes, 'parathion or dieldrin, or heptachlor'.[24] The 1965 poem 'Dry River', by the Australian poet Rosemary Dobson, alludes to 'a lost spring, dwindled to silence' and yearns for 'cool, clear notes of the bell-birds' making' that can only be an 'illusion' or 'mirage'.[25] Czeslaw Milosz's 1965 poem 'Advice' duplicates the information in *Silent Spring* by chronicling the poisoning of land and water by 'oil and chlorine and methyl compounds'.[26] These are components of the DDT whose actions are so carefully described by Carson.[27] By alluding to the 'Chemical zone of the farmers' where 'The insect and the bird are extinguished',[28] Milosz echoes Carson's argument that poisons are not selective. Ted Hughes's 1993 children's classic, *The Iron Woman*, depicts birds and fish who are dying from the chemical poisoning of their waters. This poisoning, and the ensuing silence, seem indebted to *Silent Spring*'s title image.

Like these other writers, Plath shares Carson's concern over the infiltration of the food chain by different poisons, and, ultimately, her fear that spring will be empty not only of birdsong, but of human voices too. Carson writes in *Silent Spring*:

> chemicals are the sinister and little-recognised partners of radiation in changing the very nature of the world ... Strontium 90, released through nuclear explosions into the air, comes to earth in rain or drifts down as fallout, lodges in soil, enters into the grass or corn or wheat grown there, and in time takes up its abode in the bones of a human being.[29]

Before *Silent Spring* was even published, Plath wrote to her mother in a 1961 letter, 'I hope the Strontium 90 level doesn't go up too high in milk. I've been very gloomy about the bomb news; of course, the Americans have contributed to the poisonous level. The fallout-shelter craze in America sounds mad'.[30] What Plath rejects in the 'craze' for fallout shelters is not just the potential environmental and human disaster that has precipitated their invention, and the refusal of those responsible to recognise their own culpability. She also repudiates the selfish stance of non-involvement taken by those who desire the shelters. To be safe within a fallout shelter is to lock out others, knowing that, unprotected, they will sicken and die outside. Moreover, Plath's work makes it clear that boundaries between poisons and people are always penetrable. No fallout shelter can really act as a barrier to invisible and microscopic particles of radioactive poison. As we will now see, for Plath there can be no real tourist, just as there can be no pure nationality. Fine distinctions between 'here' and 'there', and 'inside' and 'out', are not possible in this world.

From the City to the Sea

Plath's environmentalism was present from the outset of her writing career. A concern that metal and poisons have infiltrated the air and water is expressed in her early unpublished sonnet 'City Wife'.[31] The manuscript is not dated, but according to the *Collected Poems*, Plath wrote 'City Wife' before 1956.[32] In it, a 'city wife' speaks of her isolation in a desolated cityscape, and her alienation from plants and nature in a place where nothing can grow. The 'metal rain' that falls upon her must also touch the plants that she lovingly, diligently tries to foster in her 'green-painted window box'. The speaker wryly notes that only the weeds and nettles can flourish. These are strong enough to burst through concrete or move metal. By contrast, her own carefully tended sprouts weaken. Her 'red geraniums rust and bleed, / And down the sterile sidewalk blows the seed'.[33] It is as if the 'metal rain' upon which the geraniums have fed and then sickened has seeped back out of them, to recirculate the deadliness, floating it back into the air and propelling it down the street.

In a later poem, 'Waking in Winter', Plath revisits the environment-alist subject matter and imagery of 'City Wife', but develops cause and effect, moving to the next logical step in the food chain. The poem's title may refer to a nuclear winter, the aftermath of a nuclear disaster where dust in the atmosphere, shaken up by the explosion, blocks the sun's rays. Plath wrote the poem at the end of 1960.[34] It is about tourists, about characters on an excursion or holiday that does not deliver what it promises. The poem's speaker drives with her companion to a sea resort which, instead of offering healthy air and a beautiful landscape as an antidote to the polluted city, appears itself to be poisonous and deadly. The sky tastes like 'tin', as though the 'gray Chevrolet' in which they travel (American in spelling and brand name) has spat its metal pollution into the air. If, as 'City Wife' implies, the 'metal rain' is corrosive to plants, 'Waking in Winter' makes it clear that this rain is also dangerous to human beings. Moreover, the poisons of the city of the earlier poem are not contained there, but move into the country where the later poem is set. There is no place of safety; poisons cannot be sealed off. The two travellers of 'Waking in Winter' pay for the speed and convenience of their car by taking into their bodies the toxicity of the technological age in which they live. Trees that resemble 'burnt nerves' decorate the landscape, evoking the skeleton-like figures that are now familiar post-nuclear photographic images. The speaker describes items that we might find in museums dedicated to Hiroshima, such as 'Cot legs' fused into 'terrible attitudes'. Visualising the devastating and immediate effect of an atomic explosion upon the human bodies in its epicentre, she remarks, 'How the sun lit up / The skulls, the unbuckled bones'.

All elements of any ecosystem are connected (like Plath's poems themselves, 'City Wife' and 'Waking in Winter' included). This fact is made vivid in 'Waking in Winter' by the speaker's sense that she has somehow swallowed the 'Poison of stilled lawns'. It is as though rain and animals have carried pesticides into the food chain and air. While these chemicals allow the grass to attain its artificially bright colour, they also affect the bodies of the poem's speaker and companion. The poem evokes the interplay between all living and inanimate things, and makes an ecological argument about the dangers of ignoring this interaction. 'Waking in Winter' works through a series of metaphoric and gender-based indeterminacies. These indeterminacies are ecological because they are about interdependence: the multiple combinations of different, shifting elements.

'Waking in Winter' suggests that mechanisation, industrialisation and overproduction result in a nightmare of Fordist capitalism. The speaker imagines 'cut throats' in an 'assembly-line'. This is one of many points in the poem, and in Plath's writing, in which we cannot easily assign blame, because the demarcation between injured and injurer is not clear. Cut throats are objects, the wounds of mutilated victims, as well as subjects, a way of describing murderous criminals. They are also weapons – razors. Domesticity in the poem is materially and figuratively toxic; houses, or beach huts, are not described as havens, but as 'clapboard gravestones'. 'Waking in Winter' allows no simple contrast between guilt and innocence; it resists any obvious pattern in which violence must be masculine while protest must be feminine. Women are not the natural and pre-modern custodians of the earth, and men are not its industrial destroyers. The poem offers no certainty that the speaker is female, or her fellow traveller male. Even if such resolution were available, it would not help us to assign culpability, which is shared between the poem's personae. The 'beautiful rubber plants' mentioned in the poem's penultimate line may well be sacrificed to supply the coagulated juice used to make the 'rubber wheels'[35] that move cars such as the speaker's. 'Waking in Winter' suggests that to be complicit with destruction and pollution is not a morally superior position to being their direct, active cause. Nor does the poem suggest that to be oblivious to the damage one causes is to be absolved of blame. The speaker may be a passenger (rather than the driver of the car or its manufacturer), but the distinction is not important, and does not lessen her responsibility. In the most fundamental sense, 'Waking in Winter' refuses its speaker and her companion the privileged, and selfish, position of tourists who can view their surroundings as a playground that has nothing to do with them and exists only for their pleasure.

This position might be described as 'toxic consciousness', a state of awareness that we often encounter in Plath's work. 'Toxic consciousness' is Cynthia Deitering's term. She uses it to argue that much of the fiction of the 1980s reflects 'our own complicity in postindustrial ecosystems, both personal and national, which are predicated on pollution and waste'. Deitering explains: 'insomuch as they provide representations of a postnatural world, of a culture defined by its waste, and of a nation that has fouled its own nest, these novels do much to raise the environmental consciousness of the society that sees itself in the mirror'.[36] Plath's writing anticipates this 'toxic consciousness'.

However, there is a difficulty with 'toxic consciousness' – for Deitering's 1980s novelists, and for Plath. It is this: such a perspective tends to inhibit any full analysis of environmental profit, as well as loss. 'Toxic consciousness' encourages the focus to be on the negative effects of technology and on pollution, but there is a more complex sense of losses and gains in modernity than Plath often allows. Her emphasis, some may say, is unbalanced, or morbidly negative. There is little in Plath's work about the benefits to human beings of industrial capitalism, though there is a great deal about the toxicity of the twentieth century. For instance, there are few references to the improvements afforded by medical technology, or the benefits of medicine and vaccinations, or increased human life expectancy, or the narrowing of the gulf between the objects that the rich and the poor can afford to purchase. When Plath has weighed everything up, it seems, again and again in her work, that 'Loss cancels profit',[37] as the narrator of 'Green Rock, Winthrop Bay' puts it. Perhaps this is because, at the time Plath wrote, it seemed imperative to stress a point that not enough of her contemporaries had perceived. Perhaps the problem seemed so large it left little room to ask whether dirty rivers were a justifiable price to pay if mass production was to ensure that crops were not ruined and human beings did not starve.

Prose

Johnny Panic's Toxic Lake

The Lilly Library owns four undated scrapbooks in which Plath collected images. She used these books, which amount to a series of collages, as another way of telling stories and commenting on her world, cutting and pasting numerous pictures of paintings, advertisements, and even, ironically, designs and floor plans for suburban dream homes. In one of these scrapbooks, Plath arranged a picture of a man working in a factory. He is surrounded by hot, orange-red metal. Framed by a window, he wears a tank top, and gazes up and sidelong, as if wishing he weren't there. Outside this window looking in, as if sharing our perspective, is a comfortably cool-looking man. Clearly a manager and not a labourer, this man is dressed in a shirt, and, like us, stands safely outside the reach of the inferno. The caption reads: '**ELECTRIC REFRIGERATORS,** ranges and other appliances are made by Frigidaire Division in Dayton, Ohio. Here, as refrigerator freezing units move through a 37-foot water tank, inspectors look for air bubbles which betray leaks'.[38]

On its own, Plath's decision to file this picture could tell us little of her thoughts about it, or why she thought it was worth keeping. Only by its context – with two other pictures – can we begin to guess at Plath's position in relation to it. Together, these three pictures make viewers wish to dissociate themselves from the consumers they target. Together, as Plath composed them, these advertisements backfire. They force those who see them into concern for the men who sweat to produce the goods. They persuade spectators to reject the position of the complicit buyer who cravenly admires the product and desires it. The other two pictures are in the same scrapbook. They are of hygienic family dream kitchens. One kitchen is startling white, the other the pinkest of 1950s pink. Alongside the pink kitchen, Plath placed a glamorous-looking woman in housecoat and slippers, holding an open book. The woman walks with an absorbed, absent look on her face. This figure, cut from a magazine as one cuts around the contours of a paper doll, is not part of the kitchen advertisement, but from a different page or magazine altogether. Nonetheless, Plath ensured that this veritable paper doll was perfectly coordinated with the kitchen. She is dressed in silky pinky red to complement the pink-painted cupboards.

To the left of the white kitchen, Plath glued a happy mother and her little girl. Smiling at each other, the two of them wear matching blue dressing gowns that co-ordinate with the blue drapes. These figures, Plath implies, are part of the sale: accessories. But neither came with the advert. Plath found them and put them alongside, but not in the pictures; no human beings dirty or disorder what rests inside the perfect frames. The scrapbook is ordered so that the kitchens come before the Frigidaire factory. Plath couldn't have missed the contrast, indeed was surely highlighting it for herself: the underbelly of industrial capitalism, the production side of consumption. Clean, middle-class American life buys its comforts without acknowledging the price other human beings pay so that it can keep its suburban hands smooth. So indifferent, in fact, has consumer capitalism become to production and labourers, that advertisers do not even shrink from depicting the hellish scene of factory work. Instead, they safely assume that potential buyers will see only the product and its efficiency, not the workers. What the advertiser thought would-be customers would take as a virtue, Plath sees, and makes us see, as a nightmare.

Another of the art scrapbooks contains cuttings from a series of advertisements for printers. The images and rhetoric of industrial capitalism and war characterise these. One of them tells us, 'This precision machined anti-aircraft gun is as accurate in action as printing is in its sphere', and then asks, 'Are you interested in making a direct hit every time?' Another urges, 'Take a tip from the women who have always used fashion as a weapon for their personal victories. Use printing as they use style; to win!' A third offers a picture reminiscent of Edvard Munch's 1893 painting *The Scream*. A horrified man in a savage landscape holds his arms akimbo in desperate frustration as a train moves off without him. A wristwatch, bigger than the man, hangs from a tree. The watch's face shows the time: '8:16'. Below it are the words '... is much too late'. Put the two together, and the message is clear: '8:16', just one minute late, 'is much too late'.[39] The implication is that human beings are slaves to the age and its technologies. Don't be left behind, urges the advertisement.

Plath's best-known short story, 'Johnny Panic and the Bible of Dreams', is set in precisely such a terrifying, alienating world of machines and inhumanity. Written at the end of 1958, soon after Plath began working with patients' records in a Boston mental hospital, the story, like 'Waking in Winter', explores the physical and mental damage sustained by the individuals who live in the toxic, mechanised mid-twentieth century of the cold war. 'Johnny Panic and the Bible of Dreams' is typically read as yet another account of Plath's 'breakdown story'[40] and experience of electric shock therapy. One critic concludes that 'Plath writes of *her* betrayal by the woman figure' (my emphasis),[41] and identifies Plath's own psychiatrist as the monstrous secretary of the Observation Ward in the Adult Psychiatric Clinic where the narrator illicitly transcribes case notes.

Yet 'Johnny Panic and the Bible of Dreams' has an environmentalist context − a concern with individuals and their connections to their world − that moves beyond any representation of events from Plath's 'real' life. Jacqueline Rose usefully refers to the story's 'political dimension', describing it as the 'public, institutional' version of Plath's 'intimate' 'Poem for a Birthday', written a year earlier. For Rose, the poem and story both make it clear that 'the damage of electrotherapy is not just what it does *to* the speaker … but equally what it takes *away* — a negativity'.[42] In other words, electric shock treatment is not simply barbaric. If it 'cures', if it removes the dissent that is diagnosed as depression and dysfunction, it also deletes something valuable, however 'negative' that something may be. More to the point, that negative something is not Plath's alone, or, for that matter, her narrator's. It is more important than anything merely personal. During the period in which Plath worked on the story, she wrote in her journal of her job in the mental hospital: 'I feel … as if I … opened up the souls of the people in Boston & read them deep'.[43] 'Johnny Panic and the Bible of Dreams' is very much about this world, and the shared hazards of living in it. These hazards are at once psychic, social and physical: a literal and metaphoric poison that circulates between the human beings who live in post-industrial capitalist culture, and pay a high price for the privilege of technology and convenience.

If Jacqueline Rose is right in connecting 'Johnny Panic and the Bible of Dreams',[44] the link between the two texts also concerns nature, and the individual's access to it. Writing in her journals on 22 October 1959, Plath said of 'Poem for a Birthday', 'To be a dwelling on madhouse, nature: meanings of tools, greenhouses, florists shops, tunnels, vivid and disjointed'.[45] These words could double as an account of 'Johnny Panic and the Bible of Dreams'. The dreams that crowd the story's pages are of a dehumanised, mechanised existence, where human beings become part of the machinery they work:

> This one guy, for example, who works for a ball-bearing company in town, dreams every night how he's lying on his back with a grain of sand on his chest. Bit by bit this grain of sand grows bigger and bigger till it's big as a fair-sized house and he can't draw breath. Another fellow I know of has had a certain dream ever since they gave him ether and cut out his tonsils and adenoids when he was a kid. In this dream he's caught in the rollers of a cotton mill, fighting for his life. … A lot of people these days dream they're being run over or eaten by machines. They're the cagey ones who won't go on the subway or the elevators. … I wonder, now and then, what dreams people had before ball bearings and cotton mills were invented.[46]

These are the dreams of people with no access to what we might term the natural world — that is to say, to wildlife, unpolluted air, the countryside and indigenous plants and flowers. The sweating Frigidaire factory workers, like those who inhabit the nightmare landscapes of the printer ads, might have such dreams.[47]

'Johnny Panic and the Bible of Dreams' nonetheless deprives the reader of any illusion that there can be an untainted natural world. The narrator dreams of 'a great half-transparent lake', and looks down on it 'from the belly of some helicopter'. She believes the lake contains dragons that 'were around before men started living in caves and cooking meat over fires and figuring out the wheel'.

> It's into this lake people's minds run at night, brooks and gutter-trickles to one borderless common reservoir. It bears no resemblance to those pure sparkling-blue sources of drinking water the suburbs guard ... in the middle of the pine woods and barbed fences.
>
> It's the sewage farm of the ages, transparence aside.
>
> Now the water in this lake naturally stinks and smokes from what dreams have been left sogging around in it over the centuries ...
>
> ... I see whole storehouses of hardware: knives, paper cutters, pistons and cogs and nutcrackers; the shiny fronts of cars looming up, glass-eyed and evil-toothed. ...
>
> One of the most frequent shapes in this backwash is so common-place it seems silly to mention it. It's a grain of dirt. The water is thick with these grains. They seep in among everything else ...[48]

This lake seems to represent a collective dream life or unconscious. Some of what the lake contains is anterior to industrialisation (as symbolised by 'fires' and the 'wheel'). But the lake is not idealised. No mere residue of cave men, it is contaminated by the substances of the twentieth century.

The narrator hovers over the toxic water in a 'helicopter', a vehicle beyond the aspirations of prehistoric men and their wheel. The lake, whether as a storehouse of metal instruments or as a 'sewage farm', is not just a *symbol* of human distress and fear. The representation, another of those moments of 'toxic consciousness', is also literal: of the products, and poisons, of our age; of the pollutants and 'grains of dirt' we pour into the water, the by-products of all that hardware. Such a reading becomes more convincing in the context of the other departments that border the Adult Psychiatric Clinic, and sometimes even share office space and patients with it: Skin Clinic, Tumor, Nerve Clinic, Alcoholic Clinic, Amputee Clinic. Like the seeping grains of dirt, these 'rude invasions of other Clinics' and 'days of overlap'[49] where hospital space must be shared show that no boundary is impermeable. However isolated a person thinks they may be, nobody, and no thing, whether positively or negatively charged, human comfort or poison, can be held off as separate.

It is no accident that Plath chooses clinics that deal with illnesses which are often the result of environmental damage. There is a real sense that the users of these other clinics, living in the toxic twentieth century, are not simply made mentally ill by it, but physically ill too. One Catholic psychiatric patient, 'scared blue he'd go to hell … was a piece-worker at a fluorescent light plant'. The story's narrator makes up a dream for him. She imagines a Gothic cellar built of human bones and filled with laid-out corpses:

> it was the Hall of Time, with the bodies in the foreground still warm, discoloring and starting to rot in the middle distance, and the bones emerging, clean as a whistle, in a kind of white futuristic glow at the end of the line. As I recall, I had the whole scene lighted … not with candles, but with the ice-bright fluorescence that makes skin look green …[50]

Death itself is here an assembly line process. The human body, even after life, is not allowed to decay and rot 'naturally', but must be regulated by the same mechanisation that enslaved it when it was still breathing. Possibly what hastened death itself, the green fluorescence and glowing bones suggest a sort of radioactivity. The fluorescence brings to mind the cancer victims wandering through Tumor, Skin Clinic, Amputee Clinic, and Nerve Clinic. The secretary of the Adult Psychiatric Clinic's Observation Ward, Miss Milleravage, is malignant in more ways than one. She subjects the narrator to electric shock therapy, but is herself a likely future candidate for Tumor or Skin Clinic. Miss Milleravage's 'moles are noticeable mainly because the skin around them is so pallid', and she looks as though 'she'd been brought up from the cradle with the sole benefit of artificial lighting'.[51]

Yet another Clinic patient has 'an interesting notion about the filth in this world' and is terrified of 'catching cancer'. He ceases to touch anything, or leave the house, in order to avoid 'the spit and dog turds in the street'. He grows convinced that 'stuff gets on your shoes and then when you take your shoes off it gets on your hands and then at dinner it's a quick trip into your mouth and not a hundred Hail Marys can keep you from the chain reaction'.[52] This patient is duly 'cured'. To be cured is, in this story, to participate fully in consumer capitalism again, and return to one's gendered place in that system. Restored fully to manhood, he is soon 'sitting down in movie-house chairs ... and weight lifting', able even to 'shake hands with the Clinic Director'. Illness, whether physical or mental, is anything that prevents human beings from purchasing cinema tickets or behaving like 'proper' men or women, be it a tumour, a fear of contact with toxins, 'or pink affiliations'[53] that signal social and national maladjustment. The logic of the story is that this character, while in the grip of his conviction that the world is dangerous and contaminated, is right. His 'cure' takes the form of a delusion of safety.

Part of the narrator's 'illness' (or crime) is her disregard for consumer capitalism, her refusal to keep to her place in that system. Her interest in patient dreams, as well as her criticism of technology and the havoc it wreaks, is a usurpation of her position in the material economy. It is the job of the psychiatrists and doctors to 'practise their dream-gathering for worldly ends: health and money, money and health'.[54] Illness is a business. By eschewing 'worldly ends', and her humble role in helping the doctors to make their money, the typist narrator forgets her own part in that business. Her wish to 'counteract those doctors'[55] is a transgression of the highest order.

Nature as Theme Park in 'The Fifty-Ninth Bear'

Like 'Johnny Panic and the Bible of Dreams', Plath's 1959 story 'The Fifty-Ninth Bear' explores the shock experienced by individuals who resist the hegemony of consumer capitalism and its hold on the natural world. 'The Fifty-Ninth Bear' has been given little critical attention. Discussion has largely been the province of literary biographers. Lucas Myers says in his Appendix to *Bitter Fame*, 'I was surprised she made a story of the killing of a husband for her husband and their friends to see'.[56] In another version of Myers's moral judgement, Anne Stevenson chides Plath for disliking the story for the wrong reason: on literary grounds, not for regretting its 'ill will against her husband', whose 'family and friends were appalled when it appeared'.[57] Paul Alexander, while not disapproving of Plath, can find only one 'drastic difference' between the 'imagined incident' in the story and 'the real-life incident' of Hughes and Plath losing their supplies to a bear while camping in Yellowstone Park. This difference is the killing of the husband.[58] To speak of the story favourably, yet still in biographical terms, is to do no more justice to the text than the indictments against Plath for writing it at all. Like 'Johnny Panic and the Bible of Dreams', 'The Fifty-Ninth Bear' is about the impoverishment of human beings who inhabit the twentieth century and have lost all forms of meaningful contact with the natural world.

From the story's opening sentence, the young couple who travel to an American national park to 'do' nature react badly when they discover that they are part of a large crowd of tourists trying to capture the wilderness. Perhaps naively, they are startled to find that the national park is a business, a fact that Plath explored a year earlier, in her 1958 story 'Above the Oxbow', which revolves around a couple's argument with a mountain ranger. The two have walked up a mountain, and so object to paying fifty cents to park their non-existent car. Nature, the story suggests, is never free, or priceless, and cannot be idealised. Plath repeats the subject matter of 'Above the Oxbow' in a 1958 poem of the same title,[59] where 'A state view- / Keeper collects half-dollars for the slopes / Of state scenery, sells soda, shows off viewpoints'.[60] In both story and poem, as in 'The Fifty-Ninth Bear', those who 'only come to look' (to borrow a phrase from 'New Year on Dartmoor')[61] are processed like Disneyland guests. In 'The Fifty-Ninth Bear' they are steered from the 'parking lot' and 'midday crowds on the boardwalk' through attractions such as 'Dragon's Mouth' and 'Devil's Cauldron'.[62] Discussing the development of national parks and how 'tourist crowds could be controlled', Peter J. Schmitt explains that 'To offer scenic beauty without destroying the wilderness it was only necessary to build a limited but carefully designed road network between major park attractions'.[63] Plath's protagonists resist such 'control'. Like tourists photographing their children with the wobbling, pillowed incarnations of amusement park cartoon characters, the campers feed the bears, luring them 'with sugar and crackers to pose in front of the camera', even thrusting 'their children under the bear's nose for a more amusing shot'.[64] The husband recoils from the 'spiels of rangers, the popular marvels'.[65] The question 'What hadn't they seen?'[66] is aligned with the consciousness of the wife, Sadie. Here, she may be expressing a strong desire to experience nature as fully as she can, but she also seems to display a consumerist fear. Implicitly, and probably unconsciously, Sadie expresses a nagging suspicion that they have somehow not got their money's worth as travellers, an anxiety that they have missed something a more astute tourist has found. Sadie and her husband play a game of counting each bear they see, which is a way of quantifying the amount of nature they have got.

Nature itself does not simply give pleasure. Fumes from the hot spring of Devil's Cauldron nauseate Norton, the husband. The 'full noon sun'[67] gives him a headache. Material hardship does not cease in the wilderness. Somebody steals the couple's water bag, perhaps a sight-seer more selfish (and thirsty) than they are. Norton withdraws into the privacy of the car. Shielded from other people, and from any direct contact with the very wildlife and natural wonders they have come to experience, he dreams, instead, of the 'animals of the forest'.[68] There are layers of ironies here. Norton behaves like the tourists he wishes to dissociate himself from, who, as Peter J. Schmitt puts it, keep to their cars too and enjoy 'the wilderness as it was framed in their windshields'.[69] Plath keenly recognised the damage cars wreak on the environment. 'Waking in Winter', written a year later, made clear the threat cars pose to the very places they make accessible. Having travelled miles to see the national park, the husband retreats in his dreams; in them, he fantasises a different hinterland filled with creatures that may be indigenous to the place he is from, rather than the place where he is. He imagines animals as he would like them to be, rather than seeking those that actually surround him. He does not simply shun the crowds and the commercialisation of nature; he shrinks from what is unfamiliar or foreign.

Ted Hughes retells 'The Fifty-Ninth Bear' in *Birthday Letters*. His 'The 59th Bear' elaborates upon Plath's depiction of Yellowstone Park; as Hughes puts it, a 'Mislaid Red Indian Mickey Mouse America'. Like Plath's Yellowstone, Hughes's is dotted with 'Uncle Bruins in Disney-land overalls, / Who warned against forest fires'.[70] Yet, in the end, Hughes diminishes Plath's fiction, and his own fine version of it, by giving in to the impulse to diagnose Plath herself, closing down the meanings of her writing, and his own, and seeing the events as evidence of Plath's own pathology. 'I had not understood / How the death hurtling to and fro / Inside your head, had to alight somewhere'.[71]

If we return to Plath's own story, Norton (who I left asleep in the car) is snatched from dreams in which he has been in control, 'fiercely, indefatigably willing the movement of each hoof and paw'. What wakes him is the swerving and halting of the car, and his wife's excited cry, ' "Elk!" '[72] ('The Fifty-Ninth Bear' was written before Yellowstone 'adopted a policy of shooting elk in order to reduce a herd that had become far too large … in response to an earlier policy of killing the elk's predators in order to protect this popular animal'.[73]) Norton opens his eyes to find other cars 'pulling up beside them and behind them', and another mass gathering of camera-carrying tourists who wish to capture the elk for their memories, photo albums and vacation stories. Sadie joins the crowds who gape at the elk as they would an 'astounding accident', but the elk rises 'with a slow, sleepy amazement' and moves off. Norton, on the other hand, stands apart 'on the top of the slope with a quiet, insular dignity'. He takes no notice of the noisy, 'disgruntled' tourists, and composes a silent 'apology to the elk. He had meant well', only to have his thoughts interrupted by Sadie's complaint, 'I didn't even have time for a shot'.[74] This scene is certainly comic, and gently mocks Sadie's insensitivity, as well as Norton's pious snobbery. In spite of the story's seldom-acknowledged humour, 'The Fifty-Ninth Bear' is about the tensions of a marriage where there are immense cultural and philosophical differences between husband and wife. In the above passage, and throughout the story, Sadie is happy to be part of the crowd, to wield her camera and freeze nature, even to intervene in nature by scaring away the animals she and the others come to witness. Alison Byerly has pointed out that 'tourists' enjoyment of landscape' can be 'based less on an appreciation of nature itself than on the secondary image of nature that they themselves constructed'.[75] We can describe Sadie – and her camera – in this way.

The husband, by contrast, looks on disapprovingly at his tourist wife and the other sightseers. He is caught in a fantasy that he understands nature, and does not participate in its vulgar commodification. There are Romantic precedents for this in Thoreau and Wordsworth, who offer their own versions of this desire to be alone with nature, this refusal of materialism. Yet Scott Slovic reminds us that Wordsworth and 'Most nature writers, from Thoreau to the present, walk a fine line … between rhapsody and detachment, between aesthetic celebration and scientific explanation'. A 'suitable balance of proximity to and distance from nature', Slovic writes, 'results in the prized tension of awareness'.[76] It is this 'balance' or 'tension of awareness' that Norton and Sadie both lack, for he is caught in 'rhapsody' and 'proximity', while she is preoccupied with recording instead of looking. Plath reveals both omissions as dangerous. She examines the tenability of a position of special sympathy with animals in an unpublished poem, 'Zeitgeist at the Zoo'. According to the address Plath typed in the top right corner, it was written while she lived at '4 Barton Road, Cambridge, England', and therefore can be dated as 1955 or 1956. The poem is forced and trite, with overdone rhyme and cuteness, but is nonetheless about something serious. In spite of her jokey tone, the poem's speaker (unlike Sadie) recoils from the imprisonment of animals at the zoo: 'Oh, I refuse to cock my kodak / at the domesticated yak'.[77] Nonetheless, the speaker's self-conscious irony in the poem (signalled by its strained form) indicates a *mixture* of identification with and detachment from the animals.

'The Fifty-Ninth Bear' itself does not appear to sympathise with either the husband's fantasy of his oneness with nature, or the wife's readiness to see nature as a product. Plath evaluates the drawbacks of both stances, and shows that neither the wife's nor the husband's perspective on nature is sustainable. Moreover, she reveals the gendered colouring of these attitudes. Sadie 'passe[s], with a line of other tourists',[78] and without Norton, to see a boiling pool, but nature, literally, slaps her in the face, while the other sightseers prevent her from having any private experience of the wilderness:

> a freakish shift in wind flung the hot steam in her face and nearly scalded her to death. And somebody, some boy or group of boys, had spoken to her on the boardwalk and spoiled the whole thing … a solitary woman was a walking invitation to all sorts of impudence.
> All this, Norton knew, was a bid for his company.[79]

The story makes it clear that contempt for crowds is a male luxury. Many women do not feel safe enough in open spaces to commune, one to one, with nature, and so are by necessity more tolerant of the intrusiveness of crowds. In the summer of 1951, Plath wrote in her journal: 'I am a girl, a female always in danger of assault and battery … I want to be able to sleep in an open field, to travel west, to walk freely at night'.[80] It is not that Sadie wants crowds. It is that she feels she needs them, in spite of their inconvenience. Well trained in the 1950s valorisation of 'truly feminine women',[81] though, Sadie would prefer her husband, and her husband alone, to protect her. The story is not simply about Plath's marriage to Hughes, or if it is, we cannot know it. What the story does offer is an exploration of larger issues of sexual politics. Men's and women's perceptions of nature differ because of cultural preferences and experiences, and the practical, material conditions imposed by gender.

As the wife's tolerance of the crowds is punctured, so is the husband's antipathy towards the mob. Blissfully separated from the other sightseers, and reminded by Sadie of the role a husband must play, Norton regards her, 'a few yards ahead of him, invisible, swathed in a mist, but surely his as a lamb on a leash. Her innocence, her trustfulness, endowed him with the nimbus of a protecting god'.[82] After sunset, the couple drive to the lake. Uncertain of whether they have enough petrol to reach it, and finally, ironically, free of other cars, they feel that their long beams are 'no match for the dark battalions of surrounding pines'. Norton thinks 'how pleasant it would be, for a change, to see the beams of another car close behind him'. But the mirror 'brim[s] with darkness' and bears 'down on top of his skull, as if intent to crush the frail, bone-plated shell that set him apart'.[83] For a brief moment, Norton reverses his desire for isolation. To be away from the crowds of tourists becomes, when faced with running out of petrol in the middle of nowhere, a threat. Schmitt reminds us that ' "any protracted, genuine association with nature means a reversion to a state of brutal savagery" '.[84] What Norton has desired throughout the story is at last offered, but revealed as dangerous. The references in this passage to the dark, to the crushed skull, foreshadow Norton's fate. It is a fate of getting what he both wishes for and dreads: absolute union with an animal.

Away from the glare of camera flashes and sightseers, the bear, looked at only by Norton and equally intent on him, kills:

> The darkness fisted and struck. The light went out. ... A hot nausea flared through his heart and bowels. He struggled, tasting the thick, sweet honey that filled his throat and oozed from his nostrils. As from a far and rapidly receding planet, he heard a shrill cry – of terror, or triumph, he could not tell.
>
> It was the last bear, her bear, the fifty-ninth.[85]

Eating, and being eaten, is the key here. When Norton is killed by the bear, he also becomes it. As if he *is* the bear, Norton tastes 'thick, sweet honey that filled his throat' (honey is what bears are supposed to love). At the same time, Norton becomes honey, which seeps 'from his nostrils' and into the bear who feeds on him. He is consumer and consumed.

The story also associates Norton with bears, or makes him one, in a passage that Plath cut from 'The Fifty-Ninth Bear', where he 'eats' his wife. After Norton and Sadie have had sex, Norton feels as if he is coated in her 'honey and milk'. Like a bear or nuzzling animal, he sleeps and rubs his nose gently 'at her breast like a child searching out

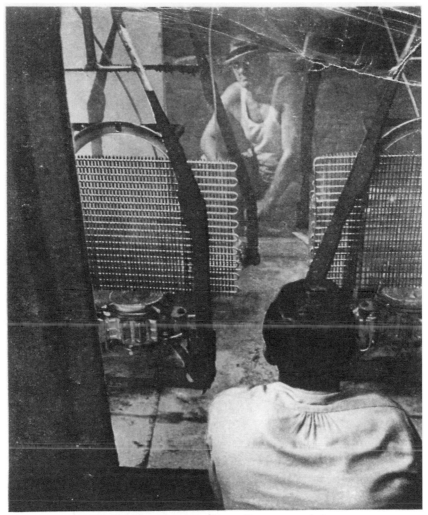

ELECTRIC REFRIGERATORS, ranges and other appliances are made by
Frigidaire Division in Dayton, Ohio. Here, as refrigerator freezing units move
through 37-foot water tank, inspectors look for air bubbles which betray leaks.

Plate 1: Electric refrigerators, ranges and other appliances are made by Frigidaire Division.

Plates 1 to 4 are taken from Sylvia Plath's art scrapbooks and are reproduced courtesy of
the Lilly Library, Indiana University, Bloomington, Indiana, and with kind permission of the
Estate of Sylvia Plath.

Plate 2: A pink dream of a kitchen.

Plate 3: A white dream of a kitchen.

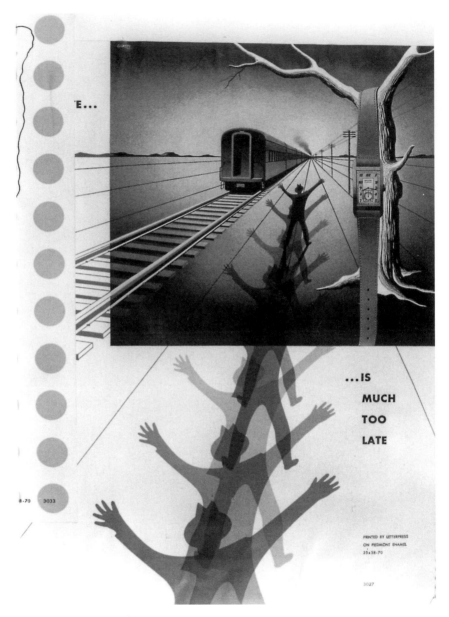

Plate 4: Advertisement for a printer.

its mother'.[86] Honey, and the sensation of eating and being eaten, is therefore also associated with sexuality in the story. Norton can taste his wife, the honey that oozes from her pores to cover him. He can even, the implication is, drink her milk. Yet Norton is also eaten, surrounded by Sadie's scents and fluids as if she has encompassed him. Desire becomes located in a traditional pairing of sex and death, the loss of self that occurs when the boundaries between two different people become blurred. But we might ask why Norton's fulfilled desire, his merging with nature and the bear, leads to his death. Within the logic of the story, he becomes the bear by becoming bear food. The bear assimilates him. Ashes to ashes. Dust to dust. There is a long-standing idea that human beings return to nature through death, feeding animals and plants as they decay back into the earth. This is connected to the Cartesian idea that people are differentiated from animals and plants by consciousness, so that thinking is a human activity. The Romantic view of nature is of a desire for unconsciousness. Plath suggests that this is a type of death wish, and a misguided one at that. Interrupted by Sadie's scream, the privacy of Norton's one and final communion with nature cannot be sustained.

Plath's typescripts for 'The Fifty-Ninth Bear' reveal systematic cuts to the story. What Plath omitted were sex scenes. These might be said to be of embarrassing women's magazine badness, but they are interesting for the way that they allow us to see Plath puzzling over what to do about male sexuality. Moreover, they cement the conceptualisation of Norton as a bear. Moving from one extreme to the other in her depiction of male sexuality, it appears that Plath was finding it difficult to represent it. In one of these cuts, the narrator tells us:

> Her fearful softness was a manna to him. He had never quite lost his awe of her body. Each time he undid her dress, unsheathed her from her electric, crackling silks and frail laces, he felt unaccountably bearish, a violator of her virginal, mauve tipped breasts, her moon curved belly, her incomparable whiteness. Even now, her veils of modesty inflamed him as on their bridal night, when she had shuddered and sprung to response under him like some wild, fine-timbered ship in a high gale.[87]

Here, in a caricature of manly strength that the male character does not wear easily, there is almost too much maleness. Here also, Norton sees himself as 'bearish' and uncivilised, an animal ready to lose control or become 'inflamed' in the face of his desire. The second cut reveals masculinity at the other pole, weakened and feminised, and again speaks of Norton as if he were a bear:

> Night after night she would yield to him with the full, somnambulant abandon of a deep-throated flower, leaving him in her honey and milk, her pungent fragrances. Yet in the very act of love he was unmanned; he nuzzled and drowsed at her breast like a child searching out its mother. [88]

These cut passages suggest that as Plath redrafted the story, she felt it important that there be no distractions from the open space that Sadie and Norton occupy. Plath dispensed with allusions to Sadie's and Norton's married life at home (in the period before they occupy Yellowstone and its wide horizons), perhaps because these do not sit easily in the world of the story. These are writerly decisions, made on literary and practical grounds.

It is worth mentioning one other passage that Plath discards from 'The Fifty-Ninth Bear':

> More and more during the second year of their marriage she seemed unwilling to go anywhere without him – to the market, to the bank, to the park. She clung to him, shy as a child, as if he provided a sanctum outside which she would be ruined, undone by brutal elements. He read her like a book. Even her tantrums were infantile, transparent. A prolonged din of pot-lids in the kitchen, a glass hurled to smithereens in the fireplace, a slammed door – these naïve stage effects testified to some straw too many in her slight load. The simplest question would free her tongue, her tears, and, after a decent interval, embraces, the act of love, would heal the last of her hurt.[89]

What Plath takes out here, besides more of the domestic context, is a reference to Sadie's own volatility and temper. Like the uncomfortable extremities of Norton's sexuality that Plath erases from 'The Fifty-Ninth Bear', this passage depicts a version of contradictory femininity that the story cannot accommodate. Here, Sadie is a baby, but also violent and sexual (just as the deletions about Norton had rendered him overly masculine yet 'unmanned'). Had this passage remained, Plath would have given us a Sadie who was less passive, more culpable and antagonistic. As the story stands, its ending – the question of whether Sadie desires Norton's death, even perhaps brings it about – is undecidable. With the above passage, the weight would have been redistributed, and the ending would be less ambiguous; Sadie would appear as an agent of Norton's death.

If Plath had retained the three cut passages, she would have diminished the intensity with which her story explores the commodification of wilderness, and men's and women's ambivalent feelings about privacy, as well as their different responses to the position of the tourist. Sadie and Norton both desire, and fear, being cut off from the crowds. The story warns that, in the end, any idealised wish to be alone and part of nature means, invariably, death. Plath's 1962 poem 'Elm' also considers the perils and pleasures of isolation, and does so in ecological terms.

Circulating Venom

Or Shall I Bring You the Sound of Poisons?

Writers have perennially spoken of the making of poetry as a sort of gestation and birthing. If you accept this metaphor, and look at Plath's manuscripts and typescripts for 'Elm', you can only conclude that the labour for the poem was long and complicated. Before she achieved its published version, Plath wrote thirteen drafts of 'Elm', and produced two typescripts. The tangles of lines and stanzas, the insertions and scribbled cross-outs, ensure that the 'Elm' manuscripts are exciting and challenging to read. What becomes clear in Plath's successive drafts of the poem is how centrally 'Elm' is absorbed by environmentalism. This is no less true of lines that Plath eventually discarded, for such lines remain in the poem as ghosts, surviving in trace within the metaphors, language and ideas that emerge in the finished version of 'Elm'.

'Elm' expresses a similar environmentalism to *Silent Spring*, and Plath and Carson write out of the same historical moment. David Holbrook, in his still influential book on Plath, reads 'Elm' as evidence that Plath was 'schizoid', and as proof of her 'anguish' and 'deep lack of satisfaction'.[90] This personal approach misses the extent of the poem's environmentalist preoccupations (and can we accurately diagnose somebody's psychological condition on the basis of a poem?). These preoccupations are indicated at the poem's most obvious level by the fact that Plath places a tree as its central persona, and by the fact that the poem's 'action' consists of the Elm describing and reflecting upon its physical situation. In a letter dated 10 October 1962, to Howard Moss, *The New Yorker* editor to whom she submitted 'Elm', Plath writes: 'I think "Soliloquy of the Elm" would be my alternate to "The Elm Speaks", but I think I like your title better. Yes, I think I do'.[91] In 'Elm', the tree merges with another of the poem's personae, a woman.

'Elm' was written on 19 April 1962, two months before *Silent Spring* was serialised in *The New Yorker*. When the elm tree asks, 'Or shall I bring you the sound of poisons?', Plath pre-empts *Silent Spring*'s central metaphor: the idea that the 'sound of poisons' is silence, or 'hush'.[92] The water that the elm tree/woman sucks with its 'great tap root' from the soil is deadly. 'This is rain now, this big hush', she comments, 'And this is the fruit of it: tin white, like arsenic'. The hush evokes not just the paradoxically noiseless sound of rain, but also the lack of animal noises caused by the poison it carries.[93] *Silent Spring* tells us that arsenic is 'the basic ingredient in a variety of weed and insect killers'.[94] The 'fruit', or outcome, of the rain is not just silence. In a more material sense, the fruit of the rain is also what the rain carries: poison, or arsenic.

Many pages of Plath's handwritten drafts for 'Elm' appear on the reverse side of early typescripts of *The Bell Jar*. Plath might have reused paper for ecological reasons: to recycle. More prosaically, Plath certainly got through a great deal of paper, and may have had financial economies in mind as well as ecological. I like Susan R. Van Dyne's speculation that one of Plath's reasons for using early manuscripts of *The Bell Jar* in this way was a 'desire for sympathetic magic'.[95] This is a sort of writer's superstition that a previously completed and successfully placed piece of writing will seep through the page to benefit one's current work. Yet the relationship between the manuscripts of 'Elm' and *The Bell Jar* is more intricate than a mere wish for luck. Plath habitually turned to a previous piece of writing – usually her own or Ted Hughes's – to revisit or argue with the earlier material, or as creative inspiration.

When Plath's narrator asks, 'Or shall I bring you the sound of poisons?' and then refers to rain and the arsenic it bears, she seems to do so in response to the scene from *The Bell Jar* that appears on the other side of the page. Here, written in Plath's hand as an insertion on the typescript, we have Esther's recollection of 'a color photograph of a beautiful laughing young girl with a black mole on her cheek. "Twenty days after that mole appeared the girl was dead," the doctor said. ... I never really found out what the mole was or why the girl died'.[96] These concerns about poisoning, about cancers and burning, percolate from *The Bell Jar* into 'Elm' – mimicking the way that poisons circulate in the poem itself. Passages from the scenes where Esther is literally poisoned at the *Ladies Day* lunch appear to leak from the earlier manuscripts into 'Elm',[97] which depicts its own brand of poisoning. Early drafts of the poem reveal how much more literal Plath originally meant that poisoning to be. While the final version of 'Elm' links the sound of the sea with the speaker's contained but still discernable 'dissatisfactions' (a traditional image of the depths of being), earlier versions make clear that this sea contains 'glittery rubbish',[98] and so is *actually* polluted and toxic.

Like 'Waking in Winter', 'Elm' plays on a common environmentalist trope of sunsets that are not quite right. Over-bright, too intense, and thus dangerous, these sunsets are artificial rather than natural. Such a response to sunset can be found as early as Thomas Hardy's writing. Hardy's 1897 novel *The Well-Beloved* refers to 'those marvellous sunset effects which, if they were not known to be made up of kitchen coal-smoke and animal exhalations, would be rapturously applauded'.[99] 'Elm' describes the effects of nuclear and chemical damage upon a tree and a woman. 'I have suffered the atrocity of sunsets', the speaker explains, and further, 'My red filaments burn and stand, a hand of wires'.[100] At the end of 1961, Plath alluded more than once to the 'repulsive shelter craze for fallout', also mentioning her inability to sleep because of 'all the warlike talk in the papers' and her fear of a nuclear attack.[101]

Long before she came to write the poems that were to make her famous, the possibility of nuclear destruction established its presence in Plath's imagination. In the winter of 1950, Plath wondered

> what would happen to us all if the planes came, and the bombs. ... But the squirrels would still be there, and the birds. Long after, unless the smoke and the radioactivity (Oh, Marie Curie, if you could know!) got them. ... In the back of my mind there are bombs falling, women & children screaming ... I think there would only be the wondering what to eat and where to sleep and how to build out of the wreckage of life and mankind. Yet while America dies like the great Roman Empire died, while the legions fail and the barbarians overrun our tender, steak-juicy, butter-creamy, million-dollar-stupendous land, somewhere there will be the people that never mattered much in our scheme of things anyway. In India, perhaps, or Africa, they will rise. ... And so I will belong to a dark age, and historians will say

> "We have few documents to show how the common people lived at this time. Records lead us to believe that a majority were killed. But there were glorious men." And school children will sigh and learn the names of Truman and Senator McCarthy.[102]

In 1951, Plath wrote:

> When I read that description of the victims of Nagasaki I was sick: "And we saw what first looked like lizards crawling up the hill, croaking. It got lighter and we could see that it was humans, their skin burned off, and their bodies broken where they had been thrown against something." Sounds like something out of a horror story. God save us from doing that again.[103]

Plath demonstrated a precocious combination of powerful imagination, historical awareness and political questioning in these passages, written when she was only at the close of her teens.

'Elm' is one of many poems in which Plath explores the consequences of isolation, and argues against the impulse to hold oneself as separate from the rest of the world (an impulse that she deplores in the craze for fallout shelters). The poem's speaker declares, 'A wind of such violence / Will tolerate no bystanding: I must shriek'.[104] The mushroom cloud, or radioactive poison, cannot be ignored. It causes injuries that cannot be endured with stoical silence. It also calls for responsibility and involvement, a willingness to 'shriek' protest, a refusal of complicit acceptance. Lines that Plath deleted from earlier drafts of the poem invite us to read the speaker's irrepressible shriek as a feminist protest. In this earlier draft, we are told that the elm/woman 'is at war with herself, she is dripping with hatreds', and that 'It is the wind she swallows mostly'. Perhaps thought by Plath to be too blatant or strident, these omitted lines appear on the back of an early typescript from *The Bell Jar*. Here, with a similarly straightforward feminism that did not make it into the published novel, Esther tells us: 'If a woman wanted to do anything interesting outside her home and pay a daily help for doing the dirty work, a man could always fix that by making her have children'.[105] What connects the poem's cancelled lines and the novel's deleted sentence is the sense of entrapment; the elm, like the women about whom Esther worries, is harmed by things that enter her without her consent. The unwanted guest may be poison carried by the wind, or it may be a baby. This is the anxiety that structures the poem, and remains its central concern from its first line until its last. We can see this preoccupation, and its genesis in *The Bell Jar*, from the very first draft of 'Elm', which begins with a line that will not appear in the poem's final version: 'She is not easy, she is not peaceful'. The line appears on the back of a manuscript page from *The Bell Jar* that refers to an infectious wasting disease sneaking into your body to inhabit you and leave you powerless. Esther recalls Buddy writing to her that '"TB is like living with a bomb in your lung ...You just lie around very quietly hoping it won't go off"'[106] not 'easy' or 'peaceful'.

Like 'Waking in Winter', 'Elm' evokes those now familiar photographic images of the visual aftermath of nuclear tests or bombs. Like *Silent Spring*, it also illustrates the consequences of the wanton use of chemicals that alter the complex ecosystem. The poem indicts any refusal to acknowledge the connections between all systems and forms of life. Its first line initiates a rhetorical pretence that the speaker is a mere third person narrator reporting the elm's words, and not sharing its perspective. Such pretence results from a need to cordon off pain and danger, to attribute them to something or somebody else (literally a third and not first person). But the attempt at self-delusion is unconvincing and unsustainable; hence the rapid slippage into the first person. Howard Moss is initially perplexed by the relationship between the third person and the first person in 'Elm'. He wonders about the identity of '"she" ... in the first line', but then answers his own question: 'perhaps the elm?'[107] The narrator clearly speaks with the elm, *is* the elm. Throughout the poem, the elm/woman confronts rather than evades the deadliness that is in her. She faces the 'snaky acids' that course through her branches or veins where sap or blood should be.

Yet in the last two stanzas, alluding to Medusa whose snaky hair resembles a tree's branches, the speaker retreats back into the third person with which the poem began. In doing so, she returns to the inherent dissociation of such a narrative perspective. This shift implies that the elm finds any further admission of the dangerous exchanges between herself and the immediate ecosystem too much to bear. Carson explains: 'no one knew that to fill large areas with a single species of tree was to invite disaster. And so whole towns lined their streets and dotted their parks with elms, and today the elms die and so do the birds'.[108] It is noteworthy that Plath, who received an A in Physical Science and sat in on Chemistry classes as an undergraduate at Smith College,[109] uses the chemical form 'isolate' in 'Elm'. The 'isolate, slow faults'[110] are the deadliest, she warns. According to Plath's own dictionary, an 'isolate' is a substance that is 'separate from all other substances' (Plath did not mark this entry). The word's more usual usage, as a verb, means to 'separate (a patient with an infectious disease) from persons not similarly infected'.[111] Plath connects isolation with death, and so remarks upon the dangers of overdependence on one species. In its depiction of the dangerous consequences of any refusal to intervene, 'Elm' echoes 'Waking in Winter' but makes the point with greater force.

Yet 'Elm' is contradictory in its analysis of the choices between isolation and hybridity, the benefits or penalties of crossing borders. Carson points out that 'The so-called Dutch elm disease entered the United States from Europe in 1930, in elm-burl logs imported for the veneer industry'.[112] 'Elm' plays ironically on what might be seen as the corruption of the new by the old, and the confusion between what is inside and outside, self and not-self, American and European. The speaker refers to a 'dark thing' that slumbers within. The incessant physical reminders of its presence, 'its soft, feathery turnings, its malignity', disturb her.[113] These lines do not make their first appearance until relatively late in the composition of 'Elm'. Exceptionally for 'Elm', when they do occur, they are typed and neat; very together compared to the long and messy tangle of handwriting that has been 'Elm' until this point. They are introduced on the back of a typescript page from *The Bell Jar* where Esther wakes up after contracting ptomaine poisoning from the crabmeat at the *Ladies Day* lunch.

> 'What's the matter with me then?'
> 'Poisoned,' she said briefly. 'Poisoned the whole lot of you. I never seen anythin' like it, sick here, sick there, what have you young ladies been stuffin' yourselves with?'[114]

The elm/woman cannot expel the distress and poison that inhabit her as Esther expels the bad fish. Yet it is difficult to imagine that it would do the elm any good even if she could. Though Esther vomits, something toxic still haunts her through the course of the novel, as if a residue of the contamination remains within her.

'Elm', like its antecedents in *The Bell Jar* and from the first moment of its composition, explores a disturbing indeterminacy between self and not-self. This indeterminacy again calls to mind Kristeva's notion of abjection. It is a state that can be initiated by the beetle that carries the Dutch elm disease and lives within the tree, by poisoning from a dirty sea or contaminated food, or by an infectious disease like TB. Or the indeterminacy may be played out through a deeper sense of some unspeakable repressed identity – the 'dark thing' within the elm/woman that resembles pregnancy. We find in 'Elm', as we did in the 1962 poem 'Cut', that what is foreign or ostensibly without has always already been within. Poisons are not simply 'out there'. Not only do they escape the boundaries of the individual into other systems, they also threaten to leave these other systems and enter that individual. Similarly, as Plath's writing shows again and again, America and Europe are not separate places with disconnected meanings. Neither people nor poisons respect borders. As Carson puts it, insecticides 'do not single out the one species of which we desire to be rid'.[115]

Death in the House

The permeability of the human body is also explored in another poem written in 1962, 'The Detective'. This poem concerns the attempts of its Sherlock Holmes like speaker (and his voiceless companion Watson) to solve a mystery not just of how a man actually or figuratively killed his female partner, but also of the degree to which environmental poisons are implicated in the crime. An analysis of this process reveals a contiguity of Plath's thought with Rachel Carson's, or even a decided debt to *Silent Spring*.

Again, the poem has mainly been read in terms of Plath's personal life. Linda Wagner sees 'The Detective' as a 'quasi-comic anti-Hughes poem',[116] while Susan Van Dyne believes that Plath here 'recasts marriage as a criminal act, an intimate violation that robbed her of her poetic voice'.[117] Whatever the validity of such interpretations, the poem undoubtedly poses questions about the environment. Such a reading of the poem depends on a literalism similar to that which Jonathan Bate deploys in *Romantic Ecology*, a study of William Wordsworth that is one of the founding texts of ecocriticism. Bate reasserts the importance of nature in Wordsworth by aligning Wordsworth studies with modern environmentalism. He observes that many recent poststructuralist readings of Wordsworth have emphasised the metaphorical at the expense of the referential. An environmentalist reading would have it that a poem may well be metaphorical, but is also about what it claims to be about. Specifically, 'nature' is not merely a vehicle for human concerns. Bate attempts to show that what 'literature [or Wordsworth] is "about"'[118] is the environment.

In an issue of *The New Yorker* that makes numerous references to the combined effects of 'radioactive particles and man-made chemicals',[119] Carson writes:

> detergents are now a troublesome and practically universal contaminant of public water supplies ... Some detergents may promote cancer in an indirect way – acting on ... tissues so that they more easily absorb dangerous chemicals.[120]

Two years before *Silent Spring*'s publication in *The New Yorker*, Plath makes a similar argument in a letter to her mother: 'Already a certain percentage of unborn children are doomed by fallout and no one knows the cumulative effects of what is already poisoning the air and sea'.[121] In the poem the Detective asks what the woman was 'doing when it blew in'. What, the reader wonders, is this mysterious 'it'? The Detective notices 'smoke rising', and a 'smell of years burning' in this death valley where the killer's eyes move 'sluglike and sidelong'.[122] These clues suggest that the murderer – or 'it' – is not necessarily (or only) a man, but may also be the radioactive fallout from a nuclear bomb or test, or a power station leak.[123] When the Detective observes that the 'case' is one of 'vaporization', he refers to the woman's physical body as much as her individuality.

Like Carson, Plath does not supply a single cause for the destruction, but emphasises the fact that different toxins and particles co-operate with one another. In the house the Detective encounters the scent of polish. 'Which of the poisons is it?' he wonders of the murder weapon. 'Which of the nerve-curlers, the convulsors? Did it electrify?'[124] The poem identifies bourgeois cleanliness with poison, criticising the ease with which all impurities, insects and invisible life forms can be deleted. Carson warns that 'Some detergents may promote cancer'.[125] Plath appears to be taking up Carson's warning when she dramatises the fact that, though deceptively harmless, the polish might kill not just because it is a symptom of imprisoning domesticity, but because it is *actually* poisonous. The symptoms described by the Detective resemble the damage to nerve tissues caused by the 'organic phosphates' Carson discusses in *Silent Spring*.[126] The line 'There is only the moon, embalmed in phosphorus' supports Holmes's conclusion that the case is one of 'vaporization'.[127] In an early draft of the poem, a comma follows 'phosphorus', then: '~~the barren queen. Her light like~~ the bright scalpel'.[128] Consequently, 'phosphorus' was modified directly (if only temporarily) by 'the bright scalpel'. The moon's sharp light cuts like a 'scalpel' through the shimmering mist or cloud that veils it on a dark, not perfectly clear night. Natural causes are not the only reasons why this moon glows, though. The moon glows because it is radioactive *and* because of the presence of vaporised organic phosphates. Carson tells us that the organic phosphates used in cleaning products, such as 'benzene hexachloride', are also 'used in vaporizers – devices that pour a stream of volatilized insecticide into homes, offices, and restaurants'.[129] If we read Carson's information alongside Plath's poem, we see that 'The Detective' examines the way that the woman is constructed as an insect, pest or germ.

For Plath, the home is metaphorically and literally toxic. For Carson, it is only the latter. Plath pushes the logic of domesticity to its extreme and finds death. Absolute cleanliness and sterility can be achieved only through the eradication of all living things. For Carson and Plath alike, the primary victims of the toxicity of housework are women and children. 'There is some evidence that women are more susceptible than men, very young children more than adults',[130] writes Carson. Holmes describes the female victim's physical damage. The effects are similar to those that might result from radiation or chemical poisoning.

Among the parts of the woman's body that are damaged is her mouth. Susan Van Dyne argues that 'The insatiable mouth recalls the conflation, frequent in the Boston journals, of emotional hungers and her appetite for artistic success, and Plath's habit of looking to Hughes to feed both'.[131] Although Van Dyne identifies the important link that Plath makes between the mouth and art, it seems reductive to place Plath and Hughes as the dramatic personae of the poem. The destruction of the woman's reproductive parts is bound up with the loss of her voice, identity and creative powers. After all, her primary organ of expression, her 'insatiable' mouth, is an 'absence', cut away and 'hung out' to 'dry' as if on a clothesline. Given the poisonous house and dangerous domesticity of the poem, this is a fitting and ironic 'punishment'. Mothering is glimpsed, here, as an oppressive situation for women and children. The Detective describes the woman's breasts as 'harder' than the mouth. The breasts are materially altered. That is, they are less soft in structure than they once were. Yet they are also harder in a symbolic sense, having resisted the effects of poison and domestic death for longer than the mouth. The implication is that the woman preserves what is essential for her children above all else. She will sooner be silent than give up her milk and abdicate responsibility for their physical needs.

113

Given the physical and emotional pressures upon her, such an effort cannot remain forever successful, for

> The milk came yellow, then blue and sweet as water.
> There was no absence of lips, there were two children,
> But their bones showed.[132]

The punished and absent mouth mentioned by Van Dyne evokes the baby's suckling lips as much as the mother's voice. The constitution of mother's milk is also ambiguous, though represented with physiological accuracy: rich liquid that, towards the end of a feed, becomes more watery; or 'yellow' colostrum that, after the first days of a baby's life, gives way to a less intense fluid. Or we could read these lines as a depiction of milk fever. These breasts produce milk that might also be read as pernicious. How can we account for the desolation evoked in the poem, the tainted 'yellow' milk and then the nutrient-free 'water' which result in the children's starvation? One explanation is that the poisoned ecosystem has infiltrated and then damaged the woman's reproductive system.[133] Karen J. Warren reminds us that 'Persistent toxic chemicals, largely because of their ability to cross the placenta, to bioaccumulate, and to occur as mixtures, pose serious health threats disproportionately to infants, mothers, and the elderly'.[134] 'The Detective' shows us, yet again, that in Plath's work there is no safe demarcation between inside and out. The Detective never does locate the vaporised woman. Within the framework of the poem, we can only imagine that she is in the air, in the soil, in the water. Perhaps she makes her way into other bodies and systems, as her poisoned milk made its way into her children, a circulation between bodies that we will now consider more fully in Plath's late 1962 poem, 'Fever 103°'.

Water, Water Make Me Retch

Like 'Elm' and 'The Detective', 'Fever 103°' dramatises the movement of dangerous substances between an individual body and a larger ecosystem. Like 'The Detective', 'Fever 103°' occupies the same ground as *Silent Spring*. As its title suggests, 'Fever 103°' concerns the very high body temperature of its speaker, and explores what might have caused this. In one breath, the poem constructs the body's relation to the environment, sexuality and the making of poetry. The speaker tells her lover, 'Darling, all night / I have been flickering, off, on, off, on'.[135] Later, she asks without a question mark (and so forces an interrogative into an imperative), 'Does not my heat astound you. And my light'. The speaker describes herself as 'Glowing and coming and going, flush on flush'.[136] Consciousness is like a light switched on and off. These lines typify the poem's strategy of linking sexual arousal and orgasm, poetic activity and brilliance, and the physical symptoms of high fever. They show that there is something very nasty in the immediate ecological, erotic and cultural systems. All of these become analogous circuits.

Robyn Marsack has demonstrated the influences of T. S. Eliot and Dante on the poem.[137] More typically, and less convincingly, 'Fever 103°' has been read as Plath's 'own suffering' raised to 'universal dimensions',[138] or as her 'retaliation against her husband for his infidelity'.[139] Van Dyne sees the poem in terms of 'Plath's stereotypical postures of victimization and the imagery of her transfiguring new poetics'.[140] I want to consider 'Fever 103°' as a politically and environmentally engaged poem that looks resolutely outward, evaluating the place of the individual in the larger world.

The poem charts the speaker's physical response to a material and cultural system that has been damaged by technology, politics and pollution:

> Love, love, the low smokes roll
> From me like Isadora's scarves, I'm in a fright
>
> One scarf will catch and anchor in the wheel,[141]

The reference to the famous dancer choked by her own scarf while driving suggests the speaker's recognition that it can be deadly for women to please men. Like the narrator of 'Waking in Winter', the glamorous Isadora Duncan submits herself to male technology – the car – as well as male-orientated female vanity. The scarf is worn to make an impression, to make her look attractive, and it kills her, strangling her like the poisonous smoke that is at once a product of her own violable body and the car's pollution. As in 'The Detective', and like *Silent Spring*, 'Fever 103°' acknowledges the particular vulnerability of the very young and old to such poisons, which the speaker imagines 'Choking the aged and the meek'. Elisabeth Bronfen reads these lines, and the poem as a whole, as evidence that the speaker's 'internal heat and her self-sufficient light turn her into an instrument of destruction' until she assumes 'divine proportions', shedding 'lovers' and 'selves'.[142]

The poem can also be read much more literally: as about poisons, and the way they circulate in the ecosystem. The poem's speaker does not simply excrete poisons. She takes them in from others, from around her, and gives them out again in a series of exchanges that are complex and circular. She does not merely injure others. She too is injured, and must be, for that is the inevitable consequence of breathing and drinking and eating in the world she inhabits. In spite of its cautions about environmental hazards, 'Fever 103°' is a potentially uncomfortable poem for feminist readers who may not wish to admit its ambivalent pleasure in the combined dangers which murder Isadora Duncan and threaten the speaker. The speaker tenderly addresses her lover: 'Love, love'. She is aware of the risks presented by a culture in which it is difficult, if not impossible, to survive without relying on technology and pleasing men. Nonetheless, she experiences these aspects of that culture as sexually exciting as well as problematic.

The suffocating pollution and 'Radiation' from 'Hiroshima ash' account for the speaker's own persistent fever, but water – one of the things most fundamental to her survival – also conspires with these poisons. Almost deliriously, she pleads and complains, 'Lemon water, chicken / Water, water make me retch'.[143] Reminiscent in cadence, image and harmfulness of that all-pervasive water in Coleridge's 'The Rime of the Ancient Mariner', this water is both treatment for and cause of her illness.[144] The lemon water treats her illness because it replenishes fluid, or makes her retch and thus expel the poison and break the fever. The water causes her illness because radiation or chemicals contaminate it. Carson frequently connects polluted water and sickness:

> many man-made chemicals act in much the same way as radiation; they lie long in the soil, and enter into living organisms, passing from one to another. Or they may travel mysteriously by underground streams, emerging to combine, through the alchemy of air and sunlight, into new forms, which kill vegetation, sicken cattle, and work unknown harm on those who drink from once pure wells.[145]

Such a poisoning of water might explain the fever suffered by the speaker of Plath's poem, who, describing her symptoms, tells us that she is made of 'pure acetylene'. Common usage of acetylene suggests a blowtorch, as Plath knew, for she underlined the definition of the word in her own dictionary:

> *Chem.* A colorless gaseous hydrocarbon ... <u>formed by the direct union of carbon and hydrogen in the electric arc</u>, by the action of water on certain carbides, etc. In a burner it produces a <u>brilliant white diffusive light</u>, and combined with <u>oxygen is used for welding</u>.[146]

To this definition, *Kingzett's Chemical Encyclopaedia* lets us add the fact that acetylene is a 'poisonous hydrocarbon'.[147]

Carson explains that the chlorinated hydrocarbons which make up widely used insecticides 'have a strong effect on metabolism; that is, ... they have the ability to cause a potentially fatal rise in temperature'.[148] The poem's speaker, misguided in her trust of the water supply, has drunk these hydrocarbons, this poisonous acetylene, and they have become a part of her, generating her unnatural heat. Ironically, Plath writes the very first draft of 'Fever 103°' – a poem filled with her knowledge of science – on the back of the typescript page from *The Bell Jar* where Esther triumphantly manipulates herself out of her required (and dreaded) college chemistry course. Instead, Esther sits in on chemistry while not enrolling in the class, and writes poems while pretending to listen to the lectures. This trick on the lecturer, and the whole college system, is enacted because Esther hates the 'hideous, cramped, scorpion-lettered formulas' of physics. She dreads the 'ugly abbreviations with different decimal numbers after them' on the 'chart of the ninety-odd elements in the chemistry lab'.[149]

Acetylene is 'unstable' and 'must be handled with unusual care for it can detonate, not only with oxygen, but also without oxygen, into its elements'.[150] We cannot know if the 'potentially fatal rise in temperature' and relentless physical and emotional experiences of Plath's acetylene speaker are a direct response to the effects of the hydrocarbons that Carson describes. At the very least, the speaker's predicament is the result of Plath's detailed scientific knowledge and more general awareness of journalistic concerns about the effect of poisons on human beings and ecosystems. The image of the speaker's body throwing off its 'beads of hot metal'[151] suggests that she is sweating out the poisons she has taken in; that there is a constant exchange of substances between individual bodies and other ecosystems. With its reference to the 'Hothouse baby'[152] who is among the most endangered, the poem makes it clear in its first half that there is no protected space, no airtight seal. Nobody is invulnerable. The poem's form duplicates this idea of connection, particularly in the very complicated end rhymes that link the ideas and words of tercets that are positioned at some distance from one another: 'fright', 'white', 'night', and 'light' appear in the fourth, eighth, tenth, and fourteenth of the poem's eighteen tercets.

The poem's images of melting and forced fusion also reflect postwar and cold war concerns with the effects of nuclear explosions on the human body. The 1959 film *Hiroshima Mon Amour*, directed by Alan Resnais and written by Marguerite Duras, seems a likely influence here (as well as on 'Elm').[153] A. Alvarez has astutely remarked of 'Fever 103°', 'perhaps she was remembering the film *Hiroshima Mon Amour*, where adultery, radiation and expiation were also joined inextricably together'.[154] The central visual image in 'Fever 103°' seems to come straight from the film's opening scenes: Plath's adulterous lovers, like the film's, expose their naked, greased skin to radioactive air motes. This 'Hiroshima ash' floats and whirls like tiny dots of light, until it finally clings to flesh, and penetrates their tangled bodies. The heroine of *Hiroshima Mon Amour* visits the Hiroshima museum, which harbours some of the terrible relics of the day the bomb was dropped on the city. These include pieces of twisted metal, often containing traces of human bodies. The body of the poem's speaker, unnaturally hot with radioactive heat, melting and producing its metal beads, appears to register such an impact. 'Fever 103°', like others of Plath's poems, reflects the horrifying and (in the early 1960s) still startling impression of black and white newsreel footage from the war: the liberation of Belsen; the twisted limbs of concentration camp victims. The connections between *Hiroshima Mon Amour* and the poem are not simply visual, but also linguistic. The film refers, like Plath's poem, to poisoned water and the dangers besetting the food chain after a nuclear holocaust. 'The rain brought fear. Ashes raining on the waters of the Pacific. The waters of the Pacific killed. … Food brought fear'.[155] The film might even be said to influence the poem's narrative structure. The film's heroine provides its narrative voiceover. Recounting what she saw in Hiroshima, she is repeatedly interrupted by her male lover's denial and contradiction. 'Nothing. You know nothing', is his refrain. Plath's heroine also addresses her lover, but in a poem that is keenly attuned to its historical moment, Plath does not allow him to punctuate, or affect, her narrator's description of personal and world history, and the connection between the two.

The Complications of Masculinity

Nervous Prostration

For many critics and biographers, the final line of 'Lady Lazarus', 'And I eat men like air', has come to represent Sylvia Plath's own stance on men.[156] Plath, the stance has it, dislikes men, is positively dangerous to them. Anne Stevenson sees 'Lady Lazarus' as one of three poems whose central personae are 'merciless self-projections of Sylvia', while in the last line, the 'Sylvia figure' is 'very dangerous indeed'.[157] Alvarez has described 'Lady Lazarus' as 'angry', as 'a declaration of war'.[158] York Notes, though not the state of the art on Plath scholarship, exert a great influence on large numbers of readers who turn to them for 'answers' – and exam success. Their assessment of 'Lady Lazarus' typifies the unashamedly biographical way the poem's famous last line has been read. 'Lady Lazarus' is 'a harshly mocking poem boasting of the poet's ability to survive accidents and suicide attempts'. The last line 'can be interpreted as either a feminist declaration or a hostile threat to all mankind'.[159] The problem here is not just the unfairness (and dubiousness) of making assumptions about Plath's personal views and lived existence because of a poem. The problem is also that this view has coloured the expectations, and then opinions, of numerous readers. Worse still, this view of Plath and the one poem expands to cover everything that Plath ever wrote.

'Paralytic', written on 29 January 1963, is one of many of Plath's poems that counter the view that her writing is hostile to men. It is one of seven poems that, according to Jacqueline Rose, are 'hardly ever talked about', in which Plath 'takes up a male persona'.[160] The poem's male speaker lies in a hospital bed paralysed, describing his hospital room and physical situation. The poem examines quite specific effects of environmental pollution on the human body. At the same time, it explores pressures exerted upon masculinity. Again, *Silent Spring* may well have been a source or stimulant.

Silent Spring chronicles the 'delayed effects' of 'damage done to the nervous system by chemicals in the environment'. Carson cites Dieldrin as having 'long-delayed consequences ranging from "loss of memory, insomnia, and nightmares to mania"'.[161] She describes the effects of organic phosphates. These 'have the power to cause lasting physical damage to nerve tissues and … to induce mental disorders. Various cases of delayed paralysis have followed the use of one or another of these insecticides'.[162] The speaker of Plath's poem exhibits similar symptoms. But his paralysis results not just from his loss of motor functions (nerve damage that might be caused by his exposure to poisons), but also from his estrangement from the mother and from femininity. He describes a movement from the primary bodily relation of the infant with the mother ('No fingers to grip, no tongue') to a relation with the male technology that has replaced her ('My god the iron lung').[163] Plath underlined the definition of iron lung in her own dictionary, which played up the elements of technology and infancy that any reference to an iron lung evokes:

> **iron lung**. A device for <u>artificial respiration in which rhythmic alternations in the air pressure in a chamber surrounding a patient's chest force air into and out of the lungs.</u> It is of special value when the nerves governing the chest muscles fail to function because of *infantile paralysis*. [my italics][164]

The speaker himself becomes an instrument. Like a vacuum cleaner, he sucks dirt and pollution out of the air and into his lungs or 'Dust bags'.[165] His alienated position anticipates Kristeva's theory that the semiotic, which is allied with the bodily and the mother, gives way to the symbolic, which is associated with the grammatical and the father. Put simply, we could see this as a movement from baby babble to carefully structured and syntactically correct sentences. Kristeva explains: 'Language as symbolic function constitutes itself at the cost of repressing instinctual drive and continuous relation to the mother'.[166] The speaker has regressed into an 'infantile paralysis' and needs an artificial mother to breathe for him, to keep him alive.

Val Plumwood has summarised the key problems of any theory that aligns men with culture and technology, and women with nature. (Plumwood calls this the 'angel in the ecosystem'.) Such theory is not only essentialist – that is to say, oblivious to cultural and material construction in favour of an assumption that men and women are 'naturally' and invariably 'that way'. Such a theory also 'fails to recognise the dynamic of power',[167] refusing to acknowledge the fact that power is unstable and shifting, and does not immutably reside with masculinity. 'Paralytic' appears to address these very tensions. After alluding to his wife and daughters, the speaker refers to his oxygen tent as 'A clear / Cellophane I cannot crack'.[168] Syntactically, we can attach this impenetrable cellophane barrier to the speaker's wife, daughters, waters and/or his own body parts. The very femininity and primary physical senses the speaker yearns for, yet is divorced from, themselves gag him. The poem begins by ostensibly positioning masculinity and femininity in opposition, but these poles soon shift. The cellophane stands in for the speaker's female family, though it is a product of medical technology that is conventionally associated with masculinity. At the same time, cellophane is also a product that is commonly associated with feminine domestic activity.

Femininity, like nature, is in this poem both what the speaker wants ('Let me relapse'), and at the same time what he is protected from ('My god … Will not / Let me relapse').[169] Melanie Klein argues that the child's ambivalence towards the mother is 'split between the good and bad breast'. For Klein, the breast is both synecdoche and metonym: synecdoche because it is a part of the mother (mammary tissue) that stands for her; metonym because it is an attribute or quality (goodness or malignity) that describes her. Plath's speaker engages in precisely this division. The good, 'gratifying breast'[170] offers unlimited satisfaction, or milk perpetually on tap. The post-semiotic (linguistically and culturally law-abiding) subject is nostalgic for such gratification. The bad breast is the persecuting, 'starched inaccessible breast'[171] of the speaker's nurse who, like the mother, has 'withheld'[172] sustenance and love, and therefore threatens destruction and alienation, leaving him a 'Dead egg' resting on a 'world I cannot touch'.[173] The breast evokes the interpenetration of bodies, the exchange of fluids. The breast is about the osmosis of substances, benign or pernicious, between two individuals and the ecosystems they inhabit.

We have not rid ourselves of the impulse to cordon off environmentally protected zones: from science fiction images of domed cities, to experiments in the 1980s with climate-controlled, puncture-proof eco-domes inhabited by human beings; from enclosed shopping malls, to contemporary nature reserves. (Pragmatically, these reserves may be the only way to protect endangered species.) Such separation, whether by an oxygen tent or a fallout shelter, is a recurrent motif of Plath's writing, which is often critical of the impulse towards such separation. 'Paralytic' suggests that however dangerous the materials outside one's own body may be, the isolation of not being able to partake in them is a torture. At the same time, such substances can sever our connection with our environment. The price of the speaker's former contact with the 'outside' is disconnection, paralysis and isolation. 'Paralytic' ends with a characteristically Plathian doubleness. It is not clear whether the speaker is a smiling and inscrutable bundle of wants and desire, or whether he smiles in the pleasure of having triumphed over his longings. The poem concludes by moving from the hospital machinery to an image of nature that is androgynous and autoerotic: a flower that is masculine and feminine, self-propagating and self-sufficient in its pleasure. But the 'claw'[174] of this magnolia can be either a piece of it, or the pull of it – the speaker's attraction to something he cannot have but yearns for.

The Surgeon at 2 a.m.

'The Surgeon at 2 a.m.' was written on 29 September 1961. To help Plath write, Ted Hughes provided her with lists of subjects for poems, and Plath used many of his suggestions, the 'Surgeon at 2 a.m.' included.[175] These lists come close to reading like the Contents pages of Plath's work. Many of Hughes's suggestions are ticked or starred or bullet pointed, as if Plath has marked them to register the fact that she has completed a poem. 'The Surgeon at 2 a.m.' is one of numerous poems (this one also with an environmental edge) whose narrator is assumed to be male. As Anne Stevenson puts it, 'he strolls like God'.[176] For Jacqueline Rose '"The Surgeon at 2 a.m." is only one of a number of Plath's poems in which she takes up a male persona'.[177] Yet the poem never allows the reader to determine whether the speaker, a surgeon on duty in the middle of the night, is male or female. This indefiniteness is absolutely intentional on Plath's part, as her successive drafts of the poem make clear.

Plath removes all traces of gender identity from the narrator, and then puts them back. She does this repeatedly. At each stage of the poem's composition, she wrestles with the one reference in the poem that makes the narrator certainly male, but in the end, she discards it. In the first handwritten draft of 'The Surgeon at 2 a.m.',[178] Plath writes the line 'I turn like St. George with my knife', but then crosses it out. Variant versions of this are written but then deleted in the second handwritten draft of the poem. These include 'I am St. George with his knife' and the sardonic 'like St. George with his little knife'. All references to the male St George are out by the third handwritten draft, but restored by the fourth, where the line 'I am St. George with my knife'[179] is written, expunged, put back just after the cross-out, then cancelled again. By the fifth, typed draft, all traces of St George are gone, and remain so through two more typed drafts until the poem's final version. Plath evidently liked these lines, and the resonance of the martyred patron saint of England, yet the reference also appears to have made her uncomfortable and uncertain. She relinquishes the allusion only after some struggle, and the surgeon's gender remains unspecified.

Plath herself said in a 1962 interview, 'I think if I had done anything else I would have liked to be a doctor. This is the polar opposition to being a writer, I suppose. ... perhaps I'm happier writing about doctors than I would have been being one'.[180] Clearly, Plath would never have regarded a career in medicine as an entirely male province, though it is hard to imagine that she would have been oblivious to the difficulties a woman would face in such a profession in the 1950s and early 1960s. By refusing to make the surgeon decidedly male, Plath challenges her readers' assumptions; many readers and critics walk right into the trap. Nonetheless, I don't think that Plath left the surgeon's gender unspecified merely because she wanted to highlight sexist assumptions, or make a political statement about professions for women. The poem makes it clear that if it leaves a space for a woman to be a surgeon, it also leaves a space for her to behave as imperialistically and power-worshipfully as any male doctor ever did.

To Plath's genderless surgeon, the human body is a terrain to be colonised: 'I worm and hack in a purple wilderness'.[181] When the rhetoric, and the attempt to gain control, cannot be perfectly accomplished, the surgeon shifts from the metaphor of the body as an unruly landscape to a metaphor of the body as a museum piece. During the first half of the poem, to the surgeon the body is a 'garden I have to do with'. Its organs are 'tubers and fruits', a 'mat of roots', a 'lung-tree' and 'orchids'.[182] The informal syntax here, the talky phrase 'have to do with' (breaking a grammatical rule and ending with a preposition) allows Plath to suggest two things. First, that the body or garden is what the scornful surgeon must put up with: a second best thing. Second, and more straightforwardly, that the body or garden is simply what the surgeon's job or business is. By the poem's second half, the body becomes a 'statue' whose veins are 'intricate, blue piping' beneath 'pale marble'. At this point, the surgeon exclaims upon his admiration for the Romans, presumably because of the perfect control they exercised over their architecture: their unmessy sculptures. This shift from speaking of the body as a wilderness to speaking of it as a statue comes at a moment where the surgeon fails to control that body. It is a moment where its messiness literally spills over: 'The blood is a sunset. I admire it. / I am up to my elbows in it, red and squeaking. / Still it seeps up, it is not exhausted.' Only when the body is regarded as a statue and no longer animate can the surgeon say in triumph, 'I have perfected it', and celebrate escaping from such messy corporeality altogether: 'Tomorrow the patient will have a clean, pink plastic limb'.[183] Plath here satirises a version of postwar consumer capitalism which has it that anything home-grown or natural must be inferior to the artificial and factory-made – the human body included. (Advertisers reversed this strategy in the 1980s and 1990s, so that 'home-grown' and 'natural' have become key terms that they assume customers will value, while merchandisers have attempted to play down anything 'artificial' about their products.) Garden or sculpture: these are the limits of what a sick person can be to Plath's surgeon. He or she refuses to see the patient as a person, and is helped in this dehumanisation by the operating theatre's procedures, the sheets that ensure 'As usual there is no face'.[184]

Feminists have often accused the male medical profession of failing to treat patients as human beings, just as they have regarded imperialism as a largely male policy. 'The Surgeon at 2 a.m.' suggests that when women are in positions of power, they are as capable as men of the desire to own and control, and as quick to trample upon anybody who interferes with this impulse. Plath only reveals the gender of the patient in the last stanza, where we learn that the cut-open body is male. By making the patient a man, Plath shuns any simplistic depiction of yet another female victim of the medical profession. At both ends of the equation, surgeon and patient, Plath rejects any stereotypically gendered relationship of power and passivity, or coloniser and colonised. At every stage of the poem, Plath's possibly female surgeon thrills at power – as in its last, startlingly sharp and beautiful lines: 'I am the sun, in my white coat, / Gray faces, shuttered by drugs, follow me like flowers'. [185] The last line finishes the only one of the poem's five stanzas that concludes without an end rhyme. Up until this point, the poem's rhyme scheme has en-sured that the last line of each stanza rhymes with at least one of the three lines that precede it, but the pattern is finally broken. This rupture seems to echo the surgeon by saying: I stand out, importantly, unattached and unrelated to anything; I am special and different. Such a perspective is the very opposite of an environmentalist view. To regard all other human beings as the inhabitants of a world from which you are entirely detached, to view them as victims of illnesses that you can control, but to which you are immune, is, in the world of Plath's poems (and in our own), delusional. Just as Robert Browning wrote dramatic monologues spoken by unreliable narrators who invited readers to resist them, so Plath does not create the surgeon to endorse his or her view, but to dramatise an outlook that is impoverishing, as well as unsustainable.

Environmentalist and Destroyer

Two poems that highlight the connection between poetic indetermin-acy and ecology are 'Pheasant', written on 7 April 1962, and 'The Rabbit Catcher', written the following month, on 21 May. 'Pheasant' is linked at composition stage to another of Plath's environmentalist poems, 'Elm'. Plath dated 'Elm' twelve days after 'Pheasant', and her handwritten drafts of the two poems are intertwined. One page of an early draft of 'Elm' contains phrases from both poems.[186] Plath draws a line beneath a section of 'Pheasant in the New Year' and continues with 'Elm' as if they are part of the same poem. It is difficult to look at these drafts and not take away an impression that Plath's environmentalist project was consistent and systematic; it is hard to see some of these environmentalist poems as separate. The connections that are so apparent in the drafts encourage us to see these poems as sections of a larger project, or even of a larger poem.

Like the final image of 'Paralytic', and like 'The Surgeon at 2 a.m.', 'Pheasant' hinges on an ambiguity of gender. After a hill walk, its speaker recalls a pheasant she or he has observed, and contemplates the legitimacy of killing or owning such an animal. 'Pheasant' complicates any assumptions the reader might have that there is a privileged kinship between women and nature. The poem begins, 'You said you would kill it this morning. / Do not kill it'.[187] Janice Markey believes that the poem's 'female narrator is forced to beg her male companion for the life of the pheasant.' However, the speaker, like the person who is asked to spare the pheasant, is of unspecified gender. Markey also argues that in this poem 'the attitudes of the speaker and the speaker's partner contrast sharply.' In an essentialist reading that assumes men are 'naturally' brutish, Markey sees the poem as depicting the 'inherent trend in men towards wanton violence and destructiveness'.[188]

The speaker, on the contrary, acknowledges in herself, or himself, the coexistence of sympathy with a supposedly masculine desire to kill and possess 'nature'. It cannot be a coincidence that Plath drafted 'Pheasant' on the back of a typescript page from *The Bell Jar* in which Esther speaks sardonically of a view that sees men and women as entirely polarised. 'The main point of this article was that a man's world is different from a woman's world and man's emotions are different from a woman's emotions and only marriage can bring the two worlds and the two different sets of emotions together properly',[189] she explains. Despite the plea, 'Let be, let be', the speaker of 'Pheasant' is not wholly innocent, not simply pleading for clemency. We cannot dismiss the yearning admiration for possession in the line 'It is something to own a pheasant', in spite of the seemingly exonerating qualification that follows it, 'Or just to be visited at all'.[190]

In fact, to own a pheasant is to be a member of the English aristocracy. Plath plays this up in an early draft of the poem, where she follows the statement 'It is something to own a pheasant' with a more precise formulation of what that 'something' would mean. It would mean you were 'Almost royal'[191] – two words Plath wrote twice, and deleted twice, keeping them out of the final version. To own a pheasant you need to own land, probably a country estate. Indeed, in some cases pheasants on a tenant's land would be the landlord's property. Seen in this way, the speaker's companion potentially transgresses the laws of class, and the speaker's attitude is ambivalent: she or he desires and admires the privileges of aristocracy, yet feels excited by the companion's possible defiance of it. While the speaker denies that the pheasant possesses a 'spirit', asserting instead that it is 'simply in its element',[192] it is worth pointing out that the pheasant is not a native bird in England (whether or not Plath realised this) and is not, therefore, 'in its element'. Moreover, pheasants can only be reared successfully if predators are ruthlessly exterminated. This is a circumstance that again links Plath's environmentalist project with the ways she dramatises the instability of national identity, and the erroneousness of assuming that anything or anyone has a 'natural' place.

Carolyn Merchant's account of the two traditional and opposing views of the natural world is relevant here. There is the view of 'nature as a nurturing mother' associated with a 'premodern organic world'. There is the male, seventeenth-century view famously propagated by Francis Bacon of a nature that, through the 'development of science as a methodology',[193] could be understood and then controlled. This is the view of nature Markey ascribes to the companion of the poem's narrator. The logic of these views for crude theories of the ways men and women might write would be that women's writing about the environment favours the organic account, and men's the scientific. Defying this logic, Plath's writing does not comply with any simple organicist view that women are one with nature and in opposition to violence and technology. Nor, at the other extreme, is there any engagement in Nietzschean power worship. There is that desire, expressed by the genderless speaker of 'Pheasant', to control nature, to 'own' the Pheasant. Yet this *coexists* with a seemingly contradictory acknowledgement of the bird's separateness, and the gesture of intervention to ensure its survival.

The eight tercets, or three-line stanzas, of 'Pheasant' are composed of perfect nine-syllable lines. The stress patterns of these lines vary according to their meaning, and the speaker's colloquial, talky voice. In the last line, however, the poem's form is broken. This final line consists of ten syllables, and the metre is perfect iambic pentameter. 'I trespass stupidly. Let be, let be',[194] the speaker concludes. This exception to the poem's measure and rhythm emphasises the ambiguity of the speaker's position. Is the speaker stupid to trespass because it is illegal and dangerous and he or she may be caught? Is the speaker stupid as in silent, stumbling along dumbly and protesting only as an unspoken wish; or stupid as in not smart, because of his or her own complicity and hypocrisy? Who is the speaker addressing, and referring to, with the final, twice repeated plea, 'Let be, let be'? The words are not attached to a subject. Are they a prayer for the speaker's own safety, a wish not to be caught by the property owners? Or are the words a prayer for the pheasant, and others like it, who are hunted?

'The Rabbit Catcher' also disorders any straightforward categorisation of Plath's writing as feminine in its construction of the relation between women and nature. Marjorie Perloff has compared the poem with Lawrence's 'Love on the Farm'.[195] In a poem that is technically more adroit than Lawrence's, Plath complicates his simplistic opposition between the hunter's masculine power and violence, and his female partner's feminine sympathy for and identification with the rabbits that her male partner catches in mechanistic 'snares' that are like his hands. Plath follows Lawrence in making the woman the narrator, and in dramatising her ambivalent fear of, and desire for, the man. Plath answers Lawrence's melodramatic and rhythmically overburdened 'To be choked back, the wire ring / Her frantic effort throttling'[196] with her own swiftly moving 'and a mind like a ring / Sliding shut on some quick thing',[197] borrowing the 'ings' of his rhyme scheme, as well as the 'ring' itself. She fills 'The Rabbit Catcher' with other objects from 'Love on a Farm' (its 'snares' and 'wires',[198] for instance) and also notes the woman's attention to the man's hands, and the tenderness and destruction of which they are capable.

Like 'Pheasant', 'The Rabbit Catcher' considers class. Snaring a rabbit is what a poacher does. A poacher, historically, is usually a member of the rural poor who, as a necessary way of supplementing a subsistence diet, breaks the laws imposed by aristocrats. Ted Hughes made this point in his own version of 'The Rabbit Catcher', writing: 'I saw / Country poverty raising a penny, / Filling a Sunday stewpot'.[199] Plath's 'The Rabbit Catcher' (like 'Pheasant') is about the taking or killing of animals by human beings who do not own them. Yet the roles of conquered animal and violent controller become ambiguous in the last stanza of 'The Rabbit Catcher':

> And we, too, had a relationship –
> Tight wires between us,
> Pegs too deep to uproot, and a mind like a ring
> Sliding shut on some quick thing,
> The constriction killing me also.[200]

Plath's use of indefinite reference makes the identity of 'we' ambiguous. 'We' can include the speaker and the 'rabbit catcher', and/or the speaker and the rabbits. Such a structure implies not just that the speaker is being killed, like the rabbits, but that the relationship is equally deadly to the Rabbit Catcher. The poem's last word, 'also', could refer to the deaths of not just the speaker and the rabbits, but the hunter too. The 'mind like a ring' belongs, syntactically, as much to the speaker as to the man. In its dismantling of the relation between women and nature, Plath's writing defies any reader who wishes to label it as straightforwardly 'feminine'. The breaking down of boundaries between inside and outside, or self and not-self, is bound up in the dissolution of oversimple oppositions between victim and oppressor, female and male, environmentalist and destroyer.

Do You Do No Harm?

Terry Gifford has argued that Plath 'uses nature imagery to externalise her inner life'.[201] Gifford does not make this point as a criticism, but it does lead us to an important question. Is Plath appropriating material and historical events – the damage to living things and ecosystems by chemicals and radiation – in a hyperbolic way, in order to wallow metaphorically in her personal subject matter? This question is raised by an environmentalist reading of Plath, and recalls the scrutiny to which her use of Holocaust imagery has been subjected.[202] The very breadth of her historical, political and cultural references goes some way towards countering the charge of solipsism. So does the important role her work can play in larger debates about ecofeminism and postmodernism. Plath's writing might be said to be environmentalist *avant la lettre*. Her work opposes the most simplistic version of what is now termed ecofeminism. Deborah Slicer has explained the primary characteristics (and problems) of ecofeminism, which argues that '"women are closer to nature than men", and that, by virtue of that alleged special relationship, women have some privileged insights into our environmental morass or at least sensibilities that are more respectful of nonhuman life'.[203] As 'The Fifty-Ninth Bear' makes clear, Plath's writing frequently rebuts any notion that there is a sacred alliance between women and the earth that is to be celebrated. It foregrounds material and cultural relations between the self and the environment, by emphasising the self as unstable and penetrable. Alfred Kazin (whom Plath knew at Smith[204]) writes unjustly that for Plath 'The world existed just to be written about', as if she saw it as unreal and nothing to do with her. In fact, Plath's writing often emphasises that such a position is untenable and dangerous. Her environmentalist writing invalidates the familiar and unjust accusation that, as Kazin puts it, 'her posthumous fame has been to celebrate so thoroughgoing a coldness, so elegantly but murderously phrased a rejection of the world'.[205] Plath's writing does anything but reject the world.

It might at first glance seem that Plath's environmentalist texts see the fragile boundaries of the self in terms that are largely fearful. This is in contrast to more recent 'postmodernist' celebrations of the self as porous, fluid and multiple – open to invasion from the outside. Terry Eagleton has expressed this 'positive' view of postmodern identity, writing: 'The dispersed, schizoid subject is nothing to be alarmed about after all'.[206] (Eagleton here borrows a term from psychiatric medicine that others have used negatively, inaccurately, or too easily, and challenges us to think about it differently.) An ecocritical account of Plath's work raises questions that are important not just to our interpretation of Plath's own writing, but also to our understanding of the relationship between environmentalism and postmodernism.

It also raises difficult questions about Plath's writing. Does Plath's work inevitably construct any possible penetration of the self or body by something from outside as a threat, as potential contamination? Are environmentalism and postmodernism antithetic in the ways they position any permeation of boundaries, so that environmentalism frowns upon such permeation while postmodernism smiles upon it? The answer to both questions is no. Toxicity and radiation are of course materially dangerous and it is logical that they should be seen as such, yet the instability of any identity or body is also frequently accepted or even celebrated in Plath's writing. We have seen how midatlantic poems such as 'Cut', 'New Year on Dartmoor' and 'Stars Over the Dordogne'

dramatise the hybridity of any national identity through a disorientation of place, self and language. Plath's interpenetrations between
body and ecosystem are often concomitant with intersections between
femininity and masculinity, or between America and Europe. These
coincidences mirror other postmodern interactions, for instance
between genres, identities and histories. Such correspondence demands
of the reader similarly pluralistic ways of reading. Environmentalism
and midatlanticism are equally global. Pressing for both is the lack of
deference to borders, the fact that people, like the components of the
ecosystem, do not exist in separate bell jars, but are constantly circu-
lating, always mixing.

If the infiltration of bodies by foreign substances is often a threat,
Plath's 1962 poem 'Poppies in July' (like 'Paralytic') counters this by
depicting the frustration of isolation, the sadness of not being able to
touch but wanting to, however dangerous such contact might be. The
speaker begins the first of the poem's seven couplets by asking the
lovingly addressed 'Little poppies', 'Do you do no harm?' Even if the
answer to the question is no, and to touch them would indeed be
harmful, lack of contact is seen as a 'colorless' death. This worry over
non-involvement – the tourist position – is made even more explicit in
Plath's drafts of the poem. In these, the question 'Do you do no harm?'
is followed by a clear reference to marginality that Plath excised from
the final draft: 'At the edge of my eye you burn'.[207] If we return to the
published version of 'Poppies in July', we see that the speaker wants to
touch what the poppies exude, their flames and opium fumes and
liquors, and in turn to give out herself. 'If I could bleed',[208] she exclaims
yearningly. But such a reciprocal exchange is not possible and can only
be expressed conditionally as a desire that cannot be fulfilled. Such a
situation, the poem implies, is to be mourned, and is certainly no antidote to the dangers of interacting with the world. The husband in 'The
Fifty-Ninth Bear' wants direct contact with an animal, but also, rightly,
fears it. For the price of that exclusive and private exchange, its material
danger, is death. So was his desire a mistake? Within the terms of the
story, the desire itself is not wrong. Rather, his refusal to follow through
the logic of this desire and imagine (or admit) where it must lead is
misguided. 'Poppies in July' ends with an isolated single line: a couplet
that cannot be finished. Thereby it breaks with the pattern that characterises the rest of the poem. The line itself, lonely and not fitting in,
mimics the position of the poem's speaker: 'But colorless. Colorless'.[209]

By contrast, though the speaker of Plath's November 1962 poem
'Thalidomide' has a protective membrane, the membrane is permeable,

and therefore does not deny her access to a larger world. She and her baby are preserved from harm by a mysterious and seemingly arbitrary 'leatheriness', a sort of shield. The speaker knows that some women, not so lucky, have taken the infamous sedative of the title, which was prescribed for morning sickness in the 1950s, until its effect of mal-forming the limbs of infants was detected in 1961. Despite her escape, the speaker expresses concern for those others, publicising and politi-cising their story while taking ambivalent pleasure in her unaccountable love for her own ungrateful baby and the substances it exudes: its 'wet eyes', its 'screech', its 'White spit'. The poem ends with an image of a broken thermometer. The breakage reflects the speaker's lack of faith in protective zones or shields, however leathery, and is mirrored in the shape of the poem itself, through a splintering of form. One couplet has been split, so that it frames twelve tidy couplets: an isolated line appears at the poem's beginning, and another isolated line appears at its end. The shattered thermometer is another of Plath's motifs of the uncontainability of dangerous substances. It echoes the concern about high temperature expressed in 'Fever 103°' only a few weeks earlier: 'The glass cracks across, / The image / Flees and aborts like dropped mercury'.[210]

Plath's poems are not totalising in their rejection of permeability. While poems such as 'Elm' and 'Thalidomide' see poisons as invasive and dangerous, they nonetheless argue that isolation is impossible as well as pernicious. 'Elm' does so through a voice that is unstable and multiple, the elm tree who speaks and/or a woman who identifies with it. The water that makes the speaker of 'Fever 103°' 'retch' leaves her body to become part of something else. The 'beads of hot metal'[211] fly off like sweat to recirculate within the system. The heat of her body (those 'low smokes' that 'roll / From me like Isadora's scarves'[212]) will return to the air to affect something or somebody else. The elm soaks up poisons that do not kill the beetle that inhabits it, but instead, leave the elm's permeable body and enter related systems, killing and silen-cing birds and other life forms.

As Carson puts it, 'The history of life on earth is a history of the interaction of living things and their surroundings'.[213] We see in Plath's poetry and prose that the insights of feminism are important to any construction of the environment, especially the notion that the self cannot be held separate from the world. Plath depicts an ecosystem which overwhelms any sense of an individual self and body, regardless of its sex. A repeated image in her work is of the movement of particles from one body to another, whatever the particulars of the exchange of fluid, though blood, milk and sweat are among her favourites. Plath is interested in the way the body is entered by different substances. No place is inviolate, or sealed by cellophane. No hospital clinic can remain cordoned off from the others, or unrelated to them. Nothing is outside the ecosystem. One must account for all waste matter. Nothing can be repressed or left behind for long.

Notes

1. Legler, 'Ecofeminist Literary Criticism', 1997: 227.
2. Marco, *Silent Spring Revisited*, 1987: xv.
3. Braidotti, *Women, the Environment and Sustainable Development*, 1994: 173.
4. Graham, *Since Silent Spring*, 1970: x
5. *Letters Home*, 92. *The Journals of Sylvia Plath*, 1982: 55. *The Journals of Sylvia Plath*, 2000: 132.
6. *Letters Home*, 345–6.
7. *Collected Poems*, 104.
8. *Ibid.*, 105. Plath first visited the subject of the green rock, and the changes wrought by time and memory, in the 1949 short story 'The Green Rock'. Plath wrote it when she was fourteen. Fourteen-year-old Susan and her younger brother visit the seaside they left five years earlier, and find they have lost childhood itself, which is symbolised by the rock they used to play on: 'Where were the castles, the sailboats, the mountains that once had been? Only the rock remained, stark and bare' (*The Green Rock*, 1982: 15; *Johnny Panic*, 257). Yet even five years earlier, the sea was not immune to contamination; five years earlier, the difference was of perception. The younger children delight in what is essentially litter: 'a piece of water-smooth glass' of which Susan's brother David says, ' "I wish I lived inside" ' (*The Green Rock*, 1982: 9; *Johnny Panic*, 254). In the end, the rock, and the childhood for which it is a metaphor, linger, but only as a trace: 'a thin line of foam remained above the spot where the rock lay, silent, dark, sleeping beneath the oncoming tide' (*The Green Rock*, 1982: 16; *Johnny Panic*, 258). The rock will disappear, but be revealed again. Plath revisited the rock in the 1956 poem 'Dream with Clam-Diggers'.
9. *Collected Poems*, 105.
10. *Ibid.*, 104.
11. *Ibid.*, 105.
12. Any quotation from *Silent Spring* will be from *The New Yorker* version. The first reference provided will be from the magazine. For those readers without access to these issues of *The New Yorker*, a subsequent reference will indicate the corresponding pages of the readily available Penguin

book. It should be noted that there are occasional differences in wording between the two versions.

13. *Letters Home*, 396, 402.
14. LILLY. Plath MSS. II, Correspondence, 1961, Jan.–May, Box 6. 9 Feb. 1961.
15. Plath's references to the 'VERY GOOD NEWS' of her 'FIRST acceptance from *The New Yorker*' in June of 1958 (*Letters Home*, 345, Plath's emphasis) and 'one of their coveted "first reading" contracts' in March of 1961 (*ibid.*, 411) are indicative of her regard for the magazine. See also *The Journals of Sylvia Plath*, 1982: 242–3, 336; and *The Journals of Sylvia Plath*, 2000: 397, 601.
16. The following poems were published in *The New Yorker* in the period running up to and just following the magazine's publication of *Silent Spring*: 'Watercolor of Grantchester Meadows', 26 May 1960, p. 30; 'The Net Menders' (hyphen omitted by *The New Yorker*), 20 Aug. 1960, p. 36; 'On Deck', 22 July 1961, p. 32; 'Tulips', 7 April 1962, p. 40; 'Blackberrying', 16 Sept. 1962, p. 48.
17. Hughes. Unpublished handwritten letter to Tracy Brain. 6 Aug. 1998.
18. Hughes, 'The Environmental Revolution', 1970, repr. 1994: 129.
19. Graham, *Since Silent Spring*, 1970: 48.
20. Brooks, *The House of Life*, 1972: 231–3.
21. Graham, *Since Silent Spring*, 1970: 31, 35.
22. *The New Yorker*, 16 June 1962, 16–35; *Silent Spring*, 22.
23. *Silent Spring*, 20.
24. Byatt, *Babel Tower*, 1996: 56–7, 356.
25. Dunn, *Beneath the Wide Wide Heaven*, 1991: 121. (Dunn takes the title for her collection from Samuel Taylor Coleridge's 1797 poem, 'This Lime-Tree Bower My Prison'.)
26. *Ibid.*, 138.
27. *The New Yorker*, 16 June 1962, 38–9; *Silent Spring,* 34–5.
28. Dunn, *Beneath the Wide Wide Heaven*, 1991: 139.
29. *The New Yorker*, 16 June 1962, 35; *Silent Spring,* 23.
30. *Letters Home*, 434.
31. LILLY. Plath MSS. II, Writings, Poetry – C, Box 7a, folder 9, 'City Wife'.
32. *Collected Poems*, 'Uncollected Juvenilia', 339.
33. LILLY. Plath MSS. II, Writings, Poetry – C, Box 7a, folder 9, 'City Wife'.
34. To some extent 'Waking in Winter' is provisional. Ted Hughes tells us in a note that the poem 'has been extracted from a tangle of heavily corrected manuscript lines, and must be regarded as unfinished'. *Collected Poems*, 290.
35. *Ibid.*, 151.
36. Deitering, 'The Postnatural Novel', 1996: 197, 202.
37. *Collected Poems*, 105.
38. LILLY. Plath MSS. II. Oversize 4–7. Art Scrapbooks. Scrapbook 2.

39. LILLY. Plath MSS. II. Oversize 4–7. Art Scrapbooks. Scrapbook 1.
40. Bassnett, *Sylvia Plath*, 1987: 125.
41. Rowley, 'Electro-Convulsive Treatment in Sylvia Plath's Life and Work', 1998: 94.
42. Rose, *The Haunting of Sylvia Plath*, 1991: 40, 57.
43. *The Journals of Sylvia Plath*, 1982: 263. *The Journals of Sylvia Plath*, 2000: 424.
44. The editorial commentary littering the 1982 edition of *The Journals of Sylvia Plath* (p. 262) points out the similarity of 'Dark House' from 'Poem for a Birthday' – 'I may litter puppies / Or mother a horse. My belly moves' (*Collected Poems*, 132) – to the patient Plath described in the Hospital Notes that also prompted her to write 'Johnny Panic': 'Might turn to animal or be pregnant, and have puppies. Turn into mule or horse' (*The Journals of Sylvia Plath*, 1982: 265; *The Journals of Sylvia Plath*, 2000: 627).
45. *The Journals of Sylvia Plath*, 1982: 324. *The Journals of Sylvia Plath*, 2000: 520.
46. *Johnny Panic*, 18–19.
47. Plath explored the dehumanising effects of industrial capitalism(using an image that may come straight from the Frigidaire picture) in her 1957 poem 'Nightshift'. Here, the speaker realises that the thudding noises he or she hears are not from his or her own heart, but from the silver factory where 'Men in white // Undershirts circled, tending / Without stop those greased machines, / Tending, without stop, the blunt / Indefatigable fact'. *Collected Poems*, 77. The connection between what human beings do and feel, between their environment and what they are able to imagine, is made explicit: the factory allows for only the 'Indefatigable fact'.
48. *Johnny Panic*, 19–20.
49. *Ibid.*, 20.
50. *Ibid.*, 22.
51. *Ibid.*, 23.
52. *Ibid.*, 27.
53. *Ibid.*, 29.
54. *Ibid.*, 26.
55. *Ibid.*, 28.
56. Lucas Myers, in Appendix 1 to Stevenson, *Bitter Fame*, 1989: 317–18.
57. Stevenson, *Bitter Fame*, 1989: 161.
58. Alexander, *Rough Magic*, 1991: 235.
59. Puzzlingly, Jacqueline Rose asserts that 'All the Dead Dears' is 'the only title that repeats itself in [Plath's] work'. Rose, *The Haunting of Sylvia Plath*, 1991: 1.
60. *Collected Poems*, 88.
61. *Ibid.*, 176
62. *Johnny Panic*, 94, 95.

63. Schmitt, *Back to Nature*, 1969, 1990: 163.
64. *Johnny Panic*, 103.
65. *Ibid.*, 96.
66. *Ibid.*, 94.
67. *Ibid.*, 95.
68. *Ibid.*, 96.
69. Schmitt, *Back to Nature*, 1969, 1990: 163.
70. Hughes, *Birthday Letters*, 1998: 89.
71. *Ibid.*, 94.
72. *Johnny Panic*, 96.
73. Byerly, 'The Uses of Landscape', 1996: 59–60.
74. *Johnny Panic*, 97.
75. Byerly, 'The Uses of Landscape', 1996: 54.
76. Slovic, 'Nature Writing and Environmental Psychology', 1996: 353.
77. LILLY. Plath MSS. II, Writings, Poetry – U–Z. Box 8, folder 5.
78. *Johnny Panic*, 97.
79. *Ibid.*, 98.
80. *The Journals of Sylvia Plath*, 1982: 30. *The Journals of Sylvia Plath*, 2000: 77.
81. Friedan, *The Feminine Mystique*, 1963: 13.
82. *Johnny Panic*, 99.
83. *Ibid.*, 100.
84. Schmitt, *Back to Nature*, 1969, 1990: 176. Schmitt is quoting T. K.
    Whipple, 'Aucassin in the Sierras', *Yale Review*, n.s. XVI (July 1927): 714.
85. *Johnny Panic*, 105.
86. SMITH. Box: Plath – Prose, Quotation. Folder: Prose Works, 'The Fifty-
    Ninth Bear', Copy 1: 10.
87. SMITH. Box: Plath – Prose, Quotation. Folder: Prose Works, 'The Fifty-
    Ninth Bear', Copy 1: 9–10. (The cut passage would appear after 'enclosed
    her' on p. 99 of 'The Fifty-Ninth Bear' in the Faber *Johnny Panic*.)
88. SMITH. Box: Plath – Prose, Quotation. Folder: Prose Works, 'The Fifty-
    Ninth Bear', Copy 1: 10. (The cut passage would appear after 'drew him'
    on p. 100 of 'The Fifty-Ninth Bear' in the Faber *Johnny Panic*.)
89. SMITH. Box: Plath – Prose, Quotation. Folder: Prose Works, 'The Fifty-
    Ninth Bear', Copy 1: 6. (The cut passage would have followed 'Norton
    knew he had disappointed her' on p. 97 of 'The Fifty-Ninth Bear' in the
    Faber *Johnny Panic*.)
90. Holbrook, *Sylvia Plath: Poetry and Existence*, 1976: 121.
91. SMITH. Box: Plath – Letters (Plath – Sylvia). Folder: Plath, Sylvia. T.L.s.
    10 Oct. 1962.
92. *Collected Poems*, 192.
93. Plath uses the 'silent spring' image again one month later, in
    'Apprehensions' (28 May 1962). Here the speaker, embedded in a distant
    and vaguely menacing environment, remarks that 'There are no trees or
    birds in this world' (*Collected Poems*, 195).

94. *The New Yorker*, 16 June 1962, 35; *Silent Spring,* 23.

95. Van Dyne, 'More Terrible Than She Ever Was', 1982: 5.

96. SMITH. Box: Plath – Ariel Poems, Daddy – Event. Folder: Ariel Poems, 'Elm', Draft 1c. P. 66 of the Faber edition of *The Bell Jar.*

97. SMITH. Box: Plath – Ariel Poems, Daddy – Event. Folders: Ariel Poems, 'Elm', Draft 2c; Draft 6c; Draft 7c; Typed Copy 1.

98. SMITH. Box: Plath – Ariel Poems, Daddy – Event. Folders: Ariel Poems, 'Elm', Draft 1b; Draft 2b; Draft 2c.

99. Hardy, *The Well-Beloved*, 1975: 165.

100. *Collected Poems*, 192.

101. *Letters Home*, 438.

102. SMITH. Journals, July 1950–July 1953. Handwritten in bound note-book: pp. 55–6. *The Journals of Sylvia Plath*, 2000: 32 (not in 1982 edition).

103. SMITH. Journals, July 1950–July 1953. Handwritten in bound notebook: p. 86. *The Journals of Sylvia Plath*, 2000: 46 (not in 1982 edition).

104. *Collected Poems*, 192.

105. SMITH. Box: Plath – Ariel Poems, Daddy – Event. Folder: Ariel Poems, 'Elm', Draft 2a. The omitted passage follows the paragraph that ends 'never had a minute's peace' on p. 89 of the Faber edition.

106. SMITH. Box: Plath – Ariel Poems, Daddy – Event. Folder: Ariel Poems, 'Elm', Draft 1a. P. 92 Faber edition.

107. SMITH. Box: Plath – Letters (A–Z). Folder: Letters, The New Yorker, T.L.s. 27 June, 1962.

108. *The New Yorker*, 23 June 1962, 46; *Silent Spring*, 112.

109. *Letters Home*, 93, 102; Wagner-Martin, *Sylvia Plath: A Biography*, 1987: 87; Stevenson, *Bitter Fame*, 1989: 39.

110. *Collected Poems*, 193.

111. SMITH. *Webster's New Collegiate Dictionary*. Springfield, Massachusetts: G. & C. Merriam Co., 1949: 447.

112. *The New Yorker*, 23 June 1962, 35; *Silent Spring*, 102.

113. *Collected Poems*, 193.

114. SMITH. Box: Plath – Ariel Poems, Daddy – Event. Folder: Ariel Poems, 'Elm', Draft 6c. P. 48 Faber edition.

115. *The New Yorker*, 30 June 1962, 66; *Silent Spring*, 99.

116. Wagner, *Critical Essays on Sylvia Plath*, 1984: 17.

117. Van Dyne, *Revising Life*, 1993: 41.

118. Bate, *Romantic Ecology*, 1991: 5.

119. *The New Yorker*, 30 June 1962, 39; *Silent Spring*, 168.

120. *The New Yorker*, 30 June 1962, 55; *Silent Spring*, 209–10.

121. *Letters Home*, 378.

122. *Collected Poems*, 208.

123. The first large-scale commercial reactor was Calder Hall, built in Britain in 1956. Bradwell Nuclear Reactor was operational in Britain in 1962.

124. *Collected Poems*, 209.

125. *The NewYorker*, 30 June 1962, 55; *Silent Spring*, 210. (The wording differs between versions, but the meaning is the same.)

126. *The NewYorker*, 30 June 1962, 42–3; *Silent Spring*, 175.

127. *Collected Poems*, 209.

128. SMITH. Box: Plath – Ariel Poems, Daddy – Event. Folder: Ariel Poems, 'The Detective', Draft 1. The cross-outs duplicate Plath's own.

129. *The NewYorker*, 30 June 1962, 42–3; *Silent Spring*, 175.

130. *The NewYorker*, 30 June 1962, 41–2: *Silent Spring*, 173.

131. Van Dyne, *Revising Life*, 1993: 42.

132. *Collected Poems*, 209.

133. *Three Women* (March 1962) also alludes to the material effects of poisons upon human beings and the environment. The Second Voice who repeatedly miscarries her babies wonders at the cause of her reproductive dysfunction: 'Is it the air, / The particles of destruction I suck up?' (*Collected Poems*, 177). Also foreshadowing the language and argument of *Silent Spring*, the First Voice, who gives birth to a wanted son, remarks, 'The rain is corrosive' (*Collected Poems*, 180). Alluding to thalidomide, she worries over 'those terrible children … / with their white eyes, their fingerless hands' (*Collected Poems*, 185).

134. Warren, 'Taking Empirical Data Seriously', 1997: 10.

135. *Collected Poems*, 231.

136. *Ibid.*, 232.

137. Marsack, *Sylvia Plath*, 1992: 9. Anne Stevenson has also picked up on the Eliot connection (Stevenson, 'Sylvia Plath's Word Games', Winter 1996/7: 28–34).

138. Butscher, *Sylvia Plath: Method and Madness*, 1976: 322.

139. Kirkham, 'Sylvia Plath', 1988: 290.

140. Van Dyne, *Revising Life*, 1993: 118.

141. *Collected Poems*, 231.

142. Bronfen, *Sylvia Plath*, 1998: 91–2.

143. *Collected Poems*, 232.

144. Similarly, the speaker of 'A Birthday Present' observes:

> But my god, the clouds are like cotton
> Armies of them. They are carbon monoxide.
>
> Sweetly, sweetly I breathe in,
> Filling my veins with invisibles, with the million
>
> Probable motes that tick the years off my life. (*Collected Poems*, 207)

145. *The NewYorker*, 16 June 1962, 35; *Silent Spring*, 23–4.

146. SMITH. *Webster's New Collegiate Dictionary*. Springfield, Massachusetts: G. & C. Merriam Co., 1949: 7. The underlining is Plath's.

147. Hey, *Kingzett's Chemical Encyclopaedia*, 1966: 8.

148. *The NewYorker*, 30 June 1962, 35; *Silent Spring*, 181.

149. SMITH. Box: Plath – Ariel Poems, The Fearful – Kindness. Folder: Ariel Poems – Drafts, 'Fever 103°, Draft 1. See p. 37 of the Faber edition of *The Bell Jar.*

150. Hey, *Kingzett's Chemical Encyclopaedia*, 1966: 8.

151. *Collected Poems*, 232.

152. *Ibid.*, 231.

153. Many thanks to Stan Smith for bringing *Hiroshima Mon Amour* to my attention.

154. Alvarez, 'Sylvia Plath', 1963: 70.

155. Alain Resnais, *Hiroshima Mon Amour*, 1959.

156. Perhaps when she wrote 'Lady Lazarus', Plath had in mind not just The Gospel According to St John, but also Sebastiano del Piombo's early sixteenth-century painting *The Raising of Lazarus*. This would have been in the National Gallery during Plath's frequent visits to London, before she moved there late in 1962 (it was the first painting the gallery ever acquired, in 1824). *The Raising of Lazarus* depicts what looks like, to use a phrase from 'Lady Lazarus', a 'peanut-crunching crowd'. One onlooker holds a cloth to his nose against the stench of the four-days-dead Lazarus (there is no reference to the smell in the Bible); Lady Lazarus reassures us that 'The sour breath / Will vanish in a day'. The commands 'Peel off the napkin' and 'unwrap me hand and foot' (*Collected Poems*, 244, 245) recall Lazarus 'bound hand and foot with graveclothes', and Jesus' order to 'Loose him' (John, 11. 44), as well as the bandages dripping from Lazarus in Piombo's painting.

157. Stevenson, *Bitter Fame*, 1989: 269, 270. See also Kenner, 'Sincerity Kills', 1989: 68–9.

158. Alvarez. Interviewed on *Voices & Visions: Sylvia Plath*. New York: Mystic Fire Video, 1988.

159. Sambrook, *York Notes: Sylvia Plath: Selected Works*, 1990: 14, 15.

160. Rose, *The Haunting of Sylvia Plath*, 1991: 134.

161. *The New Yorker*, 30 June 1962, 42; *Silent Spring*, 175.

162. *The New Yorker*, 30 June 1962, 42–4; *Silent Spring*, 175.

163. *Collected Poems*, 266.

164. SMITH. *Webster's New Collegiate Dictionary*. Springfield, Massachusetts: G. & C. Merriam Co., 1949: 445. The underlining is Plath's.

165. *Collected Poems*, 266.

166. Kristeva, *Desire in Language*, 1980: 136. While Kristeva's theories frequently open up new readings of Plath's work, Kristeva's own reading of Plath reproduces that too-common gesture of reducing Plath's poems to causal prefigurements of her own death. For Kristeva, Plath was 'another of those women disillusioned with meanings and words, who took refuge in lights, rhythms and sounds: a refuge that already announces, for those who know how to read her, her silent departure from life' (Kristeva, 'About Chinese Women', 1974: 157).

167. Plumwood, *Feminism and the Mastery of Nature*, 1993: 9.
168. *Collected Poems*, 266.
169. *Ibid*.
170. Klein, 'A Study of Envy and Gratitude', 1986: 217, 220.
171. *Collected Poems*, 266.
172. Klein, 'A Study of Envy and Gratitude', 1986: 221.
173. *Collected Poems*, 266.
174. *Collected Poems*, 267.
175. SMITH. Box: Plath – Memorabilia, Notes. Folder: Notes, Poem Subjects.
176. Stevenson, *Bitter Fame*, 1989: 228.
177. Rose, *The Haunting of Sylvia Plath*, 1991: 134.
178. In this draft, Plath calls the poem 'The Bald Truth about: The Surgeon at 2.a.m.'
179. LILLY. Plath MSS. 1961, 29 Sept. 'The Surgeon at 2 a.m.'
180. Orr, *Plath Reads Plath*, 1975: transcription from recording, mine.
181. *Collected Poems*, 171.
182. *Ibid*., 170.
183. *Ibid*., 171.
184. *Ibid*., 170.
185. *Ibid*., 171.
186. SMITH. Box: Plath – Ariel Poems, Daddy – Event. Folder: Ariel Poems, 'Elm', Draft 2c.
187. *Collected Poems*, 191.
188. Markey, *A Journey into the Red Eye*, 1993: 12, 102.
189. SMITH. Box: Plath – Ariel Poems, Nick and the Candlestick – Sheep in Fog. Folder: Ariel Poems, 'Pheasant', Draft 1. See p. 84 of the Faber edition of *The Bell Jar*.
190. *Collected Poems*, 191.
191. SMITH. Box: Plath – Ariel Poems, Nick and the Candlestick – Sheep in Fog. Folder: Ariel Poems, 'Pheasant', Draft 1.
192. *Collected Poems*, 191.
193. Merchant, *The Death of Nature*, 1989: xx, 186.
194. *Collected Poems*, 191.
195. Perloff, 'The Two *Ariels*', 1984: 12.
196. Lawrence, *Selected Poems*, 1950: 13.
197. *Collected Poems*, 194.
198. Lawrence, *Selected Poems*, 1950: 13; *Collected Poems*, 194.
199. Hughes, *Birthday Letters*, 1998: 145.
200. *Collected Poems*, 194.
201. Gifford, *Green Voices*, 1995: 150.
202. See Rose, *The Haunting of Sylvia Plath*, 1991; Heaney, 'The Indefatigable Hoof-taps', 1988; and Steiner, 'Dying is an Art', 1970.
203. Slicer, 'Toward an Ecofeminist Standpoint Theory', 1998: 49.

204. *The Journals of Sylvia Plath*, 1982: 204, 233–4. *The Journals of Sylvia Plath*, 2000: 209, 288, 347–8, 391.
205. Kazin, *Bright Book of Life*, 1971: 186, 184.
206. Eagleton, 'Capitalism, Modernism and Postmodernism', 1985: 394.
207. SMITH. Box: Plath – Ariel Poems, Nick and the Candlestick – Sheep in Fog. Folder: Ariel Poems, 'Poppies in July', Draft 1.
208. *Collected Poems*, 203.
209. *Ibid.*
210. *Ibid.*, 252.
211. *Ibid.*, 232.
212. *Ibid.*, 231.
213. *The New Yorker*, 16 June 1962, 35; *Silent Spring*, 23.

CHAPTER 4

THE ORIGINS OF *THE BELL JAR*

Brontë, Woolf and Plath

In the opening plenary session of a Virginia Woolf conference that I attended during the summer of 1996, Jane Marcus noted the interface between Virginia Woolf, Sylvia Plath and suicide. In a tone somewhere between self-knowing irony and complicity, Marcus jokingly referred to the 'dead mad-woman's poet society' to which Woolf and Plath belong. It seemed a depressing way to begin such an event. I was further dismayed to find my own paper on Plath's textual and cultural debts to Woolf grouped in a session entitled 'Suicide'. It seemed odd that the conference should be organised in a way that contradicted its primary reason for existing: that is, to give serious attention to Virginia Woolf's writing. The 'Suicide' session's first speaker began his talk on Woolf by quoting from 'Lady Lazarus': ' "Dying is an art" '

There is a common assumption – even among scholars – that the most important connection between Virginia Woolf and Sylvia Plath is the last thing that they ever did. I want to reveal the importance of the textual, psychoanalytic and even cultural links between Plath's writing and Woolf's, and between the writing of these two twentieth-century writers and their nineteenth-century literary mother, Charlotte Brontë. By evaluating the textual relationships between the work of these three writers, we can read them as literary mothers and daughters – as progenitors and inheritors. Most importantly, by studying Plath's type-scripts, and her heavily underlined and annotated copy of *Villette*, we can look afresh at the position of the mother and of the character of Buddy Willard in *The Bell Jar*. Brontë's nineteenth-century text can be read as a template for Plath's novel. Looking at *Villette* and *The Bell Jar* together enriches our understanding of both books.

A Comparison

Virginia Woolf famously wrote in *A Room of One's Own*, 'we think back through our mothers if we are women. It is useless to go to the great men writers for help'.[1] If we ask where Sylvia Plath went 'for help', we find that the answer, partly, is Woolf herself. Woolf's writing haunts Plath's. Indeed, there is a strong presence of Woolf's texts in Plath's own.

Several critics have observed that Plath and Woolf suffered from mental illness[2] and committed suicide,[3] or seen them both as self-dramatising writers.[4] Writing as though Plath were Woolf's precursor, Elizabeth Hardwick suggests that some of Woolf's last journal entries 'have in them the glittering contempt of a Sylvia Plath poem'. Hardwick concludes that, in the end, Woolf redeems herself by expressing 'apology, gratitude, and depression'[5] before her suicide; this is opposed to Plath's lack of repentance. Critics repeatedly cite Plath's boast that the Cambridge boys 'think of me as a second Virginia Woolf',[6] or her assertion that 'Virginia Woolf helps. Her novels make mine possible',[7] or her question and answer 'What is my voice? Woolfish, alas, but tough'.[8] Plath's journals and letters are crammed with lists of the Woolf novels she systematically buys and reads.[9]

Only a handful of critics have examined Woolf's textual imprint on Plath in any detail. Sandra Gilbert focuses on Plath's radio play *Three Women*,[10] and its inheritance of narrative and stylistic patterns from Plath's 'heavily underlined'[11] copy of *The Waves*. Steven Axelrod tells us that Plath more often discusses 'male writers than female', and that of the 135 books Plath kept in England, only '16 were by women – fully half of them by ... Virginia Woolf'.[12] Axelrod engages in a sustained study of Woolf's legacy to Plath. He argues that Plath's choices of character names are indebted to Woolf.[13] More convincingly, he establishes *Mrs Dalloway* as *The Bell Jar*'s 'parent text'.[14]

Plath herself offers us a blueprint for establishing Woolf's textual imprint on her writing. In her 1962 radio piece 'A Comparison', Plath explicitly invites us to liken her writing to Woolf's. The piece begins, 'How I envy the novelist!',[15] and Woolf herself appears to be the object of the envy. 'A Comparison' continues with what seems to be a parody of *Orlando*'s first sentence, copying the uncertainty of gender conveyed in Woolf's frenetic supplements and qualifications. Woolf's 'He – for there could be no doubt of his sex, though the fashion of the time did something to disguise it'[16] resonates in Plath's 'I imagine him – better say her, for it is the women I look to for a parallel'. The project of *A Room of One's Own* is passed to Plath's narrator: to 'look to' the literary mother. With the phrase 'I imagine her, then, pruning a rosebush with a large pair of shears',[17] Plath duplicates Woolf's exercise in gendered absurdity, affectionately mocking Orlando's act of 'slicing at the head of a Moor'.[18] The gardening reference may be an allusion to Vita Sackville-West, who inspired *Orlando*. Plath's narrator evokes an amusingly caricatured 'feminine' activity that also echoes Orlando's 'masculine' game of violence. Moreover, to prune a rose with shears would destroy the flower.

Using a Woolfian style, the narrator of 'A Comparison' says of her predecessor: 'Her business is Time, the way it shoots forward, shunts back, blooms, decays and double exposes itself. Her business is people in time'.[19] The pronoun 'Her' could refer to Woolf herself, while the references to time evoke Woolf's texts. There is the bulk of *To the Lighthouse* covering one day as opposed to the few pages through which decades pass. In *Mrs Dalloway*, Clarissa and Septimus occupy the same moment in different ways. Repeatedly in the novel, different characters reflect upon the same thing at the same instant from very dissimilar places, yet there is still a 'gradual drawing together of everything'.[20] This aspect of Woolf's writing made a strong impression on Plath when she was very young. As Plath put it in an unpublished high school essay on *Mrs Dalloway*, 'you jump about from one person's disconnected train of thought to another's. Imagine that you could peer into the brain of any passer-by at will'.[21] 'She can take a century if she likes, a generation, a whole summer',[22] says the narrator of 'A Comparison'. Here, she seems to speak at once of Woolf's writing, Woolf's games with time, and Orlando's romps through centuries.

This allusion to *Orlando*'s length and time frame returns us to the Woolfian question of genre implied in the title of 'A Comparison'. As opposed to the novelist, Plath's narrator quips with slangy talkiness that the poet 'can take about a minute'[23] with her necessarily economic form. This explains the emphatic beginning of 'A Comparison', 'How I envy the novelist!' The narrator of *A Room of One's Own* famously wonders what genre would best express 'the poetry in' women. She goes on to plead that 'women's books should be shorter, more concentrated, than those of men, and framed so that they do not need long hours of steady and uninterrupted work'.[24] The narrator of 'A Comparison', as if directly responding to this plea, implies that poems meet these criteria, but at a price: 'If a poem is concentrated, ... then a novel ... can touch and encompass a great deal in its travels'. While the narrator of 'A Comparison' has 'never put a toothbrush in a poem',[25] the narrator of *A Room of One's Own* implores the woman writer to explore the 'accumulation of unrecorded life', the ordinary world of 'gloves and shoes and stuffs'. In *A Room of One's Own*, Woolf puts scare quotes around the word 'novel' to 'mark ... the word's inadequacy'.[26] 'A Comparison' suggests that the genre is relative and provisional. Though poems and novels alike require patterns, Plath's narrator teases that the novel does not 'insist so much'.[27] In other words, the novel is a more expansive and mobile form. All of these tentative definitions and hypotheses about genre are nonetheless inconclusive. What both Plath and Woolf point up is the creative deadliness of rigid prescriptions, and the necessity for development. While I cannot think of a poem in which Plath literally puts a toothbrush, she does put in the grease of roasting lamb in 'Mary's Song', a Victorian nightdress in 'Morning Song', and sweat-sodden sheets in 'Fever 103°'. *The Bell Jar* can be said to explore the world of 'gloves and shoes and stuff', and show how serious, but also how absurd, a world this can be. Yet with its highly condensed, figurative language, *The Bell Jar* is in many ways as 'concentrated' as any poem. Plath's poems and prose forge new patterns, as Woolf's did before her. They make us think freshly about what subject matter and forms can be the province of literature.

We know of the anger that the narrator of *A Room of One's Own* hurls at her own predecessor, Charlotte Brontë. Brontë's crime is to write in ways that are very like Woolf's own text: with 'indignation', with the 'continuity' 'disturbed', with scarcely a hint of anything that could be described as 'whole and entire'.[28] Coming upon the literary mother one might expect the narrator of *A Room of One's Own* to welcome, she instead rejects her. In turn, Plath mimics Woolf's disaffection with Brontë. Plath admits of a daughter-like wish to outdo the mother and 'be stronger'[29] than Woolf, both as a writer and by having children. Plath's adulation melts in the face of omission: 'That is what one misses in Woolf. Her potatoes and sausage. What is her love, her childless life, like, that she misses it, except in Mrs. Ramsey and Clarissa Dalloway?'[30] But we cannot freeze Plath here any more than we can hold Woolf at that moment of rage against Brontë's anger. Plath's momentary rejection of Woolf does not cancel her previous instances of enthusiasm and respect any more than a daughter's furious hatred of her mother erases her love. What matters most is the fact that Plath's writing is the better for Woolf's examinations of mothers, literary and otherwise.

The Legacy

Plath and Woolf shared a strong ambivalence about the effects of marriage on a woman's potential creativity. Plath wonders 'if the sensuous haze of marriage will kill the desire to write',[31] while Woolf confesses that 'the extreme safeness and sobriety of young couples does apall [*sic*] me'. The two writers were as dubious about babies as they were about husbands. At one moment, Woolf scornfully refers to a 'barren wife across the passage'. At another, she writes: 'To be 29 and unmarried – to be a failure – childless – insane too, no writer'.[32] Plath's vacillation mirrors Woolf's. In the summer of 1957 Plath refers to the 'horror … of being pregnant'.[33] Two years later she records the opposite extremity of feeling. Anxious that she has not conceived within the first few months of trying to become pregnant, she writes: 'If I could not have children … I would be dead. Dead to my woman's body … My writing a hollow and failing substitute for real life'.[34]

Plath's 1956 story 'The Wishing Box' seems to be a direct revision of Woolf's story 'The Legacy'. Both plots concern the repressive effects of marriage and husbands on the wife's creativity. 'The Legacy' appeared in *A Haunted House and Other Short Stories*, a copy of which Plath owned.[35] In 'The Wishing Box', Plath cues us by approximating the name of Woolf's heroine: Agnes is a partial anagram of Woolf's Angela. 'The Wishing Box' is another of those pieces of Plath's writing that even the most accomplished of critics cannot resist reducing to the merely personal. Jacqueline Rose asserts that her 'focus is on the writing' and she is 'never claiming to speak about the life' of Sylvia Plath. Nonetheless, Rose argues that 'The Wishing Box' 'can be read as an allegory for the poetic rivalry between Plath and Hughes'. Rose says of Agnes, 'She lacks imagination',[36] but this is to take the fictional character's word for it. If we read the story as a critique of marriage, instead of biographically, it becomes clear that Plath wishes to examine the sexual and social forces which wrongly convince Agnes that she has no imagination (or that any imagination she may possess is illegitimate).

Agnes has nothing to do but domestic chores, and the result is deadly. Plath's story, like the precursor by Woolf, ends in the wife's suicide, and for similar reasons. In Woolf's piece, creativity is signalled by Angela's diary; in Plath's, by Agnes's dreams, or the lack of them. Angela refuses to let her husband see her diary, telling him '"After I'm dead – perhaps"'[37] (which is indeed when he does see it). Plath's story is structured to indict marriage. Agnes's literal and metaphoric loss of her ability to dream coincides with her 'wedding night only three months before'.[38] Agnes views the feminine, 'fragmentary'[39] dreams that occur in the '"*back* of [her] head"' as illegitimate when compared to Harold's masculine, linear '"movie-screen"' dreams on the '"front of [his] eyelids"'.[40]

We are told that Angela had a 'passion for little boxes'.[41] Boxes are obviously important in Plath's story too. Plath's title refers to the wishing boxes about which Agnes dreams as a child. These 'grew on trees' and had handles you turned 'while whispering your wish'.[42] Agnes's wishing box, like Angela's jewellery boxes, also conjures that room of one's own. In both stories, the room has either shrunk to enclose insignificant trinkets, or come to represent the deadliness of domestic space: the room not as a place for freedom and thought, but as a prison (the many and various boxes of Plath's bee poems take on a similar meaning). In fact, Agnes's room, the '*things* surrounding her', leave her feeling 'choked, smothered by these objects whose bulky pragmatic existence' threaten 'her own ephemeral being'.[43] The wishing box is also the television that represents Agnes's humiliating lack of economic power within marriage. Only 'by dint of much cajolery'[44] does she persuade her husband to buy it. Television fails to compensate for Agnes's inability to dream, and is itself implicated as dangerous to the imagination. Television comes to signify how little there is for the exclusively domestic wife to do.

Before television, Agnes turns with ironic desperation to *The Joy of Cooking* and the *Sears Roebuck Catalogue*, two icons of American house-wifery. A decade later, Margaret Atwood would use one of these icons as a key reference for her novel *The Edible Woman* (published in 1969, but written in 1965). Atwood prefaces *The Edible Woman* with a recipe for puff pastry from *The Joy of Cooking*. 'The surface on which you work (preferably marble), the tools, the ingredients and your fingers should be chilled throughout the operation ...' The idea is that the woman should become an implement to achieve domestic perfection: mindless, utilitarian, and part of the food itself. No different from instruments and flour, even her body should be chilled. The heroine of *The Edible Woman* becomes anorexic at the prospect of losing her im-agination and freedom through her impending marriage. In other words, *The Edible Woman* is about a woman who is confronted with a future like Agnes's. Considering that *The Edible Woman* was written only a decade after 'The Wishing Box', opportunities for the later heroine have not improved overwhelmingly. As Atwood herself puts it in her Introduction to the novel, Marian's choices are 'a career going nowhere, or marriage as an exit from it'.[45]

Plath's third person story privileges Agnes's point of view, for the narrator keeps close to what Agnes knows and feels. By contrast, Woolf's narrator follows the thoughts of Angela's husband as he tries to understand the life he did not attempt to decipher while she was alive. Angela is patronisingly remembered by her politician husband as wanting 'to do something – she had blushed so prettily … to help others'.[46] The dead lover whom Angela commits suicide to join is an active socialist. Seen in this light, Angela's death cannot be read as a simple romantic gesture, but must also be interpreted as a protest against her failure to do anything of serious import while alive.

Like Angela's, Agnes's death is also as much an act of subversion as it is capitulation. Her husband finds her 'dressed in her favourite princess-style emerald taffeta evening gown, pale and lovely as a blown lily', and we are told that she looks as if 'she were, at last, waltzing with the dark, red-caped prince of her early dreams'.[47] Agnes composes herself into a death pose of magazine femininity that both mocks and complies with the ideals of her time. What Agnes loses through marriage might be described as a Kristevian semiotic, or feminine unconscious and im-agination whose removal kills her. This is made most literal by Agnes's insomnia. She rejoins the fantasy prince whom she associates with the pre-marriage girlhood in which she could still think creatively and dream. Notwithstanding, this prince is a conventional figure of socially desirable masculinity. Through suicide, Agnes escapes the nightmare room and its horrifying domestic implements of 'smug, autonomous tables and chairs'.[48] Contrary to those conventional views of Plath's own supposed death drive, 'The Wishing Box' argues that death is no victory.

Woolf and *The Bell Jar*

Steven Axelrod concludes that because Plath never mentioned *A Room of One's Own* and did not annotate her copy she 'chose to ignore it'. Axelrod argues that Woolf's vision of sexual politics and women's oppression threatened Plath's own hopes for her marriage.[49] He suspects that Plath did not want to measure her work against Woolf's prescription for 'incandescent', non-angry writing,[50] and that *A Room of One's Own* positioned Woolf as a (literary) mother who exhibited 'a need to control and to withhold, a wish to reprove, and a reluctance to grant autonomy'.[51] These are important points. But they do not acknowledge the fluctuating positions of Woolf's theories on how women should write. Nor do they credit Plath with the ability to recognise those moments where Woolf loses 'control'. We might think of such moments as antidotes to the mother's supposed bossiness: those reassuring displays of anger and discontinuity in Woolf's own writing, particularly in *A Room of One's Own* itself.

A Room of One's Own is actually an *un*repressed presence in Plath's work. Woolf writes: 'Poetry ought to have a mother as well as a father. The Fascist poem … will be a horrid little abortion such as one sees in a glass jar in the museum of some county town'.[52] *The Bell Jar* examines the problem of the poet who can find no serious female role models, of the young woman writer who finds the shift from silent muse to speaking subject difficult. Like the narrator of *A Room of One's Own*, Esther lacks examples of women who successfully combine artistic achievement with wifehood and motherhood. Dodo Conway, whose education at Bernard has not been of *much* use in her life's work of producing seven children, prompts Esther to think, 'I had nothing to look forward to'.[53] Such a sentiment echoes *A Room of One's Own*, whose narrator remarks, 'bearing thirteen children – no human being could stand it'.[54] Chapter Fifteen of *The Bell Jar* opens its second section with Esther's declaration, 'I have my own room again'. Esther is talking here about her transfer from the city hospital to the private one that Philomena Guinea pays for, and alluding to differences in comfort and luxury between the two institutions. At the same time, she evokes the relative freedom of mind that the more enlightened treatment in the private hospital affords her, a freedom that is far from perfect or ideal, but nonetheless is a great improvement on the monstrous in-humanity of the city hospital. It is in the private hospital, ensconced in her 'own room', that Esther begins to improve, however costly that improvement may be. *A Room of One's Own* must also be one of Plath's many sources for the analogy between depression and a 'bell jar',[55] and for the image of 'big glass bottles full of babies'.[56] Plath uses Woolf's equation between deformed poems and dead foetuses in her 1960 poem 'Stillborn', replicating Woolf's 'Such monsters never live long'[57] with her own 'These poems do not live'.[58]

Woolf asks, 'what food do we feed women as artists upon?'[59] We might see the eponymous vegetables of Plath's 1959 poem 'Mushrooms' as women, a sort of food who themselves 'Diet on water, / On crumbs of shadow, / Bland-mannered, asking / Little or nothing'.[60] Their menu recalls the impoverishment of the dry biscuits and 'prunes and cus-tard'[61] fed to the women at Fernham. It also duplicates their quiet resistance and slow-gaining strength. At times, Esther Greenwood appears to fantasise herself as one of Virginia Woolf's heroines, aligning herself with Woolf's thought, or attempting to duplicate it. When Esther says of physics, 'What I couldn't stand was this shrinking everything into letters and numbers',[62] she may also be referring to the male science student who sits opposite the narrator of *A Room of One's Own* in the British Museum. His 'neatest abstracts, headed often with an A or a B or a C' contrast with the narrator's own 'wildest scribble of contradictory jottings'.[63] In her recoil from physics, Esther may also be rejecting the stance of Mr Ramsey, 'stuck at Q'[64] and struggling to reach R throughout *To the Lighthouse*. Plath takes Woolf's image of abbreviation and linear thinking and, like her predecessor, uses it to speculate on masculine and feminine ways of creating.

Both writers consider the policing of the feminine by the masculine,[65] as we see in *The Bell Jar*'s reconceptualisation of *Mrs Dalloway*. Elizabeth Abel observes that repeated interruptions by men rob Clarissa of any opportunity to sustain a relationship with a woman:[66] 'the jealous male attempting to rupture the exclusive female bond'.[67] The dash signalling Peter's brutal interruption of Sally's kiss[68] is much cited.[69] So too is the manner by which Peter duplicates the gesture with his unexpected visit during what seems to be Clarissa's post-climactic pleasure[70] in mending a favourite dress.[71] However unlived Clarissa's relationships with women may be, the reveries in which she contains them are of great importance to her.

The Bell Jar refigures *Mrs Dalloway*'s examination of what Elizabeth Abel describes as the 'turn from mother to father' that is produced by '[m]asculine intervention, not penis envy'.[72] Sally's counterpart is Joan Gilling, who functions as Esther's alter ego and potential lesbian lover. Though Joan is usually taken for granted by critics and readers as a 'real' character, she can be seen as a construct of Esther's imagination. Indeed, we are cued by Esther herself that 'Sometimes I wondered if I had made Joan up'.[73] One of four quarterly reports that Plath wrote on *The Bell Jar* for the Eugene F. Saxton Memorial Trust (from whom she received a Saxton Fellowship of $2,080) refers to Esther's 'sister–double relationship with Joan'.[74] Joan embodies Esther's sexual and social transgressions. As a 'physics major' and 'hockey champion' who is 'big as a horse'[75] Joan resists feminine stereotype. In a series of coincidences, she embraces Buddy Willard's mother where Esther rejects her,[76] receives the '"same"'[77] epistolary marriage proposal from Buddy as Esther, and is incarcerated with Esther in the mental institution. These correspondences are so numerous, ludicrous, and contrived, that Plath can only have meant the reader – and Esther – to regard them as symbolic, and never literal. Joan is the antithesis of the 1950s femininity symbolised by Doreen, whose compliance Esther fears she will catch and 'never get rid of' if she allows Doreen to enter her 'room'.[78] Glamorous girls, like children, make Esther 'sick',[79] but she knows this response contravenes her culture's ideology of sanctified womanhood and the American family. As Pat Macpherson argues,[80] Esther learns from the Rosenberg execution of the terrible sanctions against social misconduct and gender delinquency. The Rosenberg execution certainly does not function, as Alfred Kazin flippantly argues, 'just to remind you what year it was when "Esther Greenwood" got to New York'.[81]

The sequence of interruptions in Esther's last scenes with Joan is worth following. When Joan makes a pass at Esther, Esther needs no male policing to protect her from the seductiveness of female transgression. She tells Joan herself, 'You make me puke'.[82] Esther here is 'properly' sick. That is to say, her illness – or disgust at Joan's sexual advance – is what her culture asks of her; in the terms of 1950s America, sickness, when brought on by potential homosexuality, is health. When Esther next sees Joan, Joan asks, ' "You'll come visit me" ', and Esther does not voice her answer of ' "Not likely" '.[83] Esther leaves Joan and loses her virginity to Irwin, but visits Joan again immediately after the sexual experience, turning to Joan for help because she is haemorrhaging.[84] It is after witnessing the blood evidence of Esther's loss of virginity to a man that Joan commits suicide. Esther 'cures' herself of her incipient sexual misbehaviour by murdering the desire that Clarissa Dalloway never gives up. Unlike Clarissa, Esther herself curtails her meetings – and relationships – with women. No Peter-like character is needed in *The Bell Jar* to administer the law of the father.

Where Esther moves on at the expense of killing a part of herself, Clarissa is trapped in regression. Clarissa's lesbianism can only be experienced through memory and fantasy. Where Clarissa's access to her mother and sister has been removed by their deaths and their virtual erasure from the narrative,[85] Esther is estranged from her very present mother by the mother-fearing culture in which she lives. Abel's skilful account of *Mrs Dalloway* as a consideration of 'a lost pre-Oedipal world and the costs of its relinquishment'[86] again helps. *The Bell Jar*, as we will see, is more concerned with critiquing the forces that sever the daughter from the mother than with endorsing any resulting breach.

Rethinking Buddy Willard

In *The Bell Jar*, male and female characters alike are subject to penalties when they do not comply with accepted gender and social codes. Like much of Plath's work, *The Bell Jar* has often been regarded as unsympathetic to men, particularly in its portrayal of Buddy Willard. Again, biographical readings have tended to cloud critical judgement. Buddy Willard has been seen as Plath's resentful version of Dick Norton,[87] but *The Bell Jar*, like 'Paralytic', is actually sympathetic to the pressures upon men and masculinity, Buddy Willard included. In the fashion of a perfect 1950s man, Buddy is 'very proud of his perfect health'. Also in keeping with popular thought, he tells Esther that her sinus troubles are 'psychosomatic'.[88] Buddy's illness is not simply an ironic visitation of just revenge about which Esther can be smug. It is also a genuine examination of what happened to such a man when he could no longer meet the requirements of virile masculinity. Buddy must take a Victorian-termed 'rest cure'[89] for his TB, and is left as feminised as any nineteenth-century heroine with some unnamable ailment. *The Bell Jar*'s early typescripts contain more details about Buddy's sickness and loss of masculinity than the published version of the novel. Buddy confesses that 'medical students with T.B. aren't really eligible'[90] for the army. His predicament is similar to Esther's in this discarded passage. Both characters are 'sick', and wait in fear and horror to be decried and punished for being so. Repeatedly, Esther mentions things that make her 'sick', among them 'being electrocuted' and 'Girls like that'. Yet she knows she must hide such deviance, for 'even when they surprised me or made me sick I never let on'.[91]

Pat Macpherson has shown that at the time of *The Bell Jar* communism was equated with sickness and spoken of like a cancerous malignancy eating America alive.[92] In this context, Buddy's sickness, like Esther's, is mortifying and dangerous: a badge of mental, national and social degeneration. Esther speaks of TB as people spoke of communism: 'I edged back … it seemed to me an extremely sinister disease, the way it went on so invisibly'.[93] This in turn resembles the way others regard Esther's own breakdown. Sickness is not merely physical. Buddy's father cannot 'stand the sight of sickness and especially his own son's sickness, because he thought all sickness was sickness of the will'.[94] As a counterpart to the dangers Esther experiences of appearing too masculine, Buddy's sickness leads him to align himself too closely with femininity and weakness. Even Buddy's body betrays and humiliates him, transgressing gender codes by plumping out like a pregnant woman's. This foreshadows the changes to Esther's own body under the influence of her insulin treatments. Because Esther's treatment and cure depend upon the restoration of her femininity, and her acceptance of it, the side effect of the insulin is not just incidental. The insulin forces her 'skinny as a boy'[95] body, and attitudes, into womanly curves. An early typescript of *The Bell Jar* reveals that Buddy's feminisation was even more exaggerated in Plath's initial conception of the novel. Here, Buddy's laugh is not just 'plump',[96] as in the published novel, but also has 'a strange, fruity richness'.[97] Buddy is not merely 'convex', with a 'pot belly' and 'cheeks … round and ruddy as marzipan fruit'.[98] He is given the further indignity of 'the contours of a double chin'.[99] It is not simply the femininity of this changed body that shames Buddy, but also the way that the rhetoric which describes this body mimics the way men talk of women, or women talk of babies: as edible, delicious, sweet as candy.

One year after writing and then cutting these allusions to Buddy's compromised masculinity, Plath drafted her April 1962 poem 'Among the Narcissi' on the opposite side of the page. 'Among the Narcissi' is about an elderly man with cancer. The narrator watches him bend, weakened by age and illness, among his flowers. The poem's tone is markedly different from the earlier text. While *The Bell Jar*'s world is scornful of any loss of male rigour, the narrator of 'Among the Narcissi' speaks tenderly and respectfully of the withered man. The poem's speaker occupies an entirely different culture from the novel's. Her membership of the decade that follows Esther's affords her a tolerance and compassion that the earlier text cannot allow its heroine. Other early typescripts of *The Bell Jar* reveal that Plath diminished her heroine's violence on her way to the novel's final version, especially Esther's anger towards Buddy. Plath cuts the line, 'I felt like kicking him in the stomach'.[100] This discarded sentence is not merely a manner of speech. If we recall the fact that Buddy's newly plump body is feminised, even pregnant looking, Esther's wish to kick him in the stomach can also be seen as a wish to hit at maternity itself, and at the babies she tells us throughout the book that she hates.

The Misunderstood Mother and
The Bell Jar Manuscripts

Aurelia Plath described the 'accusation' that she was 'the model for Esther Greenwood's cold, aphorism-spouting, cut-and-dried mother' as 'unjust', but the 'accusation' to which Mrs Plath refers need not be interpreted as Mrs Plath did: as 'horrible'.[101] Mrs Greenwood is not necessarily 'a cold, unsympathetic mother' who 'would provide the conflict necessary to win sympathy for the heroine'.[102] In fact, Mrs Greenwood is a more admirable and likeable character than Mrs Plath, and most critics, have seen. As Plath herself said of Mrs Greenwood in an unpublished letter to James Michie, a Heinemann editor: 'She is a dutiful, hard-working woman whose beastly daughter is ungrateful to her'.[103] The text repeatedly signals that we should not swallow uncritically Esther's angry perceptions of her mother. These perceptions often prove inaccurate. Esther herself admits to 'surprise', for instance, when her mother agrees to get her out of the terrible mental institution.[104]

Earlier typescripts of *The Bell Jar* demonstrate Plath's intention that her readers should distrust her narrator, and learn little about what happens to Esther after her breakdown. An early draft of Chapter One's last page appears on the reverse side of an outline of the novel. Plath crosses out the final paragraph by hand, deciding against including it in the book. The cut passage reads: 'By nineteen I was an expert at finding out other people's life stories on a bus or in a doctor's office, anywhere at all. I never told anybody my life story, though, or if I did, I made up a whopper.'[105] This is a dramatic admission by Esther of her habit of lying, and her talent for doing so. Its exclusion from the book does not mean that Plath decided to make her heroine an honest paragon. As a writer, Plath may have wanted Esther's unreliability to be less crudely signposted, to be shown more than told. Another cut passage, written by hand on a page from an early typescript, gives us a similar glimpse into Esther's future. In it, she struggles to recall the name and location of a restaurant. 'I thought for a long time it was called The Seven Steps, but then when I went to look it up in a New York Phonebook a year or two later I couldn't find it; & no New Yorker I knew has ever heard of it'.[106] We can read this omitted sentence in at least two ways. First, that Esther cannot remember something perfectly (a plausible character trait). Second, that the restaurant never existed at all, but was a figment of Esther's imagination, and she entirely fantasised it.

Either way, these deleted passages indicate Plath's conception of her narrator as less than wholly reliable. Another page from an early typescript of the book refers to a bullfight Esther attends years later and finds barbaric.[107] Plath crossed out the lines about the bull fight, presumably wishing to minimise what the reader learns of Esther's later life, and also, quite possibly, to reduce the reader's exposure to Esther's good judgement and reliability. One of the few 'facts' that we are allowed to know of Esther's future in the final draft is that she has a baby. This is a significant development given Esther's admission that 'Children made me sick'[108] (the past tense of 'made' is important here, for it suggests that, beyond the events of the novel, this is no longer Esther's stance). We learn also that Esther keeps the gifts given to her by *Ladies Day*.[109] These gifts are a badge of Esther's recovery and irony. They are indicative of the sense of humour afforded her by the time that has passed between her story and its telling. The fact of Esther's own later motherhood leaves room for the reader to imagine that, with hindsight, Esther might sympathise with what Mrs Greenwood has endured.

On 29 October 1961, Plath drafted her poem 'The Babysitters'. For paper, she used pages from an earlier typescript of *The Bell Jar*. Again, these typescript pages contain passages and lines that Plath cut from the final draft of the book. Esther explains her selection of the man to whom she decides to lose her virginity. 'I also needed somebody quite experienced to make up for my lack of it, and Irwin's ladies reassured me on this head. Then, *since my mother had hinted of the thralldom a woman undergoes in the hands of her first lover,* to be on the safe side, I wanted somebody I didn't know.' (The italicised clause is crossed out in the earlier typescript, while the words in the plain print are retained between Plath's typescript and the final published version.[110]) Plath chooses to excise a passage that hints of intimacy between Esther and her mother. What Plath expunges is a reference to an earlier moment where the mother and daughter were close enough to talk about sex, however coyly. Though Esther tries to disguise this incriminating evidence of intimacy with mocking sarcasm, she nonetheless reveals her former preparedness to speak about such matters with her mother. It is an admission of closeness that Plath judges the novel, and her disengaged, angry heroine, cannot afford to retain and admit. What Plath leaves in the novel is Esther's amusing reference to 'In Defence of Chastity', a *Reader's Digest* article that her mother mails to her, but does not discuss with her directly.[111] Without the deleted passage, it is harder to appreciate the irony whereby Esther takes her mother's advice seriously, and acts on it in a way Mrs Greenwood could never have predicted.

The culture which sanctifies the mother in the home, equivalent to the angel in the house that Woolf had to kill in 'Professions for Women',[112] also blames the mother for the so-called 'defects' of its children. *The Bell Jar* is not complicit with the popular psychoanalysis that accounts for Esther's breakdown by implying her mother had not properly 'toilet trained' her. The text, unlike Doctor Nolan, does not smile approvingly when Esther says of her mother, ' "I hate her" '.[113] Plath disorientates the reader by beginning Chapter Fifteen with what at first appears to be a disembodied voice. This voice represents the culture of mother blaming. ' "Of course his mother killed him" ',[114] a blind date tells Esther. A few paragraphs later we discover that he is discussing a play – and one in which the mother's murder of her son could be seen as an act of love and mercy. The false 'logic' of the phrase 'of course' only emphasises the spuriousness of the all-too-familiar assumption that 'the mother did it'. Plath took notes on Jung, writing: 'We praise the "sanctity of motherhood", yet would never dream of holding it responsible for all the human monsters, the homicidal maniacs, dangerous lunatics, epileptics, idiots & cripples of every description who are born every day'.[115] These notes are not dated, and there is no indication of whether Plath took them for a course at school or university, or simply privately, for herself. Later, when she comes to write *The Bell Jar*, Plath appears to argue with this earlier view, be it her own, or her summation of what she thought Jung was saying. A. S. Byatt rightly predicted of *Letters Home*, 'I fear Mrs Plath's gallantry will meet with less sympathy than it should. It is easy and customary to scapegoat "the Mother" for many inner horrors',[116] and indeed, Mrs Greenwood's 'gallantry' has unfairly met with the very fate (the lack of 'sympathy') that Byatt feared for Mrs Plath. Any careful reading of *The Bell Jar*, however, must recognise that the novel exposes, rather than advocates, the view that 'it's the mother's fault'.

Sylvia Plath's *Villette*

To find *The Bell Jar*'s antecedents, we need to look further back than Virginia Woolf's work. If the numerous underlined and annotated passages of Plath's own copy of *Villette* are anything to go by,[117] Brontë's novel is yet another template for Plath's work and concerns. Plath's underlining and notes in *Villette* mark out the territory of *The Bell Jar*, its questions, and the matrix of its characters. It may at first seem strange to juxtapose Brontë's story of an English Victorian girl with Plath's of a 1950s American college student, but many aspects of *Villette* equally characterise *The Bell Jar*. The two novels are narrated through a reflective retrospective perspective. In both books, the reader is given few significant facts about the years that follow the main events of the story. *Villette* and *The Bell Jar* both end ambiguously. We have already observed *The Bell Jar*'s complex position on mothers, and its relationship to Woolf's texts. By looking at *The Bell Jar*'s considered relationship to *Villette*, we can move beyond the view that Plath's novel is nothing more than her 'usual facile use of every bit of her experience'[118] (to use Alfred Kazin's phrase), or 'a horrific autobiographical novel'[119] (to use Elisabeth Bronfen's).

Like Brontë's, the first time Plath's heroine ever names herself in the book, she does so in the context of a lie. To Lucy's fervent and fanciful 'I, Lucy Snowe, plead guiltless of that curse, an overheated and discursive imagination'[120] (Lucy is characterised by exactly this sort of imagination), Massachusetts-born Esther Greenwood gives us ' "My name's Elly Higginbottom ... I come from Chicago" '.[121] Artistic temperament also establishes Lucy Snowe as Esther Greenwood's precursor. Plath underlines Lucy's confession, 'I never had a head for science, but an ignorant, blind, fond instinct inclined me to art'.[122] (Next to this Plath writes in the margin, 'moi?') Plath gives Esther the same antipathy towards science. Esther describes physics as a 'death' that made her 'sick',[123] and believes chemistry will be 'worse'.[124] Lucy tries 'pretty hard'[125] to learn German but finds it 'difficult of mastery',[126] as if she has 'drunk brine to quench thirst'.[127] Esther also attempts German, despite the fact that 'the very sight of those dense, black, barbed-wire letters made my mind shut like a clam'.[128] Both heroines try too hard to align themselves with feminine modes of thought and behaviour. In each case, the attempt collapses. Monsieur Paul polices Lucy for any 'contraband appetite for unfeminine knowledge' such as 'science in the abstract'. The 'injustice' of this proscription stirs in Lucy 'ambitious wishes' and 'aspiration'[129] that she did not previously possess. Monsieur Paul tells Lucy that a ' "woman of intellect" ' was a 'luckless accident ... wanted neither as wife nor worker'[130] (though Lucy's cleverness and independence are precisely what draw Monsieur Paul to her).

Similar pressures and ambivalence are brought to bear on Esther Greenwood's conceptions of femininity in *The Bell Jar*. Esther's alter ego Joan Gilling is made to represent the woman who trespasses into the male sphere through her masculine inclinations. Joan is a cliché of maladjusted femininity. She is 'president of her class and a physics major and the college hockey champion. ... She was big as a horse, too'.[131] By hiving off these tendencies and depositing them in Joan, Esther attempts to deny them in herself, and thereby escape punishment for them. To understand this impulse, we need to bear in mind the historical background of *The Bell Jar*: the Rosenberg execution and its allusions to, in President Eisenhower's words, Ethel Rosenberg's 'strong and recalcitrant character'[132] – a description that would fit Esther or Lucy.

Lucy's and Esther's breakdowns are similarly recounted. Esther's own 'sickness', or crisis, occurs when her period of employment as an editor of *Ladies Day* ends and she is rejected from the writing course she had counted on as 'a bright, safe bridge over the dull gulf of the summer'.[133] For Lucy Snowe, too, when 'the prop of employment' is 'withdrawn' and she is faced with the long autumn school vacation, she grows 'miserable' and feels only a 'sorrowful indifference to existence'. Life, Lucy comes to feel, is 'but a hopeless desert: tawny sands, with no green field, or palm-tree, no well in view'.[134] Plath uses a similarly arid figurative language for Esther, who sees 'day after day glaring ahead of me like a white, broad, infinitely desolate avenue'.[135] Neither heroine can sleep, and both are drawn to darkness and death. Lucy says of the sun and moon, 'I almost wished to be covered in with earth and turf ... for I could not live on their light, nor make them comrades, nor yield them affection',[136] while Esther comes to think that 'the most beautiful thing in the world must be shadow'.[137] At the end of the last chapter of Volume I, Lucy's collapse and loss of vision, in which she seems 'to pitch headlong into an abyss',[138] are followed by disorientation. As Lucy recovers from her fainting episode at the beginning of the next chapter, she finds herself in a strange room, and only gradually orientates herself. Esther's loss of vision and consciousness in the basement after her suicide attempt at the end of Chapter Thirteen is followed by confusion and the slow regaining of her senses at the beginning of Chapter Fourteen, when she awakens in the hospital in a strange room. These collapses and recoveries are strikingly akin in sequence and image.

Feminine selflessness is a pressure that is implicated in the illnesses of both heroines. In her copy of *Villette*, Plath draws a line vertically alongside the margin where Monsieur Paul says to Lucy, '"Women who are worthy the name ought infinitely to surpass our coarse, fallible, self-indulgent sex, in the power to perform such duties"'.[139] Monsieur Paul here refers to Lucy's horror and disgust at having to nurse the school-girl Marie Broc, whose 'mind, like her body', is 'warped'. 'Attendance on the crétin deprived me often of the power and inclination to swallow a meal, and sent me faint to the fresh air',[140] Lucy tells us. Esther has a similar failure of will in *The Bell Jar*, when, in the midst of her depression, she volunteers to work in a hospital because 'My mother said the cure for thinking too much about yourself was helping somebody who was worse off than you'.[141] Plath cut a passage from an early typescript of *The Bell Jar* that might be a read not just as a description of Esther, but also as a comment about – and sanction of – Lucy's disinclination towards selfless charity in *Villette*. 'I could never be a nurse', Esther explains. 'The idea of noble service to the sick and the injured and the crippled and all the aborted monsters hidden darkly away in public or private brick buildings has always appealed to me, but when it comes to the test, I turn my back. They disgust me so profoundly I lose my humanity.'[142]

Esther and Lucy both live in worlds where women are scrutinised for 'unfeminine' attitudes and behaviours. Lucy remarks of Madame Beck, ' "Surveillance," "espionage," – these were her watchwords', and Plath underlines the sentence in her copy of the novel.[143] Plath puts an explanation mark in the margin alongside Lucy's description of Madame, who 'would ... glide ghost-like through the house, watching and spying everywhere, peering through every key-hole, listening behind every door'.[144] Lucy lives 'where no corner' is 'sacred from intrusion'.[145] Esther, too, has no place to escape regulation and surveillance. Whether an inmate of the Amazon hotel, the mental institution, or her mother's house where 'anybody looking along the sidewalk could glance up at the second story windows and see just what was going on',[146] Esther's world, like Lucy's, contains few spaces where she can hide. Mrs Ockenden and Dodo Conway look in at Esther through the windows, driving her to take cover absurdly, 'behind the silver pickets of the radiator'.[147] With sinister self-righteousness and (amusing) blindness to her own invasive behaviour, Mrs Ockenden even complains to Esther's mother that she has once witnessed Esther kissing a boy, and another time observed her 'half-naked getting ready for bed'.[148]

At least twice in *Villette* Lucy refers to herself, or her story, as 'heretic', using the word as an adjective. Had Lucy again visited the Catholic priest, Père Silas, she muses that she might have become a nun instead of 'writing this heretic narrative'.[149] Much later in the text, sardonically (and rather proudly) referring to herself as she imagines Père Silas might secretly think of her, Lucy calls herself 'the heretic Englishwoman'.[150] Lucy fully realises that she inhabits a culture to which she must be a threat, a heretic, by virtue of her Protestantism, her financial independence, and her refusal to behave as a passive, weak woman.

These are precisely the impulses in Lucy that make those around her spy upon her all the more, for their own, and supposedly Lucy's, protection. Yet Lucy manages to resist rehabilitation by this culture, and remains outside of it until the novel's end. Esther's position in *The Bell Jar* is similar. But what threat, we might ask, is being monitored in Esther Greenwood's 1950s America? What is Esther's heresy? The answer, as in the case of Lucy Snowe, is that women who do not fit in with 'normality', who appear 'sick' or 'unfeminine' or 'strong', are perceived as threats. Put more exactly, Esther and Lucy are monitored for female desire and independence, whether these be sexual, financial, intellectual, or emotional.

Like Brontë, Plath examines social and economic systems whose values and materials are not equally distributed, and shows how such a system invariably pits women against one another. Esther is made to feel ambivalent about Doreen, and especially about the way that men respond to Doreen's sexuality and dependence. This is because Esther does not like the possible identity that Doreen represents; what Esther herself might be, if she so chooses. Doreen is also a competitor. She takes for herself male attention and, by association, male powers, so removing from circulation patronage and sexual affirmation that might have otherwise been available to Esther. Lucy's attitude towards Ginevra is similar to Esther's towards Doreen. Another potential identity is offered to Esther in the form of Betsy, Doreen's foil. A veritable incarnation of innocence, Betsy makes Esther uncomfortable. Similarly, Ginevra's antithesis, Polly, produces complex feelings for Lucy. Plath puts an exclamation mark in the margin alongside Dr John's ludicrously misconceived address to Lucy on the subject of Ginevra: ' "She is so lovely, one cannot but be loving towards her. You – every woman older than herself, must feel for such a simple, innocent, girlish fairy a sort of motherly or elder-sisterly fondness" '.[151] After Lucy learns of Ginevra's marriage to De Hamal, she teases the reader, 'Of course, a large share of suffering lies in reserve for her future'. Plath underlines this, as well as Ginevra's triumphant declaration, ' "I have got my portion!" '.[152] Lucy's caustic disgust, her pleasure in the probability of Ginevra's future downfall, and her puritanical disapproval mirror Esther's towards Doreen. Enmity and rivalry between women does not disappear between *Villette* and *The Bell Jar*. Nor does the cultivation of this enmity by male characters.

Even in her beauty, Ginevra is somehow overblown and repellent. Lucy feels Ginevra's body as a 'fatiguing and selfish weight',[153] a 'charming commodity' she wishes 'there had been less of'.[154] In the same vein, Esther perceives Doreen as 'warm and soft as a pile of pillows' and 'much too heavy ... to budge down the long hall'.[155] Alongside a passage from *Villette* that might double as a representation of Esther's differing regard for Doreen and Betsy, Plath draws a vertical line, and writes, 'Polly & Ginny' in the margin as if the two characters were her old friends. This glossed passage contrasts 'Ginevra's dress of deep crimson' and 'rose-like bloom' with 'Paulina's attire' of a 'texture clear and white'. It concludes that 'Nature' has 'traced all these details slightly, and with a careless hand, in Miss Fanshawe's case, and in Miss de Bassompierre's wrought them to a high and delicate finish'.[156] Like Ginevra's, Doreen's femininity is somehow over-ripe; like Paulina, Betsy is almost exaggerated in her contrasting innocence. It is no accident that Betsy (or 'Pollyanna Cowgirl', as Doreen nastily calls her) has a 'bouncing blonde pony-tail and Sweetheart-of-Sigma-Chi smile'. One of the few carefully chosen facts that Esther reveals about the events which occur after the period of her breakdown is that Betsy becomes a successful model, a 'cover girl' whom Esther can 'still see ... smiling out of those "P.Q".s wife wears B.H. Wragge" ads'.[157] It seems likely that Betsy does not simply act out what she imitates – that is to say, an expensively dressed, unthreatening, happy, healthily consumer capitalist *'wife'* – but also *becomes* one. Clean, beautiful Betsy is a 1950s dream girl whose image can be used to represent what American woman should aspire to economically, socially and aesthetically. Like Polly, Betsy is (literally) the model others can emulate.

Not every woman has the bone structure, breeding and money of a Polly or a Betsy, or wishes to trade on these through marriage even if she does. *The Bell Jar*, like *Villette*, addresses the question of what a woman can do to become independent, economically as well as artistically and imaginatively. Plath draws a line beneath the passage 'I could teach ... but to be either a private governess or a companion was unnatural to me. Rather than fill the former post in any great house, I would deliberately have taken a housemaid's place, bought a strong pair of gloves, swept bedrooms and staircases, and cleaned stoves and locks, in peace and independence. Rather than be a companion, I would have made shirts and starved'.[158] Later in *Villette*, Monsieur Paul tells Lucy he will not write because he dislikes 'the mechanical labour; I hate to stoop and sit still. I could dictate it, though, with pleasure to an amanuensis who suited me'. Though tempted 'to gather and store up those handfuls of gold-dust',[159] Monsieur Paul's stories, this is nonetheless an honour Lucy politely declines, and may well be the genesis of Esther's famous declaration against shorthand: 'I hated the idea of serving men in any way. I wanted to dictate my own thrilling letters'.[160] To serve a man as a secretary or typist in the 1950s is a socially sanctified equivalent to Brontë's nineteenth-century working girl, the 'governess' or 'companion'.

What also remains between *Villette* and *The Bell Jar* is the heavy proscription against young women who exhibit disrespect for a man's mother. Plath heavily emphasises this aspect of *Villette*, as if marking out a series of notes and reminders to herself on a subject that she intends to revisit. Esther knows that her dislike of Mrs Willard borders on the criminal, and that Mrs Tomolillo is institutionalised for sticking her tongue out at her mother-in-law, or in other words, for derision towards the mother of her husband, and by extension, insolence towards her husband himself. Dr John is finally cured of his love for Ginevra when she exhibits irreverence towards his mother. Plath underlines every step of his conversion, as she does his admission to Lucy that '"I never saw her ridiculed before. Do you know, the curling lip, and sarcastically levelled glass thus directed, gave me a most curious sensation?"'[161] (Plath writes in the margin alongside this, 'It's about time!') In the following passage, Plath underlines just the word 'mother': '"She might have scoffed at *me* ... through myself, she could not in ten years have done what, in a moment, she has done through my mother."' She also marks Graham's declaration that '"The merry may laugh *with* mamma, but the weak only will laugh *at* her"'.[162]

Plath does not highlight Graham's comment that '"Ginevra is neither a pure-minded angel nor a pure-minded woman"'.[163] Nonetheless, she provides a twentieth-century twist on such nineteenth-century rhetoric in *The Bell Jar*, with Mrs Greenwood's fixation on Buddy Willard being a 'fine, clean boy' whom 'a girl should stay fine and clean for'.[164] What finally repels Graham from Ginevra is his perception that she is 'neither girlish nor innocent'. He observes Ginevra giving De Hamal a 'look marking mutual and secret understanding' and concludes that 'No woman ... who could give or receive such a glance, shall ever be sought in marriage by me'.[165] The imputation of Ginevra's sexual knowingness, and possibly bodily experience, is clear. She is not, to use Plath's language, 'fine and clean', or, to use Brontë's, 'pure-minded'. With 'a smile so critical, so almost callous', Graham Bretton gives Lucy his opinion of an actress. He 'judged her as a woman, not an artist: it was a branding judgment'.[166] In the 'slutty'[167] or 'tarty' waitress Buddy Willard sleeps with but won't take home to meet his mother,[168] Plath gives us a 1950s version of the woman who, by class and profession, is not deemed by the middle-class man to be worthy of his respect or marriage. 'I hate public opinion for encouraging boys to prove their virility & condemning women for doing so',[169] Plath wrote in a 1952 letter.

Plath's interest in this sexual double standard was evident in her response to Henry James's 1877 novel *The American*. Again, Plath's heavy annotations and underlining demonstrate an engaged, energetic feminism in her reading, and seem to map out her future interests and writing. A former salesman and manufacturer of washtubs, the eponymous hero of *The American* is Newman, a young American abroad in Europe. Despite his wealth and his enthusiasm for Europe, Newman is disadvantaged by the unfamiliar subtleties and hierarchies of class in which he finds himself immersed, and oblivious to the awkwardness and naïveté of his position and behaviour. Plath marks Newman's plans for the future: 'I have succeeded, and now what am I to do with my success? To make it perfect, as I see it, there must be a beautiful woman perched on the pile, like a statue on a monument. She must be as good as she is beautiful, and as clever as she is good. ... I want to possess, in a word, the best article in the market'. Next to this mock-fairytale passage, Plath glosses the margin with the words 'commercial parlance'.[170] In a similar vein, Plath also puts a line beneath the words 'he [Newman] had already begun to value the world's admiration of Madame de Cintré, as adding to the prospective glory of possession'. Close to this Plath writes, 'Typical'.[171] Plath draws an exclamation mark alongside a passage concerning Newman's idealistic friend and fellow traveller Babcock: 'his most vivid realization of evil had been the discovery that one of his college classmates ... had a love affair with a young woman who did not expect him to marry her'.[172] Newman affects disdain for Babcock's unworldly view of women, but it is a view Newman shares. Women in *The American* are deified 'like a statue' if they are sufficiently beautiful, rich and virtuous. If they appear to enjoy relationships with men, but entertain no economic aspirations towards marriage, they are derided. These are the very hypocrises and contradictions that Plath explores in *The Bell Jar*.

Too much desire disqualifies a woman from male middle-class approval and support, both social and economic. Yet for Esther, too little desire is also a sort of crime. To scorn a man's sexual attractiveness is as much a taboo as giving in to it. By the standards of her day and, paradoxically, through her *lack* of desire too, Esther fails. Her dereliction is made all the more taboo for its coupling with a disdain not just for the man's mother, but, worse yet, for his own sexuality. Esther famously scoffs at Buddy's naked body, remarking that all she 'could think of was turkey neck and turkey gizzards'.[173] In an early typescript of the novel, Plath deletes a sentence in which Esther acknowledges the transgressiveness and, to 1950s double thinking, abnormality of such a stance (however funny it may be). When Buddy invites Esther to undress too, Plath crosses out her heroine's thoughts on the proposition: 'I thought there must be something wrong with me. I just wanted to go home'.[174]

In her copy of *Villette*, Plath underscores Lucy's allusion to Dr John's 'masculine self-love' and writes in the margin 'R?'[175] Here, Plath signals her recognition that certain forms of male behaviour and privilege have persisted from the nineteenth-century into her own history and culture. 'How I love to read D. & P. into Dr. John!' she writes in the margin at the end of *Villette*'s Chapter XIX.[176] Buddy Willard is certainly a 1950s version of Dr John. Both characters have been friends with the heroine since childhood; both have close connections to her family, notably a friendship between their mothers. Lucy says of Dr John, 'he regarded me scientifically in the light of a patient'. Plath draws a line beneath these words, and another alongside the margin where the passage continues, 'and at once exercised his professional skill, and gratified his natural benevolence, by a course of cordial and attentive treatment'.[177] Dr John, like Buddy Willard, regards the woman as an object or case. She is something to study or cure or teach. No longer a threat to him or to society in its larger sense, he can congratulate himself for making the woman reasonable, for improving her and bringing her under conventional control, no longer neurotic or delusional. Buddy himself, Esther tells us, is 'always trying to explain things to me and introduce me to new knowledge'.[178] Lucy asserts that 'doctors are so self-opinionated, so immovable in their dry, materialist views'.[179] Plath highlights this assertion, as she does Lucy's assessment that 'Dr. John, throughout his whole life, was a man of luck – a man of success. And why? Because he had the eye to see his opportunity, the heart to prompt to well-timed action, the nerve to consummate a perfect work. And no tyrant-passion dragged him back; no enthusiasms, no foibles encumbered his way'.[180] Such smug certainty, valorised by the very different times and cultures, is repellent to both heroines; their revulsion towards this aspect of masculinity is what marks Lucy and Esther as different from their female contemporaries, and threatening to their respective cultures.

Lucy assesses Dr John's view of Paulina, and Plath points up this assessment. 'The pearl he admired was in itself of great price and truest purity, but he was not the man who, in appreciating the gem, could forget its setting'. 'Setting', here, is the matrix of money and social class that support Paulina, who would not appear so beautiful to John in the context of poverty. Dr John wants the 'adjuncts that Fashion decrees, Wealth purchases, and Taste adjusts'. Next to these words, Plath states the obvious, jotting 'John's standards materialistic'.[181] Lucy Snowe worries that Paulina and her father, the Count, will cool towards her once her 'grade in society'[182] is discovered by them, and Plath marks this in her copy of the book. Plath, like Brontë, asks where a woman might fit when her education and company differ from the social and economic class she is born into, or falls into. Both novels situate themselves as anti-fairy stories, as variants of, or, rather, challenges to, 'Cinderella', that most famous of tales of a woman's social mobility. As Ginevra puts it to the miraculously transformed Lucy, '"It seems so odd … that you and I should now be so much on a level, visiting in the same sphere; having the same connections"'.[183] Ginevra asks, '"Who *are* you, Miss Snowe?"' as if Lucy really is a strange princess who has turned up for the ball, and Lucy can only tease, '"Perhaps a personage in disguise. Pity I don't look the character"'.[184] Esther too is out of her element, confessing that she 'hadn't been out of New England except for this trip to New York. It was my first big chance'. The society girls who are 'bored with yachts and bored with flying around in aeroplanes and bored with skiing in Switzerland at Christmas and bored with the men in Brazil' wrong-foot Esther.[185]

The 'Cinderella' aspect of *The Bell Jar* is made more explicit in two sentences that Plath crosses out in an early typescript of the novel (she later uses the reverse of this page of the typescript for a draft of 'Stopped Dead'). 'Jay Cee didn't have any children, but that didn't matter. It might make her just that much more willing to adopt somebody like me.'[186] In true fairy tale fashion, Jay Cee, Philomena Guinea, and Doctor Nolan are potential fairy godmothers about whom Esther feels strongly ambivalent. These surrogate mother figures echo *Villette*'s Madame Beck (the proprietress of the school where Lucy teaches), Miss Marchmont (the elderly, crippled woman to whom Lucy is briefly a companion and friend), and Mrs Bretton (Dr John's mother). Lucy says of Miss Marchmont, 'Even when she scolded – which she did, now and then, very tartly – it was in such a way as did not humiliate, and left no sting; it was rather like an irascible mother rating her daughter, than a harsh mistress lecturing a dependent'.[187] Plath placed an exclamation mark in the margin by this passage.

Jacob and Wilhelm Grimm published the first two volumes of their fairy tales in 1812 and 1815, just before Charlotte Brontë's birth in 1816. Included in these editions were versions of those famous stories about bad relationships between mothers and daughters, 'Cinderella' and 'Snow White'. In true fairy tale fashion, Miss Marchmont represents the good, lost mother, who, like Cinderella's mother, firmly but lovingly instructs the young woman to 'be good and pious', promising to 'look down from heaven and take care' of her.[188] Miss Marchmont makes a similar speech to Lucy before dying, only to return from the dead – again like Cinderella's mother – with a much-needed gift some time later. (In Cinderella's case, these gifts are beautiful dresses to wear to the prince's three-day festival, and the exposure of the stepsisters so that Cinderella can become a bride. In Lucy's case, the gift is of 'an additional hundred pounds',[189] which she uses to set up her school and home, and, with Monsieur Paul's probable death at sea, to survive independently.) Madame Beck, on the other hand, is the bad, threatening mother figure. Like the stepmother trying to prevent the '"true bride"'[190] from claiming her rightful place, Madame Beck jealously stands between the heroine and her 'prince', or in the case of *Villette*, between Lucy and Monsieur Paul. Madame Beck even gives Lucy a version of the lentils Cinderella must sort before she can go to *Villette*'s adaptation of the ball. An opiate ('I was to be held quiet for one night'[191]) nearly stops Lucy from attending the Midsummer night festival or 'land of enchantment',[192] where she watches her friends and acquaintances as if in a dream.

Fairy tales frequently split the good and bad aspects of a mother into separate characters. In Grimm's 'Snow White', the good mother must die, leaving the child subject to the envy and aggression of the stepmother. Clearly, these counterparts of real and false mother are one and the same, crudely split. The wicked queen repeats the words of Snow White's natural mother, '"White as snow, red as blood, black as ebony!"'[193] How could the wicked queen know these words, and echo them? The answer must be that she herself uttered them in the first place, when she made her original wish for a beautiful daughter: the good, supposedly 'dead' mother and the wicked queen are one and the same. Early translations of such fairy tales did not bother to disguise real mothers as stepmothers. Only the later versions imposed the separation of good and bad, real mother and surrogate, into discrete characters. Brontë, like the authors of the later tales with which she would have been familiar, similarly apportions a mother's love and hate into distinct figures.

As if to signal further her intent that Miss Marchmont and Madame Beck should be read as diametrically opposed versions of the mother, Brontë fleetingly refers to their first names: both are called Maria,[194] as if after the holy mother (and perhaps Brontë's own dead mother and elder sister). In my discussion of Plath's 'Paralytic', I spoke of Melanie Klein's idea of the good and bad breasts, which represent, respectively, the polar opposites of good and bad mothers. The good mother, or good breast, like Miss Marchmont, and like Cinderella's mother (who posthumously clothes her daughter, looking after her in the most fundamental of ways), provides love and sustenance that can be relied upon. The bad mother, like Madame Beck, takes what is most valuable for herself, leaving the younger woman scraps at best, and poison at worst, but never anything approaching mother's milk; the only fluid Madame Beck can offer is toxic. As Lucy puts it, 'To be left to her and her cordial, seemed to me something like being left to the poisoner and her bowl'.[195] Mrs Bretton, the third of Lucy's mother figures, is also a good mother. She is, in fact, literally Lucy's godmother, preserving a link to Lucy's real parents as well as the higher economic and social position Lucy once held. By contrast to Madame Beck, Lucy tells us, 'Food or drink never pleased me so well as when it came through her hands'.[196]

Plath invokes this opposition between the good and the bad mother in *The Bell Jar*. If we measure the depictions of Esther's first and second experiences of electric shock treatment against each other, we see that Plath renders Melanie Klein's ideas about good and bad breasts actual as well as symbolic. In the first instance, Esther describes the preparations for her treatment:

> The nurse started swabbing my temples with a smelly grease.
>   As she leaned over to reach the side of my head nearest the wall, her fat breast muffled my face like a cloud or a pillow. A vague, medicinal stench emanated from her flesh.[197]

This is the bad breast at its worst. Instead of feeding and sustaining, the nurse's motherly body, her mammary glands, here literally suffocate. Feminine flesh is not inviting but, rather, repulsive with its unnatural 'medicinal stench'. This scene can be read as the mother/child encounter gone wrong, inverted into pain, fear and death. It is a scene of the bad or threatening mother exacting revenge, and it ends with Esther stating, 'I wondered what terrible thing it was that I had done',[198] asking like a child why she is being punished by the terrible parent. The first shock treatment is what precipitates Esther's famous suicide attempt, which is followed by her rescue by the emergency services at the start of Chapter Fourteen. Ending with Esther's cry, ' "Mother" ',[199] the rescue reads like a squeeze through the birth canal as much as a ride in an ambulance and a rush through hospital corridors.

The second electric shock treatment occurs after another, very different, mother/child encounter, also told with an emphasis on nurturing and food that is in keeping with Melanie Klein's theories. Esther, fattening on insulin as if it were mother's milk, wakes one morning 'warm and placid in my white cocoon'[200] like an infant in her cradle, only to discover that there is to be no breakfast, no 'fat blue china cream jug'.[201] The bad breast threatens again. No breakfast means electric shock treatment, and Esther curls like a sulking child in 'the alcove with the blanket over my head', furious at Doctor Nolan's 'treachery'[202] in not warning her in advance. Doctor Nolan's response to Esther, however, is played out as the response of the good, reassuring parent: she 'put her arm around me and hugged me like a mother'. Echoing the sort of promise a mother would make to a child who has had a bad dream, or fears the first day of school, Doctor Nolan tells Esther, ' "I'll be there when you wake up, and I'll bring you back again" '. ' "Promise you'll be there" ',[203] Esther woefully presses in a sentence that can only be read aloud in a small child's voice, to which Doctor Nolan accedes once more. The treatment itself, awful as it may be, is handled with gentleness and care, with Esther's fear acknowledged. Keeping to her vow, Doctor Nolan is by Esther's bed when she wakes, like a mother watching over her sick child.

To look at *The Bell Jar's* relationships to other texts, and Plath's to Woolf and Brontë, is to discredit from yet another angle that now familiar accusation that Plath's writing is always (and only) personal. (As Stevenson puts it in the much-read *Bitter Fame*, 'she never quite abandoned her self preoccupation'.[204]) To read Plath in this way also counters the related and often-stated criticism that she too often indulges in abject imitation, that her work is too derivative of writers such as Lowell and Roethke,[205] from whom she learns 'how to include her life in poetry'.[206] Plath's writing should not be disparaged for its textual exchanges with other writers; we have seen how Plath's work itself argues that borders are not solid or stable, whether these borders are of countries, ecosystems, or cultural identities. The same can be said of Plath's own literary texts. Already I have suggested that it is sometimes fruitful to regard Plath's poems not as separate, but as connected parts of a larger entity. In a similar vein, Plath speaks to and from the writers who preceded her, particularly Woolf and Brontë. As we will now see,

Plath's writing can also be viewed as part of a dialogue with the work of her contemporaries, notably with the poetry of Ted Hughes. Evaluating Plath's work in this way, as part of a conversation, helps us to dispel further the notion of her alleged self-absorption and lack of connection to any world or thing that is not her own.

Notes

1. Woolf, *A Room of One's Own*, 1992: 99.
2. Axelrod, *Sylvia Plath: The Wound and the Cure of Words*, 1990: 100.
3. Bassnett, *Sylvia Plath*, 1987: 153. Axelrod suggests that Esther's failed attempt to drown herself in *The Bell Jar* may be a rewrite of Woolf's own suicide by drowning (Axelrod, *Sylvia Plath: The Wound and the Cure of Words*, 1990: 101).
4. Butscher, *Sylvia Plath: Method and Madness*, 1976: 190.
5. Hardwick, 'On Sylvia Plath', 1985: 105, 106.
6. *Letters Home*, 230. Gilbert, 'In Yeats' House', 1984: 216.
7. (*The Journals of Sylvia Plath*, 1982: 168. *The Journals of Sylvia Plath*, 2000: 289.) Axelrod, *Sylvia Plath: The Wound and the Cure of Words*, 1990: 102.
8. (*The Journals of Sylvia Plath*, 1982: 186. *The Journals of Sylvia Plath*, 2000: 315.) Axelrod, *Sylvia Plath: The Wound and the Cure of Words*, 1990: 4; Wagner-Martin, *Sylvia Plath*, 1987: 156.
9. (*The Journals of Sylvia Plath*, 1982: 152, 305, 306–7. *The Journals of Sylvia Plath*, 2000: 269, 286, 485, 494. *Letters Home*, 305, 322.) 'Have read three Virginia Woolf novels this week and find them excellent stimulation for my own writing' (*Letters Home*, 324) is typical of these comments.
10. As Gilbert describes them, the three voices of Plath's characters are: 'First', a woman who gives birth to a wanted baby and is like Susan a 'nurturing mother'; 'Second', a woman who repeatedly miscarries and like Rhoda lacks 'appropriate femaleness'; and 'Third', a woman who has her baby adopted and like Jinny lives 'seductively but without attachments' (Gilbert, 'In Yeats' House', 1984: 217). Gilbert's textual evidence is persuasive. For instance, Plath's infertile Second Voice 'fears that "the streets may turn to paper suddenly"' (*ibid.*: 218; *Collected Poems*, 187) while Rhoda 'imagines her defiance as "a thin dream … a papery tree"' (Gilbert, 'In Yeats' House',1984: 217–18; Woolf, *The Waves*, 1992: 213).
11. Gilbert, 'In Yeats' House', 1984: 217.
12. Axelrod, *Sylvia Plath: The Wound and the Cure of Words*, 1990: 36.
13. Perhaps tenuously, he points out that Victoria Lucas, the pseudonym under which Plath first published *The Bell Jar*, has 'an identical number of letters' (Axelrod, *Sylvia Plath: The Wound and the Cure of Words*, 1990: 115)

to Virginia Woolf; and that Virginia and Victoria end with the same four letters. He observes also that in the typescript for *The Bell Jar* the heroine was called Victoria Lucas, and that the fictional Victoria names her own fictional heroine 'Virginia' (*ibid*.: 115). Readers who find such name games persuasive might consider also the heroine of Plath's 1957/8 story 'Stone Boy With Dolphin'. Dody Ventura, an aspiring poet, falls for another poet called Leonard, who might be named after Leonard Woolf.

14. Axelrod, *Sylvia Plath: The Wound and the Cure of Words*, 1990: 116.
15. *Johnny Panic*, 56.
16. Woolf, *Orlando*, 1992: 13.
17. *Johnny Panic*, 56.
18. Woolf, *Orlando*, 1992: 13.
19. *Johnny Panic*, 56.
20. Woolf, *Mrs Dalloway*, 1992: 18. We can see the influence of Woolf's stream of consciousness, and use of water, in Plath's 1952 story 'A Day in June'. The heroine has gone canoeing with her friend Linda:

> the hot touch of sun on your skin … blinding arrows of sunlight glancing off the deep glassed blue of the water … the exhilaration … bubbles rising, bursting … the gliding motion … the liquid singing of water past the bow … shifting specks of color dancing: all this to love, to cherish. Never again such a day!!
> You paddle to a cove … you drift … you lie back and close your eyes against the sunlight, hot upon the lids … you squint into the sunlight and there are webs of rainbows on your lashes. Lulled by the rhythmic lapping of waves against the prow, the rocking … the gliding … you drift near shore (Plath, 'A Day in June', 6; *Johnny Panic*, 247).

21. LILLY. Plath MSS. II, Memorabilia. Smith College – Papers, Eq–Z. Box 10, folder 8. '*Mrs. Dalloway*. Virginia Woolf'.
22. *Johnny Panic*, 56.
23. *Ibid*.
24. Woolf, *A Room of One's Own*, 1992: 101.
25. *Johnny Panic*, 57.
26. Woolf, *A Room of One's Own*, 1992: 117, 100.
27. *Johnny Panic*, 58.
28. Woolf, *A Room of One's Own*, 1992: 90.
29. *The Journals of Sylvia Plath*, 1982: 165. *The Journals of Sylvia Plath*, 2000: 286.
30. *The Journals of Sylvia Plath*, 1982: 307. *The Journals of Sylvia Plath*, 2000: 494.
31. *The Journals of Sylvia Plath*, 1982: 37. *The Journals of Sylvia Plath*, 2000: 100.
32. Woolf, *Congenial Spirits*, 1989: 69, 61, 64.
33. *The Journals of Sylvia Plath*, 1982: 171. *The Journals of Sylvia Plath*, 2000: 294.
34. *The Journals of Sylvia Plath*, 1982: 312. *The Journals of Sylvia Plath*, 2000: 500.

35. SMITH. Woolf, Virginia. *A Haunted House and Other Stories*. London: The Hogarth Press, 1944, 1953. Plath did not underline or annotate 'The Legacy'.

36. Rose, *The Haunting of Sylvia Plath*, 1991: xi, 179, 181.

37. Woolf, *The Complete Shorter Fiction*, 1989: 281.

38. *Johnny Panic*, 48.

39. *Ibid.*, 50.

40. *Ibid.*, 52.

41. Woolf, *The Complete Shorter Fiction*, 1989: 281.

42. *Johnny Panic*, 50.

43. *Ibid.*, 53.

44. *Ibid.*, 54.

45. Atwood, *The Edible Woman*, 1980: 6, 8.

46. Woolf, *The Complete Shorter Fiction*, 1989: 284–5.

47. *Johnny Panic*, 55.

48. *Ibid.*, 54.

49. Axelrod, *Sylvia Plath: The Wound and the Cure of Words*, 1990: 107, 112, 108.

50. Woolf, *A Room of One's Own*, 1992: 74, 109–13.

51. Axelrod, *Sylvia Plath: The Wound and the Cure of Words*, 1990: 113.

52. Woolf, *A Room of One's Own*, 1992: 134.

53. *The Bell Jar*, 123. Esther recalls 'Buddy Willard saying in a sinister, knowing way that after I had children I would feel differently, I wouldn't want to write poems any more' (*Ibid.*, 89).

54. Woolf, *A Room of One's Own*, 1992: 28.

55. *The Bell Jar*, 197.

56. *Ibid.*, 65. Plath must also have chosen the title and central image of her novel for its association with bee-keeping. Bee-keepers encourage their bees to put their comb honey in a 'bell jar ... surrounded by glass wool insulation and a fitting empty brood box to keep warm and dark'. Brown, *Beekeeping*, 1985: 92.

57. Woolf, *A Room of One's Own*, 1992: 134.

58. *Collected Poems*, 142.

59. Woolf, *A Room of One's Own*, 1992: 68.

60. *Collected Poems*, 139.

61. Woolf, *A Room of One's Own*, 1992: 22.

62. *The Bell Jar*, 37.

63. Woolf, *A Room of One's Own*, 1992: 36, 38.

64. Woolf, *To The Lighthouse*, 1992: 49.

65. Plath looks at this problem repeatedly in her work. See for instance the 1959 poem 'The Colossus' or, again, 'The Wishing Box'.

66. The text discloses that Sally has her own male interruptions, ironically, ' "five enormous boys" ' (Woolf, *Mrs Dalloway*, 1992: 225).

67. Abel, *Virginia Woolf and the Fictions of Psychoanalysis*, 1989: 32–3.

68. Woolf, *Mrs Dalloway*, 1992: 46.
69. Many critics have noted the images of sexual climax which surround the midday reverie of the kiss. Clarissa thinks of 'a tinge like a blush which one tried to check and then, as it spread, one yielded to its expansion, and rushed to the farthest verge and there quivered and felt the world come closer' (Woolf, *Mrs Dalloway*, 1992: 41).
70. Axelrod, *Sylvia Plath: The Wound and the Cure of Words*, 1990: 119.
71. The sewing is oft quoted: 'drawing the silk smoothly to its gentle pause' (Woolf, *Mrs Dalloway*, 1992: 50).
72. Abel, *Virginia Woolf and the Fictions of Psychoanalysis*, 1989: 32.
73. *The Bell Jar*, 23. Axelrod observes that 'Clarissa and Esther symbolically undergo their death by means of a double, who represents, enacts, and purges their suicidal impulses' (Axelrod, *Sylvia Plath: The Wound and the Cure of Words*, 1990: 121).
74. SMITH. Box: Plath – Prose – *The Bell Jar*. Folder: Prose Works – *The Bell Jar*, Progress Report, 1 Aug. 1962.
75. *The Bell Jar*, 61.
76. *Ibid.*, 23.
77. *Ibid.*, 229.
78. *Ibid.*, 23.
79. *Ibid.*, 4, 123.
80. Macpherson, *Reflecting on The Bell Jar*, 1991: 1–5, 28–40.
81. Kazin, *Bright Book of Life*, 1971: 185.
82. *The Bell Jar*, 232.
83. *Ibid.*, 237.
84. Sue Roe noted Clarissa's 'virginity preserved through childbirth' (Woolf, *Mrs Dalloway*, 1992: 40; Roe, *Writing and Gender*, 1990: 89). Plath's own examination of Esther's burdensome and very bloody virginity in *The Bell Jar* may be a revision and recantation of this aspect of Woolf's text.
85. Woolf, *Mrs Dalloway*, 1992: 101.
86. Abel, *Virginia Woolf and the Fictions of Psychoanalysis*, 1989: 29.
87. Van Dyne, *Revising Life*, 1993: 122–3. She writes: 'When Buddy Willard (the fictionalised Dick Norton) recites his mother's advice … Esther Greenwood contemptuously dismisses the feminine role'.
88. *The Bell Jar*, 75.
89. *Ibid.*, 93.
90. SMITH. Box: Plath – Ariel Poems, 'A Birthday Present' – 'Cut'. Folder: Ariel Poems, 'Crossing the Water', Draft 2. The cut sentence is adjacent to Buddy's 'I may yet lose a rib or two' on p. 97 of the Faber edition of *The Bell Jar*.
91. *The Bell Jar*, 1, 4, 14.
92. Macpherson, *Reflecting on The Bell Jar*, 1991: 33.
93. *The Bell Jar*, 96.
94. *Ibid.*, 95.

95. *Ibid.*, 8.
96. *Ibid.*, 94.
97. SMITH. Box: Plath – Ariel Poems, Amnesiac – Berck-Plage. Folder: Ariel Poems, 'Among the Narcissi', Draft 1.
98. *The Bell Jar*, 94.
99. SMITH. Box: Plath – Ariel Poems, Amnesiac – Berck-Plage. Folder: Ariel Poems, 'Among the Narcissi', Draft 1.
100. SMITH. Box: Plath – Ariel Poems, Amnesiac – Berck-Plage. Folder: Ariel Poems – drafts, 'The Arrival of the Bee Box', Draft 1. The excised line appears between 'innocent' and 'Tell me about' on p. 72 of the Faber edition of *The Bell Jar*.
101. LILLY. Plath MSS. II, Correspondence, 1974, Box 6a. Aurelia Plath to Ted and Carol Hughes. Not dated. Sent 28 Nov. 1974.
102. SMITH. Box: Plath – Biography. Folder: Biography, Plath, Aurelia Schober, 'Biographical Jottings' About SP.
103. SMITH. Prose Works – *The Bell Jar* – T.L. 14 Nov. 1961 to James [Michie], editor for *The Bell Jar*.
104. *The Bell Jar*, 190.
105. SMITH. Box: Plath – Prose – *The Bell Jar*. Folder: Prose Works – *The Bell Jar* – Outline of Chapters.
106. SMITH. Box: Plath – Ariel Poems, Nick and the Candlestick – Sheep in Fog Folder: Ariel Poems, 'Pheasant', Draft 1. This cut sentence would follow 'seven dimly lit steps into a sort of cellar' on p. 81 of the Faber edition of *The Bell Jar*.
107. SMITH. Box: Plath – Ariel Poems, 'A Birthday Present' – 'Cut'. Folder: Ariel Poems, 'The Courage of Shutting-Up', Draft 1.
108. *The Bell Jar*, 123.
109. *Ibid.*, 3.
110. LILLY. Plath MSS. 1961, 29 Oct. 'The babysitters'. *The Bell Jar*, 240.
111. *The Bell Jar*, 84.
112. Woolf, 'Professions for Women', 1979: 58–60.
113. *The Bell Jar*, 215.
114. *Ibid.*, 163.
115. SMITH. Box: Plath – Memorabilia, Notes. Folder: Notes, Jung.
116. Byatt, 'Sylvia Plath: *Letters Home*', 1976: 251.
117. LILLY. Brontë, Charlotte. *Villette* (1853). London: J.M. Dent & Sons, Everyman's Library, 1909, 1949.
118. Kazin, *Bright Book of Life*, 1971: 185.
119. Bronfen, *Sylvia Plath*, 1998: 35.
120. Brontë, *Villette*, 1990: 14.
121. *The Bell Jar*, 12.
122. LILLY. Brontë, Charlotte. *Villette* (1853). London: J.M. Dent & Sons, Everyman's Library, 1909, 1949: 178. Brontë, *Villette*, 1990: 248.
123. *The Bell Jar*, 36.

124. *Ibid.*, 37.
125. Brontë, *Villette*, 1990: 334.
126. *Ibid.*, 376.
127. *Ibid.*, 334.
128. *The Bell Jar*, 34.
129. Brontë, *Villette*, 1990: 441.
130. *Ibid.*, 445.
131. *The Bell Jar*, 61.
132. Quoted in Macpherson, *Reflecting on The Bell Jar*, 1991: 38.
133. *The Bell Jar*, 120.
134. Brontë, *Villette*, 1990: 193.
135. *The Bell Jar*, 135.
136. Brontë, *Villette*, 1990: 196.
137. *The Bell Jar*, 155.
138. Brontë, *Villette*, 1990: 202.
139. LILLY. Brontë, Charlotte. *Villette* (1853). London: J.M. Dent & Sons, Everyman's Library, 1909, 1949: 184. Brontë, *Villette*, 1990: 255.
140. Brontë, *Villette*, 1990: 195.
141. *The Bell Jar*, 171.
142. SMITH. Box: Plath – Ariel Poems, Amnesiac – Berck-Plage. Folder: Ariel Poems, 'Among the Narcissi', Draft 2. The cut passage would have followed the phrase, 'as if the corners of his mouth were strung up on invisible wire', on p. 94 of *The Bell Jar*.
143. LILLY. Brontë, Charlotte. *Villette* (1853). London: J.M. Dent & Sons, Everyman's Library, 1909, 1949: 62. Brontë, *Villette*, 1990: 89.
144. LILLY. Brontë, Charlotte. *Villette* (1853). London: J.M. Dent & Sons, Everyman's Library, 1909, 1949: 63. Brontë, *Villette*, 1990: 90.
145. Brontë, *Villette*, 1990: 290.
146. *The Bell Jar*, 121.
147. *Ibid.*, 123.
148. *Ibid.*, 122.
149. Brontë, *Villette*, 1990: 201.
150. *Ibid.*, 526.
151. LILLY. Brontë, Charlotte. *Villette* (1853). London: J.M. Dent & Sons, Everyman's Library, 1909, 1949: 135. Brontë, *Villette*, 1990: 186.
152. LILLY. Brontë, Charlotte. *Villette* (1853). London: J.M. Dent & Sons, Everyman's Library, 1909, 1949: 434. Brontë, *Villette*, 1990: 594.
153. Brontë, *Villette*, 1990: 468.
154. *Ibid.*, 475.
155. *The Bell Jar*, 23.
156. LILLY. Brontë, Charlotte. *Villette* (1853). London: J.M. Dent & Sons, Everyman's Library, 1909, 1949: 284. Brontë, *Villette*, 1990: 389.
157. *The Bell Jar*, 6, 7.

158. LILLY. Brontë, Charlotte. *Villette* (1853). London: J.M. Dent & Sons, Everyman's Library, 1909, 1949: 271. Brontë, *Villette*, 1990: 371.

159. Brontë, *Villette*, 1990: 478.

160. *The Bell Jar*, 79.

161. LILLY. Brontë, Charlotte. *Villette* (1853). London: J.M. Dent & Sons, Everyman's Library, 1909, 1949: 196. Brontë, *Villette*, 1990: 272.

162. LILLY. Brontë, Charlotte. *Villette* (1853). London: J.M. Dent & Sons, Everyman's Library, 1909, 1949: 197. Brontë, *Villette*, 1990: 273.

163. Brontë, *Villette*, 1990: 274.

164. *The Bell Jar*, 70–1, 71.

165. Brontë, *Villette*, 1990: 281.

166. *Ibid.*, 325.

167. *The Bell Jar*, 73.

168. *Ibid.*, 74.

169. SMITH. Box: Plath – Letters (Plath – Sylvia). Folder: Plath. A.L.s. Jan. 1952.

170. LILLY. James, Henry. *The American* (1877). New York: Rinehart & Co., 1949, 1953: 34, Chapter Three.

171. LILLY. James, Henry. *The American* (1877). New York: Rinehart & Co., 1949, 1953: 125, Chapter Ten.

172. LILLY. James, Henry. *The American* (1877). New York: Rinehart & Co., 1949, 1953: 64, Chapter Four.

173. *The Bell Jar*, 71.

174. SMITH. Box: Plath – Ariel Poems, Amnesiac – Berck-Plage. Folder: Ariel Poems – drafts, 'The Bee Meeting', Draft 2.

175. LILLY. Brontë, Charlotte. *Villette* (1853). London: J.M. Dent & Sons, Everyman's Library, 1909, 1949: 178. Brontë, *Villette*, 1990: 247.

176. LILLY. Brontë, Charlotte. *Villette* (1853). London: J.M. Dent & Sons, Everyman's Library, 1909, 1949: 186. Brontë, *Villette*, 1990: 258.

177. LILLY. Brontë, Charlotte. *Villette* (1853). London: J.M. Dent & Sons, Everyman's Library, 1909, 1949: 231. Brontë, *Villette*, 1990: 318.

178. *The Bell Jar*, 70.

179. LILLY. Brontë, Charlotte. *Villette* (1853). London: J.M. Dent & Sons, Everyman's Library, 1909, 1949: 233. Brontë, *Villette*, 1990: 321.

180. LILLY. Brontë, Charlotte. *Villette* (1853). London: J.M. Dent & Sons, Everyman's Library, 1909, 1949: 290. Brontë, *Villette*, 1990: 396–7.

181. LILLY. Brontë, Charlotte. *Villette* (1853). London: J.M. Dent & Sons, Everyman's Library, 1909, 1949: 336. Brontë, *Villette*, 1990: 463–4.

182. LILLY. Brontë, Charlotte. *Villette* (1853). London: J.M. Dent & Sons, Everyman's Library, 1909, 1949: 259. Brontë, *Villette*, 1990: 354.

183. Brontë, *Villette*, 1990: 382.

184. *Ibid.*, 383.

185. *The Bell Jar*, 4.

186. SMITH. Box: Plath – Ariel Poems, Stings – Years. Folder: Ariel Poems, 'Stopped Dead', Draft 1. The cut passage would have followed 'Then I'd know what to do' in *The Bell Jar*, 40.

187. LILLY. Brontë, Charlotte. *Villette* (1853). London: J.M. Dent & Sons, Everyman's Library, 1909, 1949: 30. Brontë, *Villette*, 1990: 45.

188. 'Cinderella', in Grimm, *The Complete Fairy Tales of the Brothers Grimm*, 1992: 86.

189. Brontë, *Villette*, 1990: 614.

190. 'Cinderella', in Grimm, *The Complete Fairy Tales of the Brothers Grimm*, 1992: 92.

191. Brontë, *Villette*, 1990: 562.

192. *Ibid.*, 566.

193. 'Snow White', in Grimm, *The Complete Fairy Tales of the Brothers Grimm*, 1992: 202.

194. Brontë, *Villette*, 1990: 50, 88.

195. *Ibid.*, 600.

196. *Ibid.*, 225.

197. *The Bell Jar*, 151.

198. *Ibid.*, 152.

199. *Ibid.*, 181.

200. *Ibid.*, 221.

201. *Ibid.*, 222.

202. *Ibid.*, 223.

203. *Ibid.*, 224.

204. Stevenson, *Bitter Fame*, 1989: 287.

205. Kenner, 'Sincerity Kills', 1989: 72.

206. McClatchy, 'Short Circuits and Folding Mirrors', 1989: 84.

CHAPTER 5

A WAY OF GETTING THE POEMS

In his poem 'The Tender Place', Ted Hughes takes the line 'Over-exposed, like an X-ray'[1] verbatim from Plath's 1962 poem 'Medusa'. One way of accounting for the duplication is to see it, not as a theft, but rather as a cue. In a moment that can only be aware of its import, Hughes signals to the reader that his poetry speaks both to and from Plath's. This relationship between the two *oeuvres* was made explicit in 1995, when Hughes published a section of 'Uncollected' poems in his *New Selected Poems* and included 'The Tender Place'. It has been made still more obvious with the publication in February 1998 of *Birthday Letters*, which the book's cover advertises as Hughes's 'personal account'[2] of his relationship with Plath, and where we find numerous other echoes of Plath's lines.[3] Further still, Hughes has published eleven little-known poems about Plath in a limited edition of only 110 numbered copies. The collection is called *Howls & Whispers*, and it was published in the summer of 1998. It puts paid to the idea that *Birthday Letters* was Hughes's 'final work on his relationship with Sylvia Plath'.[4] (If the posthumous publication history of Plath's own writing is anything to go by, it would be rash to discount the likelihood that further new works by Hughes will appear.) These eleven *Howls & Whispers* poems are, as it were, *Birthday Letters* poems not published in *Birthday Letters*. 'The Minotaur', for instance, appears in *Birthday Letters*, while Hughes places 'The Minotaur 2' in *Howls & Whispers*. 'The Minotaur 2' follows the regular quatrains of the *Birthday Letters* poem, as well as its idea that writing can be destructive to real life. The poems in *Howls & Whispers* were among the last that Hughes published in his lifetime. They represent the most recent development in the careers of two writers whose literary conversations with each other are, to use a phrase of Hughes's, 'a way of getting the poems'.[5]

The Critics on Hughes and Plath

If we are to understand the undeniable textual relationship between Plath's work and Hughes's, it is instructive to begin by looking in detail at the way that Hughes scholars have treated Sylvia Plath. Some simply pretend that she never existed. Craig Robinson's 1989 monograph ignores Plath altogether, while Nicholas Bishop's 1991 book on Hughes makes just one reference to her, and does so only for the purpose of providing a relative temporal and thematic context for *Wodwo*.[6] Few Hughes scholars have acknowledged the extent to which Hughes makes Plath into his subject matter and draws on her work in his own. Still fewer have argued for any reciprocity of influence and assistance between the two.

It is difficult not to feel that a love of Hughes's work (and some form of relentless loyalty) leads many of Hughes's critics to deride Plath's writing and life. Hughes, the reasoning seems to go, cannot be good if she is not bad. One cannot help suspect, reading Keith Sagar's work, that Plath simply cannot do anything right. Even her taste in poetry must be disdained. Hence Hughes's '"Fire-Eater" ... seems to me a bad poem, though Sylvia Plath thought it the best poem in *Lupercal*'. Sagar's instinct seems to be to neutralise anything negative he wishes to say about Hughes's work by ending on a note that finds fault with Plath. In opposite excess, Hughes 'is a good judge of his own work'; he is a 'great poet'.[7]

Nicholas Bishop's single reference to Plath in his 1991 monograph comes in a book whose very first sentence is a grateful tribute to Hughes for his 'continual generosity in answering all my queries, conversationally and by letter'.[8] There is something personal in all this, though perhaps unavoidably so. The critic's feelings about Hughes, and his or her actual contact with him, become part of the making of the book. Ekbert Faas tells us with the passion of someone converted, 'even our first three-hour discussion in March 1970 was enough to turn me from an admirer of his poetry into a witness of an interior saga'.[9] However irrelevant to her review of *Birthday Letters*, Heather Neill cannot resist parading her own meaningful exchange with Hughes, who 'recommended Lorca's essay about "duende" to me'.[10]

Ekbert Faas's essay 'Chapters in a Shared Mythology' is worth looking at closely, for it typifies a powerful strand of Hughes criticism. Faas's piece declares that its central aim is to evaluate the two poets together. Yet 'Chapters in a Shared Mythology' is misleadingly titled. A work that promises a fair consideration of the exchanges between Hughes's and Plath's work proves to be quite something else. Instead, Faas argues that Hughes succeeds where Plath fails. A reference in his last paragraph to 'Hughes's development and how it stems from Sylvia Plath's'[11] is baffling, or perhaps disingenuous, because Faas argues instead that Plath's writing, like her life, stalled or reached an impasse. Hughes, by Faas's invidious contrast, 'makes real what in "Lady Lazarus" and other of Plath's poems remains an ineffectual gesture'.[12]

In Hughes, Faas tells us, the 'demonisation of the female which in "Lady Lazarus" or "Purdah" remains a largely histrionic gesture, has reached a forcefulness reminiscent of Euripides' *The Bacchae*'.[13] Along these same lines, Faas believes that 'Hughes avoids the facile rebirth symbolism of poems like Plath's early "Wreath for a Bridal"'.[14] The failures (in Faas's judgement) of Plath's poetry are attributed to her lived inadequacies: 'Plath's sojourn on the other side of sanity and life had left traces not to be erased by a mere new philosophy of life'.[15] By contrast, Hughes's personal life is never used by Faas to explain Hughes's writing. The sole 'facts' of Hughes's life to which Faas refers are those which demonstrate the poet's generosity towards Plath. Given the advantages afforded her by this generosity, Faas insinuates that Plath's failures as a poet and woman seem all the greater. Hughes 'encouraged his wife ... by hypnotising her', 'taught Plath not to read novels and poems only', and 'Even more crucial was Hughes' role in freeing her imagination and hence unleashing her worst nightmares'.[16] This is a familiar narrative: Plath herself alludes to it in her journals and correspondence, and Hughes repeats the story in *Birthday Letters*. I cannot and would not wish to dispute it, but I would wish to highlight the very different treatments of the two writers by one critic.

By contrast, what has Plath given Hughes? According to Faas, they share a theme of rebirth, but Hughes 'owes little to direct borrowing'[17] and Plath has only affected him through 'subliminal transference'.[18] Faas displays an unselfconscious confusion about just what confessionality may be. He tangles his arguments and unfairly wields two very different methodologies. 'Though hardly confessional in content', he writes, 'Plath's mature poetry stems from a clearly biographical impulse'.[19] Faas speaks as though 'confessional' and 'biographical impulses' are entirely unrelated, and assumes his readers will also find the distinction transparent.

Unlike Plath, Hughes has not fared badly at the hands of his own critics. Take for instance M. L. Rosenthal's malicious comparisons of Plath to superior male poets in his essay 'Sylvia Plath and Confessional

Poetry'. Rosenthal denies Plath's 'technical' and 'intellectual' abilities, and emphasises her attention to the personal. His account of Plath's use of personal material is a mainstream critical view: Plath's 'range of technical resources was narrower than Robert Lowell's, and so, apparently, was her capacity for intellectual objectivity. ... She chose ... the one alternative advance position to Lowell's along the dangerous confessional way, that of literally committing her own predicaments in the interests of her art until the one was so involved in the other that no return was possible'.[20] By contrast, Hughes scholars, while occasionally and tentatively alluding to links between his life and work, stick largely to the latter. Thomas West briefly states that 'the eloquence of his laments ... in *Wodwo* ... suffices in the way of personal testimony'[21] about Plath's suicide. West says no more than this, and otherwise eschews biographical correlations in his study of Hughes.

A handful of Hughes's critics have read his poems biographically, though usually hesitantly, and under the pretence that they are doing something else altogether. Leonard M. Scigaj argues that *Wodwo* (1967) presents 'no direct biographical referents',[22] though Scigaj does assert that *Remains of Elmet* (1979) is Hughes's own 'two-way journey', which partly consists of 'releasing the spirits of Edith Farrar Hughes, Sylvia Plath, and other departed relatives into a heaven ...'.[23] Scigaj describes poem 19 of *Gaudete* as

> Hughes's first direct treatment of Plath's suicide, almost a decade and a half after the event. ... The number three refers to the third death alluded to in Plath's 'Lady Lazarus,' after her father's death when she was eight (1940) and her first, unsuccessful suicide attempt while an undergraduate at Smith College (1953). The Hughes poem continues with the persona kissing the Goddess's (Plath's) forehead in the morgue, in a mood that combines deep sadness with infinite tenderness.[24]

With respect to Plath's work, such a biographical autopsy is familiar. To read Hughes's work by means of a literary post-mortem, so that every element of the poem must be attached to some real event or thought, is similarly limiting.[25] It is significant that only in relation to Plath and her death does Scigaj engage in such a reductive way of reading Hughes; Scigaj's work is otherwise careful and illuminating. Possibly, even unconsciously, Scigaj has absorbed the notion that Plath is free territory. Elsewhere, he avoids biographical criticism.

Dennis Walder acknowledges a 'remarkable, and intensely productive partnership'[26] between Hughes and Plath, but warns that,

> Inevitably, there is a strong temptation to link the poetry of Ted Hughes and Sylvia Plath, which shares an extremism, an insistence on facing the worst. But it is a temptation to be resisted since, as Plath herself remarked, 'we write poems that are as distinct and different as our fingerprints themselves must be.' More important here is the link between what happened to Plath and its effect upon the development of Hughes's poetry.[27]

Walder asserts also that 'Hughes is not, like Plath and some of her American mentors (such as Robert Lowell), a "confessional" poet, tracing his own life and circumstances explicitly in his work'.[28] Seemingly contradicting this denial of Hughes's confessionality, Walder later writes that Hughes's 'Heptonstall Cemetery'[29] 'itemises the poet's personal attachments (which include Sylvia Plath), as it suggests their immortalisation'.[30] For Walder, Plath's confessionality is a stable given. Hughes, on the other hand, is not confessional in one breath, yet is in the next. Walder's work is sensitive, but exemplifies a conundrum of contradictory assertions and denials in which even excellent scholars can find themselves caught when considering confessionality – and especially the alleged confessionality of Hughes or Plath.

Hughes's Story

Whether or not the publication of *Birthday Letters* will lead scholars to treat the issue of Hughes's own supposed confessionality with less delicacy, and less paradox, remains to be seen. When *Birthday Letters* first appeared, commentary on the book was largely the province of journalists. Perhaps influenced by old stories, and by the frequent references to 'Daddy' in *Birthday Letters* itself, the press largely reiterated the stereotypes of Plath as a mad woman whose marriage fell apart because she loved her father too much and was obsessed with death. This is not surprising given the fact that such a story is likely to sell newspapers. Heather Neill wrote: 'After her death – and perhaps, for her, before that – "Daddy" and Hughes became synonymous, a fact acknowledged here in "A Picture of Otto"'.[31] To speak of Plath and

Hughes, the front cover of the *Sunday Times* books section invoked a tabloid rhetoric of soap opera violence and 'true life' stories of disputes between sports heroes and their wives. '*Fatal Attraction*',[32] screamed its headline in red ink.

Ironically, *Birthday Letters* advertises itself as confessional poetry with a certainty that Plath's so-called autobiographical poems never have. The poems, announces the blurb inside the front cover of *Birthday Letters*, 'are addressed, with just two exceptions, to Sylvia Plath'.[33] Yet the 'you', the 'Plath' so incessantly addressed by Hughes's speaker, is a poetic character who is no more stable or real as 'Plath' than the object of any intensely felt love poem – or love letter. And *Birthday Letters*, in spite of its title, wriggles out of any simple definition as poem or letter. Like a letter, these poems are spoken to somebody else. Unlike a letter, their object can never read or hear them. Perhaps this makes no difference. As Terry Eagleton has shown so convincingly, those who write letters can be more preoccupied with talking to themselves than with the person they are addressing. Eagleton explains:

> Writing as communication threatens to become a mere pretext for writing as invention, the sober end sheer occasion for self-gratifying means. ... Writing must officially have a point, as self-exhortation or moral *aide-mémoire*; even where it is self-communion, and so prone to the dangers of narcissism, it must mime a public 'compact', provide a mirror before which the author may unite with an 'ideal ego'.[34]

Self-exhortation, memory aid, moral investigation, inner examination, private communication made public – *Birthday Letters* might be described as any or all of these. Reading the poems carefully, it is hard to imagine that Hughes himself would have quibbled with these descriptions. Above all, he seems to invite such an account of the poems as subjective. We have seen again and again in this book how slippery any biographical truth can be, how almost anything that is said or written reveals more about the person who speaks than about the one who is spoken of. This is not less true of a letter or a poem than it is of a biography.

Hughes himself is self-conscious about his own narrative fallibility in *Birthday Letters*. The first line of the collection's first poem begins with a question that dramatises the struggle to dredge up memory: 'Where was it, in the Strand?'[35] At the outset, Hughes foregrounds the imperfect process of recollecting past events. This gesture of discounting his own authority is repeated in the collection's second poem, whose first line also begins with uncertainty, with a question: 'What were those caryatids bearing?'[36] *Birthday Letters* is filled with questions – questions that are symptomatic of Hughes's unease about freezing the past categorically, or speaking for those who may have experienced it differently. The book is distinguished by Hughes's disinclination to petrify his own contradictory and changing thoughts. 'Was that a happy day?'[37] he asks at the start of 'Flounders'. 'What did they mean to you, the azalea flowers?' he wonders at the beginning of 'Child's Park'.[38] 'You needed an earth', he declares in 'The Rag Rug', before recanting any certainty about his own judgement with the next word: 'Maybe'.[39] This constant questioning, this refusal of any one meaning or privileged viewpoint, may be the source of *Birthday Letters'* power. Even on those occasions where I resist Hughes's stories or interpretations, he buys my tolerance because he owns them as partial. *Birthday Letters* is dotted with tentativeness about fact. Again and again the poems disclaim any pretence of absolute truth. In 'Fidelity' he wonders whether to feel jealous of or sorry for himself.[40] In '18 Rugby Street' he confesses, 'I cannot remember / How I smuggled myself, wrapped in you, / Into the hotel'.[41] These lines dramatise the tangled excitement of lovers, and the difficulty of committing to memory the precise choreography of an unfolding physical encounter. More literally, these lines admit the slippery nature of the past, and the imperfection of reflection.

Hesitant words and questioning syntax are a striking feature of the first half of *Birthday Letters*, as if to emphasise Hughes's position as a witness who can only describe the way things appeared from one vantage point. It is at the moments where Hughes seems to forget this that I like the poems less. More often than not, though, Hughes seems to say, I can only provide my own interpretation, I am rarely sure of anything: 'It did *seem* / You disturbed something just perfected';[42] your tears '*might have been* tears of joy, a squeeze of joy'[43] (my italics). One of the *Birthday Letters* poems, 'A Short Film', is explicit about the problem of memory: the human inability to anticipate the importance of an event, and pay attention while it happens. Therefore, we do not record these events for history, or if we do, we cannot understand their full implications. We certainly cannot control the way such evidence will be used. The home movie of Hughes's poem

> ... had been made for happy remembering
> By people who were still too young
> To have learned about memory.

The film, over time, becomes a 'dangerous weapon',[44] something which can be anatomised for the roots of inevitable tragedy, for the pathology of its star (the dancing child), or to criticise the parents who made it. Reviewers, in spite of the many cues to read *Birthday Letters* as a fallible set of recollections, have professed that Hughes, at last, has told his story. He has given them a heavy dose of indisputable fact: 'Some Home Truths About Sylvia Plath',[45] as one headline succinctly put it.[46]

In *Howls & Whispers*, that limited edition of *Birthday Letters* poems not published in *Birthday Letters*, those who treat poems as biography will find fresh material. At this point in time, we can only speculate as to why Hughes published these poems separately, and in such an obscure edition. In their chronology and subject matter, the *Howls & Whispers* poems could easily be woven into the fabric of *Birthday Letters*. I'd go so far as to suggest that there are gaps in *Birthday Letters*, gaps that can only be filled by the poems in *Howls & Whispers*. My theory is that Hughes held the poems back because they dramatise greater extremes of emotions and interpretation than anything in *Birthday Letters*. Erica Wagner tells us in *Ariel's Gift* that 'another poem, "The Laburnum"',[47] appeared in the contents page of the first proof of *Birthday Letters* that she saw in her role as Literary Editor of *The Times*, which serialised some of the poems just before the book came out. In the end, 'The Laburnum' appeared in *Howls & Whispers*, and not in *Birthday Letters*. This indicates that Hughes may have decided to hold the poem back, and other or all of the *Howls & Whispers* poems, at the last minute. As far as supposedly confessional writing goes, Hughes may have regarded the 'confessions' in *Howls & Whispers* as more sensational than those in *Birthday Letters*. Perhaps he did not feel ready to go public with them in any large way. Perhaps some day there will be a posthumous edition in which all the poems will be printed together and entwined; Hughes may have left instructions for this, and a record of an intended order, just as Plath left evidence of the sequence she had planned for *Ariel*.

Birthday Letters and *Howls & Whispers* are noteworthy for their almost novelistic natures. That is to say, both books develop the long story of a relationship over time, a story that is stronger, in a way, than death, and does not end with the death of one of the doomed lovers. Hughes divides his poems not just into verses and stanzas, but also sometimes sets them out in what has the appearance and purpose of prose paragraphs, beginning a new idea or turn of his thought on a fresh, indented line. This narrative quality, as well as the fame of the Hughes and Plath myth, has undoubtedly been a strong factor in the huge readership that *Birthday Letters* has attracted (it was the third highest selling hardback book of 1998 in Britain[48]).

As in *Birthday Letters* also, Hughes questions the reality of events as he remembers them and stresses the fictional aspect of any account he can give. Recall Hughes's wry observation in *Birthday Letters* that 'It is only a story. / Your story. My story',[49] an idea that resonates in *Howls & Whispers* too. Hughes reminds the reader that historical events cannot be made into reliable facts by anybody, even those who lived them, but that they nonetheless had material effects on real human beings. It seems mean to criticise Hughes for inconsistency as he moves between anger, distress, love, and self-justification, however much the reader may, at given moments, think irritably, 'Oh why bring Daddy into it again?' or, 'Can't we ease up on the belief in fate?' These contradictory perspectives are likely to excite compassion. Who does not have such ambivalent thoughts about those they love and lose? Yet who is also brave enough, and intelligent enough, to admit their compromised position? The fact that Hughes does both is what makes it likely that *Birthday Letters* and *Howls & Whispers* will endure.

Both books are filled with startling, surprising lines. Think for instance of the end of the *Birthday Letters* poem 'The Shot'. Here, the bewildered narrator sees his troubled lover as a bullet, and sadly, guiltily muses that someone else

> Might have caught you in flight with his bare hands,
> Tossed you, cooling, one hand to the other,
> Godless, happy, quieted.
> > I managed
> A wisp of your hair, your ring, your watch, your nightgown.[50]

There is tenderness here, and immense sorrow. These emotions feel larger, more permanent, than any biography we can reduce the poem to, any story we can make it fit. *Birthday Letters* and *Howls & Whispers* both work at their best when they are not authoritative, and when they are kind in their memories of Plath, rather than angry or looking for someone or something else to blame.

It is interesting that Hughes privileges the poem 'Howls & Whispers' by giving its name to the collection as a whole. Is this a way of disclaiming responsibility for the content and nature of the poems? Or is it an attempt to anticipate any reservations readers may have about the book, and nullify them in the same breath? Is it a way of saying, I cannot be held responsible for this in artistic, moral, or intellectual terms? Is it a way of saying, these poems are not poems? They are howls and whispers, cries and words spoken at the extreme poles of loudness and softness. Howls and whispers do not get through to those at whom they are aimed because they are garbled or indecipherable. Moreover, Hughes's do not get through to the woman to whom they are spoken because she is dead. Is it a way of saying, because howls and whispers are not forms of communication that are effective at getting the message across, and are often discounted as illegitimate because they are uncontrolled and emotional, you cannot criticise or canonise me on the basis of this content? Too little control, too much emotion: these are phrases, or accusations, frequently levelled against Plath's writing, and Plath herself. This raises yet another question. Who is howling and whispering, Hughes or Plath, speaker or spoken to? The answer, as I think Hughes must have meant it to be, is surely both.

If we turn to 'Howls & Whispers' itself, we find a poem that is about miscommunication. It is a poem of letters within letters, in which Hughes describes and quotes from the correspondence of Plath's friends and family during the months and weeks before she died. Whispers, in this poem, take on another meaning. They are nasty and unsubstantiated bits of gossip that do harm. The letters are *about* Hughes and the breakdown of the relationship, but not *to* him. They are letters that Plath left for him to find and read after she was dead. Terry Eagleton is again helpful here. Writing, and especially epistolary writing, he reminds us,

> is a matter of record and contract, seal and bond, tangible documentation which may be turned against its author, cited out of context, deployed as threat, testimony, blackmail. It is the 'iterability' of script – the fact that its materiality allows it to be reproduced in changed conditions – which makes it such an efficient instrument of oppression. The free utterance of the heart, once taken down in writing, may always be used later in evidence against the speaker.[51]

'Howls & Whispers' operates through an especially complex arrangement of fiction, real letters, and poetry. It illustrates how letters can indeed 'be used later in evidence against the speaker' and 'reproduced in changed conditions', even read by someone for whom your words were not intended (in this case, the last person for whom your words would have been intended). Knowing this, Hughes made sure before he died that *Howls & Whispers* itself could not be reproduced in changed conditions.[52] To retain my discussion of *Howls & Whispers*, I have excised all quotations from the poems and replaced them with paraphrase. This is never a satisfactory thing to do. Rewording someone else's poetry inevitably results in distortion and robs the reader of the opportunity to make his or her own judgements about the work. I hope that readers will bear with me for the next few pages, and that at the very least this discussion will make them want to seek out one of the 110 copies of *Howls and Whispers* to see the poems at firsthand.

In 'Howls & Whispers', Hughes is explicit about his resentment of and anger towards Plath's mother. He alleges that Mrs Plath wrote to her daughter, urging her to revenge herself against him by taking his money, and that Mrs Plath celebrated the end of her child's relationship to a man whom she regarded as a piece of dirt or a germ, of whom she never approved. Plath's analyst instructed her in a letter written on 26 September 1962 to 'Keep him out of your bed'.[53] Hughes puts this very phrase into 'Howls & Whispers'. These words of Plath's mother and therapist might be regarded as the passionately protective and angry statements of those who felt great loyalty towards her; those who loved her. Ugly as they may be, unfair or partisan as they may be, they are typical of the supportive rage family and friends feel for a loved one whose relationship has broken down. How would your best friend or mother or sister or brother speak of your husband or wife or lover if your relationship had ended in an ugly, unhappy way? Few of us could assert that they would behave with balance, with circumspection. There is no right or wrong here. Understandably, Hughes was not in a position to look on these comments with equanimity. His rage at discovering these remarks, at catching these women talking behind his back, is also part of a familiar human story, and one in which most of us have participated. Yet Hughes can express a sad and wry recognition that he and Plath, rather than speak to each other, had only these variously misguided, well-meaning, self-interested and misinformed advisers. The howls and whispers circulate. They are not just Plath's and Hughes's, but are the untrustworthy and ineffectual (or perniciously effectual) cries and innuendoes of family and friends too. Hughes insinuates, but does not name, those who needed to play a role in the drama, whatever the cost, for instance the messenger or negotiator who wanted to show off to herself and other people that she was a central player as the crisis between the couple unfolded. For Hughes, this woman lost her humanity. He envisions her in the poem as an insect between his sheets, or crouching by Plath's side to gain her confidence and poison her thoughts. Such people, the narrator claims, are responsible for Plath's death. This story (that 'they' did it, or drove Plath to her death) is no more convincing than the more familiar story that Hughes did. Only the grief and anger and need to blame someone else make sense; they are the only true thing.

Any sense of biographical fact becomes more slippery in the final four poems of the collection, which advertise the contingency of the relationship between words and events. Like the collection's title, these last poems seem to warn us: do not trust what we say; we do not speak of the quantifiable; we cannot be held accountable for this. These opaque poems are not so much about any events concerning Plath's death as they are about her afterlife. In them, Plath might be described as a ghost who takes different forms. Intimacy between Hughes and Plath cannot be ended by death in the world of *Howls & Whispers*. We will see that this closeness takes the form of imaginary conversations, dreams, and even Hughes's encounter with Plath's ghost.

In 'The City', Hughes imagines Plath's poems as the centre of a dark town, while her prose forms its outskirts. There is a value judgement here, in which the poems matter more than the prose suburbs. This city is populated by academics and devotees. At night Hughes wanders through it all reading Plath's work, or thinking about it. Occasionally he glimpses a lost-looking Plath. Grown old, she freezes as if in a nightmare and searches faces in the hope that she will find someone she knows. The implication is that Plath is present in her writing, but not easily recognised, and not cognizant herself. She is distorted and changed. She is uncertain and confused, even frightened. Plath does not exist in any stable or perfect form in this writing, this city. Hughes dramatises her tendency to slip away: the complex relationship between life and work, identity and writing.

I have argued that 'Howls & Whispers', through its very title, cautions us to treat with circumspection any 'messages' in Hughes's poems about Plath. 'Howls & Whispers' warns us to take note of the sort of language we are hearing, a language we may not be able to discern and then interpret accurately: involuntary 'howls' or untrustworthy 'whispers'. The poem asks us to treat these cries and murmurs accordingly. 'The City', with its representation of Plath's shape shifting, echoes this warning. So does the poem that follows it, 'Moon-Dust', where we again see how elusive 'Plath' can be, and how full of holes stories are, even when told by those who lived them. The poem's first stanza describes the numerous and at least once-removed ways that we access stories: we hear or read about them second-hand instead of hearing or reading them ourselves; we conjecture rather than know or experience directly. Plath's narrative is compared to a moon full of craters. On this moon Hughes's own story sits, small and precarious. From it he can only retrieve a small number of stones, using tongs. Even Hughes cannot touch directly; he himself must mediate his contact with Plath's story through an instrument – tongs – even where, or especially where, this story touches his own. Here, Hughes the narrator disclaims any myth of his own free access or perfect understanding: he examines the rocks, as if searching for information and comprehension that he does not inherently possess. Hughes likens himself to a flower that rests lightly on the rocks as a breeze bends and sways it. As far as his own authority and comprehension about Plath's story is concerned, he is vulnerable and unstable, blown by the wind, subject to forces outside himself, and only achieving fleeting, imperfect contact.

In the final analysis, Hughes's self-consciousness about the vagaries of his own subjectivity is moving and modest. It is a stance that Hughes repeats in his mysterious poem 'The Offers', which was published in the *Sunday Times* ten days before his own death.[54] In 'The Offers', Plath is a ghost who haunts Hughes on the tube, in her home, as he steps into his bath. 'The Offers' is positioned late in the sequence of *Howls & Whispers*; it is the penultimate poem. *Howls & Whispers* carefully builds up Hughes's rhetorical tendency to indicate (or inadvertently reveal) doubt. Therefore, the impact of uncertainty in 'The Offers' is stronger when the poem is read as part of the collection than when it is read in isolation. Such indefiniteness is indicated especially with the word *seemed*, which evokes the dream-like, mysterious and supernatural state of affairs of which the poem speaks. *Seemed* is one of those words (like *perhaps* and *appears* and *evidently* and *maybe*) that people use when they don't want to take responsibility for what they are saying, or when they want to signpost indeterminacy. *Seemed* is a sort of get-out clause. In 'The Offers' it appears five times, and signals Hughes's awareness of his imperfect ability to perceive, to make sense of what he sees and trust it. He uses *seemed* when speaking about Plath herself, his memories of her, and his fantasies about her.

'The Offers' is a riddle poem. What is Plath offering? What does she mean when she startles Hughes on her third and final visit, as he lowers himself into the bath? These lines are especially difficult to paraphrase, but she tells him in the pressing, imperious voice he knows so well that she will make no more appearances, and/or he will not have another chance and therefore must not fail her. Readers and critics will have their own theories and debates about what 'The Offers' 'means'. Yet if Hughes himself rightly refuses authority over meaning and perception in this poem, how can we assert these with any confidence? I can offer my own interpretation of what those offers might be – not to do so would be a cop out – but I do this tentatively, even shyly. Those offers may have been a promise of reincarnation (note my own 'may have been' – and my 'might have felt' and 'could be' in the next sentences). I think what Hughes might have felt Plath was saying was that she was coming back, though in what form I cannot tell. Or the poem may be about reincarnation of a different and less otherworldly kind: it could be that Plath is asking Hughes to readmit her into 'life' by speaking publicly, by publishing his poems about her.

With the strengths of Hughes's declarations of uncertainty comes weakness, for at times Hughes risks a poetic voice that is inflexibly authoritarian and Bardic. Judging from the poems to and about Plath, Hughes appears to have a two-pronged notion of what writing is. Writing is a sacred vocation, and this is an immense claim to make for writing. The poet is seen, or sees himself, as a sort of priest who speaks to a reverent and grateful public. He attempts to use his art to renew dying myths for a tribe (his readers) that has grown alienated from its beliefs and stories. (Craig Robinson has stressed this Bardic aspect of Hughes by calling his book *Ted Hughes as Shepherd of Being* – where Hughes's readers are presumably the sheep.) Paradoxically, writing is limited in what it can say and who it can reach, because its purpose is to find words for one's own feelings and perceptions. Hughes's is certainly an idiosyncratic vocabulary. He aligns his story with myth in *Birthday Letters* and *Howls & Whispers*. Some readers and critics may accuse him of mistaking a private rhetoric for a public one, using mythological references (for instance to Frigga and Loki in the last poem of *Howls & Whispers*, 'Superstitions') as if everyone would recognise them, and adopting a mono-logic tone that owes much to D. H. Lawrence. By mono-logic, I mean that despite Hughes's admirable refusal to claim authority about facts and truth, Hughes nonetheless uses a voice that does not admit of interruption, and *is* thereby authoritarian (in a sense, any form of writing or speech whose audience cannot answer back is authoritarian in this way).

Birthday Letters has been applauded by critics, and deservedly so. Whether this admiration has always come for the right reasons, however, is debatable. Possibly, this extreme feeling has prevented readers from looking carefully at the work itself, as it has with Plath's. In the months just after the publication of *Birthday Letters*, a tacit emotional blackmail operated. Hughes, the blackmail reasoned, has spoken, at last. He has spoken of deep pain. It would be churlish to use anything less than overstated praise when discussing this writing. Sarah Maguire, in an otherwise intelligent and temperate review, concludes that *Birthday Letters* is 'the most moving and vital book written by the greatest living English poet'.[55] 'It seems inappropriate, sacrilegious almost', Heather Neill gushes in a similar vein, 'to respond to *Birthday Letters* in ordinary limping prose'.[56] There is a consensus that it would be unseemly to rate *Birthday Letters* as anything less than 'a great book',[57] or make the poems accountable to the usual critical questions. Karl Miller can acknowledge that *Birthday Letters* 'is ... a work of art, and none the less so for being personal',[58] but still stops short of evaluating Hughes's poems *as art*, or in terms that extend beyond the biographically descriptive. Edna Longley has been a rare dissenting voice in her assessment of *Birthday Letters*. 'There is crude, bad writing' in it, she asserts, wondering, 'Is Hughes's reputation being talked up in some mysteriously collective way, and to hell with critical judgement, to hell with poetry ("The press was squared / The feminists were quite prepared")?'[59] Longley seems to be suggesting here that *Birthday Letters* was cynically released at a moment, and in a manner, that ensured its positive reception, so that even Hughes's former enemies (the 'feminists') could be manipulated into adulation. Undoubtedly, reaction to *Birthday Letters* has been strong, approval close to unanimous. But to imply that an omnipotent Hughes has set all this up as a sort of large-scale exercise in brainwashing is cheap and ridiculous. Who, after all, can predict and control the press to this extent? Critical and journalistic responses to *Birthday Letters* are worth examining, but surely Hughes himself cannot be held personally responsible for them?

It is an affecting (though some may say entirely coincidental) fact that Hughes died from cancer ten months after the publication of *Birthday Letters*, on 28 October 1998, the day after Plath's birthday. (I must confess that I cannot think of these dates as mere chance. My own tendency to find stories where I can, and make things up, tempts me to imagine that Hughes waited until 27 October was over before he died, so he could leave Plath's birthday as her birthday, and not take it over as his death day.) With hindsight, we might describe the critical glorification of the *Birthday Letters* poems, their privileging over some of Hughes's other important work, and the reluctance of critics to submit *Birthday Letters* to the usual critical questions, as a sort of collective and premature funeral eulogy. Since Hughes's actual death, this trend has only accelerated, as the title of one newspaper article recognised: 'The Rise and Rise of Ted Hughes, Deceased'.[60] When discussing the 1998 Whitbread Poetry Award, and the likelihood that *Birthday Letters* would win this as well as the Whitbread Book of the Year Award, Faber and Faber's chairman Matthew Evans went so far as to declare, ' "It almost seems churlish not to give him an award" '.[61] (*Birthday Letters* did indeed win the Whitbread Poetry Award, and went on to win the Whitbread Book of the Year, as well as the T. S. Eliot Prize.) I am not suggesting that *Birthday Letters* did not deserve to win these awards. Rather, I am suggesting that the criteria should be those of literary merit. Victory and esteem should not come from an explicit blackmail that it would be 'churlish' – ill-mannered or insensitive – not to honour a given book. And Hughes himself might have had reservations about the ways *Birthday Letters* has been discussed. Few serious writers want literary acclaim out of obligation or charity; they want literary acclaim because they have written good books.

The Reciprocity of Influence between Plath and Hughes

To deny that Hughes influenced Plath would be absurd. On the other hand, few of Hughes's critics allow that influence can move in the other direction, from Plath to Hughes. Not many acknowledge the reciprocity between the two. Unusually, Valentine Cunningham goes some way towards conceding such interplay when he asks, 'Does her "Sow", for instance, feed his "View of a Pig" or vice versa?'[62] But with his implied assumption that one poem must have decidedly preceded and then influenced the other ('or vice versa?') Cunningham wants to settle the question of what came first. For me, this influence is rarely of one poet or poem over the other, but much more mutual, dynamic, and complex in its string of causes and associations, as Erica Wagner has repeatedly acknowledged in *Ariel's Gift*.

In *The Art of Ted Hughes*, Keith Sagar makes a comment that goes against much of what has been said about Plath's tendency to use other poets as her template. He states that Plath was 'on the whole, resistant to influences', though he makes an exception for Hughes himself as Plath's role model. Sagar states that 'His was the stronger, surer poetic voice, and the immediate effect was of ventriloquism'.[63] For Sagar, Plath's 'Spinster' is a 'variation on' Hughes's 'Secretary' and 'echoes the vocabulary' of Hughes's 'Fallgrief's Girl-friends'[64] (all of these poems were written in 1956). Sagar argues that Plath's 1956 poem 'Strumpet Song' concludes 'with a passage of pure Hughes, the wrenched syntax, the savage consonants, the pounding monosyllables'. In a language that verges on accusing Plath of violence, Sagar writes that she '*seized* on "View of a Pig", "The Green Wolf", "Out" and several other poems in *Wodwo*' (my emphasis).[65] Yet the dates that Sagar plays with are suspect, for Hughes was reading Plath's work before they actually met at the *St Botolph's Review* party in February of 1956,[66] just as she was reading his.[67] The Hughes poems that Sagar accuses Plath of 'seizing on' for 'Strumpet Song' are actually dated later than Plath's poem. This is not to say that Hughes's poems could not have been written earlier, but rather to stress that Plath and Hughes were writing alongside each other. The question of which poet took what from whom cannot be resolved with any certainty. The qualities of 'Strumpet Song' described by Sagar as 'pure Hughes' might just as readily be seen as 'pure' Plath (if you accept such extremism at all).

Gifford and Roberts are generous in their ability to credit Plath without fearing they have somehow slighted Hughes. 'The mutual influence between Sylvia Plath and himself', they write, 'contributed importantly to the development of both poets: it seems to us likely that the greater rhythmical freedom, compression and elliptical language of Hughes's poetry from *Wodwo* onwards owes something to the example of Sylvia Plath's later work'.[68] Scigaj establishes a textual link between Plath and Hughes without feeling the need to attribute to one at the expense of the other. He alludes to *Gaudete*'s ' "baboon beauty face, / A crudely stitched patchwork of faces" – as in "The Disquieting Muses," the surrealist painting by de Chirico that inspired Plath's eerie poem of the same title'.[69]

The difficulty of pinpointing origin and echo is apparent if we look at the similarities between 'Lady Lazarus' (October 1962) and Hughes's radio play 'The Wound',[70] which 'was first broadcast by the BBC ... on 1st February 1962'.[71] Similarly, Hughes's 'Crow's Song About England'[72] (1971) and Plath's 'The Detective' (October 1962) find textual and structural mirrors in each other. A simple chronological logic would have it that 'Lady Lazarus' borrowed from 'The Wound', and 'Crow's Song About England' from 'The Detective'. Yet this would be crude and misleading. When two poets live and work together for as long as Plath and Hughes did, it would be ludicrous to assume that because one piece appears before another it was actually composed first. Conversations and influence can pass unrecorded. The fact that

Plath was the first to write something down does not preclude the possibility that Hughes's idea or suggestion prompted her to do so, or vice versa. It is less important to determine who or what came first, than to identify the reverberation and evaluate it; the poems are best regarded as fragments of a continuing conversation.

We have seen already that 'The Detective' can be read as an environmentalist poem. The detective narrator implies that the missing woman has been regarded as a pest or germ, and that she has been eradicated like the victim of chemical or radioactive poison. Dangerous substances have passed between her body and the larger ecosystem. The poem's last line reads, 'There is only a crow in a tree. Make notes'.[73] 'Crow's Song About England' might be those 'notes'. It is as if the crow has flown from the tree, out of Plath's poem and into Hughes's, replacing the detective's investigative questions with the statements of a witness who is no less authoritative for his 'Once upon a time' beginning. Plath's detective can only piece together events from an aftermath, while Hughes's crow has watched the drama unfold from the vantage point of his tree.

Hughes's crow confirms the detective's assumption that the assailant is male, and implicated in a crime that is not just of physical violence, but of emotional and domestic tyranny too. In 'The Detective' the female victim's assault stems from domestic intimacy and sexuality. This is also the case in 'Crow's Song About England'. Whether the woman of Hughes's poem tries to 'give' the parts of her body and what they symbolise, as she does in the first nine lines, or whether she tries to 'keep' them, as she does later, the result is the same. Her 'mouth' is 'snatched from her and her face slapped'. Her 'eyes' are 'knocked to the floor' and 'crushed' by the 'furniture'. Her 'breasts' are 'cut from her and canned'. Her 'cunt' is 'produced in open court she was sentenced / She did life'.[74] The pun is at least triple here. Most obviously, 'She did life' suggests a prison sentence. It also means the very opposite. To 'do life' is to enjoy and *live* it, to have sex with life, literally and metaphorically. Finally, we can read the pun at still another level of contradiction. 'She did life' implies also that she betrayed it, shunning the opportunities and privileges that being in this world offers. The body parts in Hughes's poem ('mouth', 'eyes', 'breasts', 'cunt'), and the creativity and sexuality associated with them, are like those described in Plath's 'The Detective'. 'The Detective' gives us the woman's 'insatiable' 'mouth' cut and 'hung out' as punishment for its hungers and words, its taking in and giving out. Her breasts are also dispensed with, and, in the end, her entire body is vaporised.

If critics have at times unfairly read Plath's poetry as hostile to men, they have been just as ready to charge Hughes with misogyny in his representations of women. Since Plath's death, Hughes's position has not been an easy one. As Nathalie Anderson rightly puts it, 'That a chill exists separating Ted Hughes from the feminist ... community hardly needs documenting'. Yet as Anderson also notes, the designation of blame as Hughes's is not simply the province of feminists or Plath fans, or even unheard of in those who admire Hughes. 'This,' Anderson writes, 'for many quite ordinary, unimaginative, non-vindictive people, is the accepted wisdom: Hughes kills. Hughes is inimical – no, downright dangerous to women'.[75] 'Crow's Song About England', for its dialogue with 'The Detective', and for its seeming confirmation of the earlier poem's argument, allows us to see Hughes's writing differently. The conclusion of his poem, 'She did life', is as critical of the literal and symbolic deaths that domestic relationships exert upon women as Plath's own poem. Indeed, Hughes may have seen the female victim in his poem as Plath herself.

The Question of the Confessional

Like those of many critics, Hughes's own comments about Plath's use of autobiography have been contradictory. Some might remark that this is odd considering his closeness to her. Others might come to the opposite conclusion: that such contradiction was inevitable because of the closeness. On the subject of Plath, Hughes is at his strongest, I think, in his poetry, where he foregrounds the unreliable nature of his claims, and does not pretend to speak impartially. Rather, he lets rip his side of the story, his love and anger, without apology. (Such an uncontrolled outpouring is just what Plath herself has so often been accused of.) There is no pretence in Hughes's poems that this is impersonal, businesslike, or professional. Yet the 'truth' is not to be found in his supposedly more trustworthy essays (trustworthy because expository). In these, Hughes is as mixed up as any of us.

In his Introduction to the first American edition of *Johnny Panic and the Bible of Dreams*, Hughes wavers between convicting Plath of confessionality and denying that she uses the personal. Approximately six pages, or two-thirds, of this Introduction are cut from Faber's British edition of *Johnny Panic*. This material, though important, is seldom talked about. Hughes writes of Plath's attitude towards Devon, 'She planned to case the whole region, with the idea of accumulating details for future stories'. The description is of a criminal plotting her illicit thefts like a professional burglar. Hughes refers with a mixture of pity, scorn and impatience to Plath's 'laborious tenacity'[76] over detail, and, in the guise of a compliment, says of her stories:

> They seem livelier now, in some ways, than they did when she wrote them. And their vitality comes from the very thing she was always striving to escape: the themes she found engaging enough to excite her concentration all turn out to be episodes from her own life; they are all autobiography. They have the vitality of her personal participation, her subjectivity.[77]

At this point in the Introduction Hughes appears to be praising autobiography as the very thing that makes Plath's writing vital. Two pages later, by contrast, he alludes to 'This limitation to actual circumstances, which is the prison of so much of her prose'. He asserts that in Plath's writing, 'The blunt fact killed any power or inclination to rearrange it or see it differently' (retained in the Faber edition).[78] Almost in the same breath, Plath is commended for the 'vitality' that came from using what was real, then criticised for the dullness and 'limitation' of such material.

Plath cannot win here. Her writing is faulted for its fidelity to the real – to too much fact – or deprecated for being insufficiently imaginative, too unoriginal, a sort of cheat. 'What is interesting now about some of these descriptions is the way they fed into *Ariel*', Hughes argues. 'They are good evidence to prove that poems which seem often to be constructed of arbitrary surreal symbols are really impassioned reorganizations of relevant fact ... A great many of these objects and appearances occur somewhere or other in the journals.'[79] The cumulative impact of these contradictory comments is to suggest that Plath's writing does not deserve the high regard in which it is held. Even the *Ariel* poems can be disparaged, somehow tainted by what Hughes sees as the problems of the shorter prose pieces and their grounding in 'facts'.

Hughes's attempts to control interpretation of Plath's work can be very direct. In his 1988 prose piece 'Sylvia Plath: The Evolution of "Sheep in Fog"', he attempts to pin down the meaning of every word in Plath's poem, leaving no room for other interpretations. Contrast this with his hesitation about explaining *Gaudete*: 'My own opinion I withhold. …. As far as interpretation goes – I leave all options open'.[80] If Hughes's comments on confessionality have been inconsistent, this is certainly understandable. In an interview, he said: 'Poems come to you much more naturally and accumulate more life when they are part of a connected flow of real narrative that you've got yourself involved in'. 'So', the interviewer concluded from this, 'the underlying story would be some kind of autobiographical myth.' 'Why autobiographical? It's just a way of getting the poems',[81] Hughes replied. I have used this last phrase of Hughes's as the title of this chapter of my book, using it to signal Hughes's seeming impatience with this readiness to take his words as a licence to read narrative as personal myth. I have used it also to suggest that Plath's and Hughes's literary relationship was a way of getting poems, and an inevitable one at that, however impossible it may be for us, or even for them, to untangle the complex network of influences.

In Hughes's comments, the use of the personal can be admitted, but only pushed so far. It is less difficult, and perhaps less threatening, for Hughes to acknowledge the poet's use of the personal when the poet is someone other than himself or Plath.

> Yeats's life is not the less interesting half of his general effort, and one wonders what his poetry would amount to if it could be lifted clear of the biographical matrix. Quite a lot, no doubt. But how much less than at present! With poets who set their poetic selves further into the third person, maybe the life is less relevant. But [Dylan] Thomas's life, letters and legends belong to his poetry, in that they make it mean more.[82]

These remarks are interesting given the appearance of *Birthday Letters*. Yeats, Hughes seems to say, is a better poet for his use of the personal, and we can appreciate his poetry better if we make meanings of it in this light. Without knowledge of the biographical facts, our understanding of Yeats would be impoverished, Hughes suggests. Yet how do we know if a poet sets his or her 'poetic selves further into the third person', so that their 'life is less relevant'? What data and criteria are there to establish what is 'real' in a given poem? A third person poem may be more strongly rooted in 'truth' and connected to the poet's life than a first person poem. We have access only to the words on the page, and not the poet's brain. Notably, when Hughes speaks of Plath's use of the personal, it is to downgrade her poems, not to praise them, as he does with Yeats and Dylan Thomas.

Before *Birthday Letters*

What happens when Hughes himself turns to 'facts' to make his poetry? Hughes's more recent, self-declaringly confessional poems allow us to look at the question of Plath's supposed use of her own life from a new perspective. Yet the *Birthday Letters* poems are not new revelations. Eight of them appeared in 1995, in Hughes's *New Selected Poems*.[83] The history of this publication, like the limited number of copies of *Howls & Whispers*, indicates that Hughes was reluctant to publish poems about Plath, and took care when he did. Evidently, Hughes was highly ambivalent about the whole business, wanting the poems to be out there, but (understandably) quailing at the exposure. Simon Armitage was one of the few reviewers to make the point that *New Selected Poems* offers 'snippets of personal information'. Other than a brief but suggestive discussion of 'The Earthenware Head', in which he observes that Hughes's sequence is 'reminiscent of Robert Lowell's poems about Jean Stafford', Armitage does not go into much detail about Hughes's use of the personal. Intriguingly, Armitage alerts us to the fact that the published version of *New Selected Poems* includes material that did not appear in the proof copy sent to reviewers. Perhaps the decision to put the Plath poems in the public domain was 'left until the eleventh hour',[84] or perhaps Hughes kept them out of the review copies so he could reduce the amount of publicity about the poems; reviews are usually written just before books come out. The publication of *New Selected Poems* was an important moment in literary history, but Hughes was writing to and out of Plath's work long before its appearance in 1995. 'Narcissi', 'The Honey Bee' and 'Big Poppy' (1986)[85] are only a few of a number of poems in which Hughes rewrites Plath's own flower and bee poems to engage with her arguments against individualism and comment upon her death.

'You Hated Spain' refers to Hughes's honeymoon with Plath. The poem appeared even earlier than the 1995 *New Selected Poems*, in 1982, in Hughes's *Selected Poems: 1951–1981*. Dennis Walder has acknowledged, with the tentativeness that characterised the pre-*Birthday Letters* days, that the poem is 'evidently addressed' to Plath.[86] Yet 'You Hated Spain' is interesting for reasons that go beyond biography. It plays out the tensions and attractions between Hughes's versions of working-class masculinity and Plath's own ideas about class and national identity. 'You Hated Spain' also sets up a crude polarity between stereotyped American and European identities. The poem fixes Plath as an outsider who is insensitive to what is important and oversensitive to trivia, while Hughes is someone who intrinsically belongs. The positions of the male and female personae of this poem (the male embracing an unfamiliar location and culture, the female recoiling from it) reverse those that we saw Plath setting up in 'The Fifty-Ninth Bear'.

It is worth noting that the Rhino of Hughes's 1989 poem 'The Black Rhino'[87] is male at the poem's beginning, but female by its end. Nathalie Anderson has read the change in pronoun as a 'shift from strength to vulnerability'.[88] Leonard M. Scigaj has seen the poem as 'ecologically activist',[89] while Rand Brandes has emphasised its avowal of the 'irreversibility of history'.[90] These are important points, yet 'The Black Rhino' tells another story too. The Rhino can also be seen as an allegorical representation of Plath. Both are icons. Both are isolated, and soon-to-be extinct figures who continue to affect the living: 'The Black Rhino is vanishing. / Horribly sick, without knowing, // She is vanishing ... ////// ... She has blundered somehow into / man's phantasmagoria, and cannot get out'.[91] Such a reading of 'The Black Rhino' raises questions about the way people, and especially writers, use animals. To say that the Rhino is Plath is to undermine the animal's value as being itself. More productively, we can say that the narrator is able to appreciate the animal's value and meaning because of the similar feelings a human being has evoked for him.

With hindsight, and no risk of 'you' answering back, the poem's narrator explains the Rhino to the Rhino in a direct address:

> You have nailed your strength
> To Eden's coffin
> Tree, the tree
> Of Sophistry,
> Too solidly
> To tug yourself free.
> So now you die[92]

The Rhino would conventionally be seen as a stupid animal, powerful but blundering, charging blindly, unable to see its own interests. Sophistry, a clever and subtle but perhaps misguided reasoning, replaces the tree of knowledge which was 'Eden's coffin / Tree' (the tree whose fruit tempted Eve, and caused the end of Eden and innocence). The Rhino's innocence rests in its inability to know that it is a species in danger of extinction. It has great strength, but uses it unwisely, nailing it to Sophistry. Within the framework of the poem, the allegory may be that Plath herself, in her life, and in her writing, uses her genius and powers forcefully but wrongly, destructively and dangerously. The Rhino is a kind of tragic hero, and then heroine. Unable to adapt to the new conditions that threaten its life, it is unable to show evolutionary flexibility. The manner and tone of the narrator's second person explanation of the Rhino to the Rhino foreshadow the narrator of *Birthday Letters* and the way he explains Plath to herself. 'The Black Rhino' connects to the *Birthday Letters* poems in argument (death results from too much devotion to a misguided set of beliefs) as well as images (trees, coffins, wood and tables). Addressing 'Plath', the narrator of the *Birthday Letters* poem 'The Table' says of the desk he made for her of 'coffin timber': '... I did not / know I had made and fitted a door / Opening downwards into your Daddy's grave'.[93]

A handful of critics have alluded to the effect of Plath's life and death on Hughes's writing. Dennis Walder has credited Plath's influence on Hughes, suggesting that the 'modern quality' of his writing owes much to 'poets not operating within the English traditions: the Americans ... and, of course, Sylvia Plath'.[94] Nick Bishop has smoothly assumed that Hughes draws on his life with Plath, writing that 'Bawdry Embraced'[95] 'celebrates their relationship'.[96] Stan Smith says of the poems Hughes published in the late 1970s, they 'speak of a world in which the worst has already happened ... The personal experiences that culminated in the suicide of his wife Sylvia Plath in 1963 may provide the harrowing private source of this mood'.[97]

Certainly the poems that comprise Hughes's 1978 collection, *Cave Birds: An Alchemical Cave Drama*, are filled with probable references to Plath's life, and more obvious echoes of her poetry. 'She seemed so considerate' could be read as a man's protest at or explanation of his wife's inadequacies, his description of the embarrassment and burden she became: 'She seemed so considerate // And everything had become so hideous / My solemn friends sat twice as solemn / My jokey friends joked and joked'.[98] *Bitter Fame* alleges that Plath was mortifyingly rude to Hughes's friends and family.[99] It is a situation that echoes the one of 'She seemed so considerate'. Yet to draw such analogies between Hughes's writing and life is to do to him what I am trying to avoid doing to Plath. To justify a reading which has it that Hughes's poetry is 'about' Plath, one might argue that such an enterprise has not yet been attempted. Now that Hughes has died, critics will no doubt exploit his absence. Legally, the 'dead cannot be libelled or slandered. They are without legal recourse',[100] as Janet Malcolm reminds us. Even if such biographical criticism is easier to get away with, it is not what I want to do. Licensed or not, it still poses considerable methodological, and moral, problems.

Textual Relationships and Poetic Conversations

It is less important to see Hughes's work as 'his side of the story' than as part of a continuing conversation between his poems and Plath's. Plath's late 1962 poem 'The Applicant' appears to address Hughes's earlier poem for radio, 'The Wound', which was broadcast in February of 1962. In turn, Hughes reworks 'The Applicant' in 'Bride and groom lie hidden for three days', from his 1978 collection *Cave Birds*. The echoes are not simply of subject matter, though all three poems evaluate the social functions of men and women in marriage. All three anatomise the cultural, psychic, historical and sexual forces that bring men and women together in the first place. Hughes and Plath make clear that their brides and grooms are products who must sell themselves, and buy each other. The worlds of these poems are worlds of loose body parts and amputations, worlds where men and women try to manufacture one another, attempting to create ideals to order, but instead making monsters. The influence here is not just of the war-wounded with whom Plath and Hughes would have been so familiar, but also must surely be 1940s and 1950s films that retell Mary Shelley's *Frankenstein* story – especially those in which Frankenstein makes a bride for his creature.

Gender floats unassigned and unresolved in 'The Applicant'. Plath's narrator is a sort of salesman or woman addressing a potential groom. By the poem's end, the groom's persona merges with a potential bride's. The poem's opening line – 'First, are you our sort of person?' – could be read as an initiation test for a secret society. At the same time, the question is a challenge or warning that equally haunts men and women (as it haunts Esther Greenwood in *The Bell Jar*). 'Sort of person' is a euphemism for a married, heterosexual, middle-class, anti-Communist consumer. Both sexes are subjected to the pressures of 1950s normality and conformity. Unlike 'The Applicant', gender is stable in 'Bride and groom lie hidden for three days'. Hughes gives us a 'He' and a 'She' who are clearly separate. Contact between his couple is not mediated by a sort of marriage broker, as it is in Plath's. His bride and groom seem designed to fill the gaps and empty spaces evoked in 'The Applicant'. Plath's narrator asks, 'Do you wear / A glass eye, false teeth or a crutch', and orders 'Open your hand. / Empty? Empty. Here is a hand'.[101] As if answering the job advertisement described in Plath's poem, we are told of Hughes's bride, 'She gives him his eyes' (extricated as if from a 'rubble' of war), 'She has found his hands for him', and 'She gives him his teeth'. Hughes's bride 'stitches his body here and there';[102] repairing her groom by sewing with her own hands in what we might describe as a 'natural' or traditional feminine productivity. Plath's bride, by contrast, enacts her 'feminine' labours by becoming a conveyor belt automaton: 'It can sew, it can cook, / It can talk, talk, talk'.[103] 'Bride and groom lie hidden for three days' does pick up on Plath's industrial capitalist metaphor of production, but associates such mechanisation with the man. Hughes's groom 'assembled her spine' and 'oils the delicate cogs of her mouth'. This is in opposition to his bride's more domestic labours; she 'stitches', 'gives' again and again, and 'inlays'.

Hughes's groom 'sinks into place the inside of her thighs',[104] while Plath's bride and groom are told by the narrator of 'The Applicant', 'You have a hole, it's a poultice'.[105] It is difficult to tell who possesses this 'hole'. Does the female applicant own her body? Does the hole belong, post-marriage, to the groom? Plath's poem works by unsettling and confusing. Hughes's poem creates its own uncertainties. Does the groom penetrate the bride, sliding into his natural 'place', or does he build her, putting her 'thighs' 'into place'? While opening up new questions, Hughes's poems seems also to want to seal up the ambiguities of 'The Applicant', placing the male and female personae more securely, and healing the wounds Plath's own text creates – and which he himself created, years earlier, in 'The Wound'. 'The Applicant' gives us a nightmare world of a nightmare marriage. 'Bride and groom lie hidden for three days', on the other hand, takes the ingredients of Plath's, but seems to present an old-fashioned, even archetypal, relationship between a man and woman that the poem would wish to endorse. His bride and groom 'bring each other to perfection';[106] as the title implies, they are on their honeymoon.

'Bride and groom lie hidden for three days' is not the only one of Hughes's poems to open up a conversation with the language and questions of 'The Applicant'. Though it wasn't published until 1967, Hughes's verse play 'The Wound' was performed in early 1962, eight and a half months before Plath wrote 'The Applicant'. Looked at as a dialogue that stretches beyond two poems, we can see Plath answering 'The Wound' with 'The Applicant'. Hughes then replies years later with 'Bride and groom lie hidden for three days', as if he's had further thoughts on the subject. 'The Wound' is the story of Ripley, a badly injured soldier who staggers for nine miles across a landscape devastated by war, seeking refuge. He finds (or hallucinates) a domestic interior, a nightmare chateau filled with women who are everything he fears and desires (the poem is rather like a precursor to the popular 1976 song *Hotel California*, by the Eagles).

It would be easy, and too crude, to read 'The Wound' as misogynous. Rather, the poem sets the problem that 'The Applicant' and 'Bride and groom lie hidden for three days' subsequently consider: the difficulties imposed by war and culture upon men and women who wish to live together (or feel pressured to do so). If 'The Applicant' evaluates the post-war culture that urges men to be real men and women to be feminine women, 'The Wound' considers the events that led to this state of things. 'The Wound' is about the trauma of a man who has experienced the war at first hand. Ripley has been 'properly' masculine and brave, and paid a high physical and emotional price for being so. He cannot settle easily into an interior space and simply regard women as sanctuaries. 'If I ever had a home, I'm forgetting it',[107] thinks Ripley, making explicit the difficulty of moving back into the domestic sphere which both threatens and lures the potential husband and wife of Plath's 'The Applicant'. For Ripley, a domestic environment filled with women, even in the form of a fantastic chateau, is a place in which he cannot breathe: 'This place is too hot. This place is airless. This place is like a tomb in a desert'.[108]

Like 'The Applicant', 'The Wound' makes it clear that the trauma and violence of the twentieth century affect men and women both. The body parts that litter 'The Applicant' and 'Bride and groom lie hidden for three days' also litter 'The Wound'. Something is 'wrong with [Ripley's] walk ... something wrong with his head'.[109] Something is wrong with his vision, his 'eye', and there are 'no spares available'.[110] As if in answer, Plath creates spares in 'The Applicant': 'A glass eye, false teeth or a crutch'.[111] Ripley's 'eyebrows recently burned off', and he possesses 'one gold filled molar'.[112] We might read the narrator's opening questions in 'The Applicant' as an interrogation of the shell-shocked and battle-scarred Ripley himself: 'Do you wear / A glass eye, false teeth or a crutch?'[113]

The women whom Ripley encounters in the chateau bear injuries that are similar to his. Theirs are not sustained in direct battle, but are the result of the medical and sexual violence and experimentation often experienced by women both in times of war, and, as Plath's writing makes clear (for instance in the nightmare childbirth scene in *The Bell Jar*), also in times of peace. The women discuss what has happened to them:

Fourth: And what did they find did they find what they hoped for.
   First: Lusted for.
Second: Sliced me for.
   Third: Did they find the gold teeth.
Fourth: The plastic gums.
   First: The glass eyes.
Second: The steel skull–plates.
   Third: The jawbone rivets.
Fourth: The rubber arterics.
   First: The rings.[114]

The first line of the above passage contains no commas, and uses a full stop where we would expect a question mark. Thereby Hughes dramatises the woman's battle-stunned trauma, the dulling of her reactions, as if even her voice can no longer care. Jacqueline Rose has seen these lines as 'a representation of what civilization and science does *to* women', while also worrying that the poem suggests 'they finally have only themselves to blame'.[115] 'The Applicant' and 'The Wound' diagnose men's and women's desire and antipathy for each other as historical and cultural, not as biological or essential (because men and women are 'just made that way'). 'The Wound' prefigures the refrain of 'The Applicant': 'Will you marry me',[116] Ripley asks three times, using a question mark only the third, and then changing from a question to a command ('Marry me'). He moves from recoil to hypnotised need. The last words the audience hears from Ripley, when the soldiers find him delirious, are his final 'Marry me'.[117] Is Ripley saying this because he wishes to? Or is he echoing what has been asked of him? The impression is that, however much he has resisted it, marriage offers the only hope and cure. Plath picks up on this brainwashing in the concluding line of 'The Applicant': 'Will you marry it, marry it, marry it'.[118] In both poems, the question is smoothed into an order that afflicts and drives men and women equally.

Bleeding Through the Page

We have observed repeatedly that there is an important relationship between what happens on one side of a page of Plath's manuscripts, and what happens on the other. This is certainly true of the back-to-back relationship between Plath's work and Hughes's. The successive manuscripts of Plath's August 1962 poem 'Burning the Letters' are written on the reverse sides of typescripts of some of Hughes's earlier poems: 'Toll of Air Raids', 'The Thought-Fox', 'A Fable', 'Cradle Piece', 'Unknown Soldier' and 'Poltergeist'. It is as if, at each stage of composition, Plath's poem is driven by a conversation with what is happening on the reverse side of the page. Hughes's 'Toll of Air Raids' begins with an image of human sorrow, and shows how people try to ignore their own distress by pushing themselves through the everyday and ordinary: 'These are the aged who hide their sadness / And deaths in rinds of bacon'. On the reverse side of 'Toll of Air Raids', in lines that Plath discards from the first page of Draft 1 of 'Burning the Letters', she writes:

> This is what it is to be loveless!
> Sealed in a cement box, pouring the hissing water
> In to white china cups that will not crack[119]

Like Hughes, Plath gives us human despair, and the attempt to hide or seal these feelings by moving through domestic life in a routine way. This may be by breakfasting on rations of bacon rinds (too poor in money or comfort or the privations of war to waste them), or by pouring hot water into invincible teacups.

The next page of the first draft of 'Burning the Letters' appears on the back of Hughes's 'The Thought-Fox', which gives us an image of a still night through which 'Cold, delicately as the dark snow, / A fox's nose touches twig, leaf'. On the back of Hughes's picture of snowy England, as if in argument with the earlier poem, Plath writes, but then cancels, the lines

> It never snows in this county. That is the trouble.
> There is never a gallon of white on the doorstep
> The rain drags its rags, the lukewarm droplets[120]

I have already examined Plath's interest in challenging complacent views of Englishness and English landscapes by writing from the cool and very different perspective of the foreigner. These deleted lines give us the view of somebody who is fed up with the myth of chocolate box snowy countryside, somebody who is all too familiar with unwelcome and relentless English rain.

To destroy further the image on the other side of the page, Plath writes the line 'The dogs are tearing a fox, my love. This is what it is like —'.[121] The syntax here is ambiguous. It could be that 'my love' is the speaker's unfaithful lover, and that she tells him the news of the torn fox, or it could be that 'my love' *is* the fox, the animal itself. In either case, it is difficult not to see this cut line as a signal that Hughes's fox, setting his 'neat prints into the snow', is done for. To show that 'biographical events and earlier texts deeply interpenetrate each other', Susan Van Dyne has analysed the relationship between 'Burning the Letters' and 'The Thought-Fox' in great detail. For Van Dyne, the fox represents 'Hughes's poetic agency'. He is 'set upon and destroyed by his own deception'. The speaker, by contrast, 'stands by unbloodied and yet unequivocally avenged'.[122] Hughes's poem famously ends with the lines, 'The window is starless still; the clock ticks, / The page is printed.' If this line were to bleed through the paper, onto the reverse side, we would see below it Plath's own handwritten and then crossed-out line, 'Rising & flying, but blinded, & with no message'.[123] Plath's discarded line does not just describe the burnt letters, or carbon birds, lifted by the flame into the air with their words no longer visible. It also seems to be saying: the words on the back of this manuscript are meaningless; they are saying nothing; they cannot see how things really are. Again and again, Plath's poem seems to be speaking to Hughes's, whispering, I'll show you what things are really like ('This is what it is like —'), and tear you to pieces, or burn you up, in the process.

'Burning the Letters' is at the extremity of the most fundamental and physical sense in which Plath's work is related to Hughes's. It is a sense that cannot be disclosed by the published versions of their poems, removed as these are from the original drafts and typescripts. Yet 'Burning the Letters' is not the only one of Plath's poems in which, at each stage of composition, she seems to be answering or arguing with or taking up whatever poem or line or idea Hughes's work presents on the reverse side of the paper. It is as if Plath picks up an abandoned draft or piece of scrap paper, reads whatever appears on it before putting it in the typewriter or picking up her pen, and then begins, prompted by or unable to forget the words that came before. This must be the case with her 1961 poem 'Widow', which was written during the spring that Plath began *The Bell Jar*. I have already discussed the sympathy that the book asks of the reader for Mrs Greenwood, just as I have tried to establish the clarity with which the narrative demands that Esther's view of her mother be challenged. With more explicitness than *The Bell Jar*, 'Widow' looks from a different angle at what was obviously preoccupying Plath in her writing of that period: the position of a character in Mrs Greenwood's circumstance; 'Widow' evaluates the situation of a woman bereft of her husband. Through its title, the poem makes such a woman central to it in a way that Mrs Greenwood, relegated as she is to the periphery of Esther's drama, cannot be. What, asks 'Widow', is to be done with a woman who is past childbearing age, a woman who is not attached to a man anymore?

The first two handwritten drafts of 'Widow' appear on the reverse sides of typed drafts of 'My Father', a section from Hughes's humorous children's book *Meet My Folks!*. Hughes's subject seems to have seeped through the paper and into Plath's, where the situation is given a very different treatment. Any father in Plath's poem can only be an absence, the very man whose death allows Plath's central figure to assume her label and role. Plath's poem, at least implicitly, is about the father, or male partner, who isn't there, and the woman who is left on her own. Plath also gives us an adult perspective, instead of the child's perspective of Hughes's children's book. While the father of Hughes's book is a 'Chief Inspector of Holes'[124] and 'clefts in the wall',[125] Plath metaphorically opens up the cleft left by the husband's absence in 'Widow'. 'The dead syllable, with its shadow / Of an echo, exposes the panel in the wall / Behind which the secret passage lies – stale air'.[126]

Appropriately, the third (handwritten) and fourth (first typed) drafts of 'Widow' are on the back of 'My Mother' from *Meet My Folks!*. Like the writing that appears on the reverse, Plath's poem also evaluates family positions, and especially the mother's. The zany mother of Hughes's book stands in her kitchen, in a chaotic crowd of family members who adore her. She cooks them marvellous, absurdly named dishes. By contrast, Plath's widow is alone in a 'gray, spiritless room' that she fears her husband's soul 'looks in on, and must go on looking in on'[127] while she lives, wishing to see or hear him, but unable to. Plath's poem is sympathetic to the position of the woman alone, and to the grief and loneliness of a middle-aged or elderly woman. The narrator of 'Widow' can afford to demonstrate compassion for the widow: 'The way she laid his letters, till they grew warm / And seemed to give her warmth, like a live skin. / But it is she who is paper now, warmed by no one'.[128] The half-rhyme of 'skin' with 'again' in an earlier line from this stanza seems to mimic the hopeless repetition of the widow's gesture. This imperfect rhyme also dramatises the poem's idea of what a compromised, incomplete and unsatisfying thing such pretence of contact must be. Esther Greenwood, in her depression and self-obsession, cannot express such sympathy for the mother without breaking the strictures of narrative perspective and character plausibility. Despite the sympathetic perspective towards the widow in Plath's poem, it is, in the end, a pessimistic and even patronising account of late widowhood, which need not consist of mournful repetitions, but could involve, to name but two possibilities, travel or further education. 'Widow' seems to suggest that to be anything worthwhile, a woman needs a man; or, at the very least, the poem reflects the view of its time: that this is so.

The Future

Simple as this assumption may seem, I have argued from the outset of this book that in spite of the volumes that have been written about Plath, much of what is central to her writing has been missed. This book, I hope, is only the first of many critical attempts to uncover what is in the work, and yet, because of the persisting and powerful fixation on Plath's biographical drama, has not yet been seen. There is a second and more literal sense of what remains to be uncovered: writings that simply are not available to the public at all.

On 14 September 1998, a few weeks before his death, Ted Hughes unsealed sections of Plath's journals that he had originally planned to keep locked up until 2013, or as long as Plath's mother and brother remained alive (Mrs Plath died in the mid-1990s). Once unsealed, these sections were published in Karen Kukil's 2000 edition of the *Journals*. Kukil has provided a scholarly transcription of all of Plath's personal papers that Smith College holds. She has preserved Plath's spelling, syntax, capitalisation, and punctuation, and wisely refrained from interrupting Plath's text with her own, thereby allowing readers the freedom to interpret Plath's words as they choose. Yet Kukil provides readers with the information they require. She has kept each journal separate, and used her endnotes to describe the formats and physical characteristics of the sources from which the transcribed material was taken. Given the variety of forms Plath's physical papers take, this has been no small challenge. The word 'journals' itself might be put in scare quotes. Plath's 'journals' include handwriting in store-bought bound and spiral notebooks, typing on miscellaneous pieces of paper, and scrawls on sheets of varying degrees of size, colour, type and formality. Some of these are difficult to date precisely, or even to narrow to a reasonable range of years. While the 'journals' are officially lodged in Smith College's Rare Book Room, the Lilly Library also possesses papers and small calendars in which Plath jotted her thoughts. These might also, legitimately, constitute Plath's 'journals'. I think we must accept at the outset that, even with the best will and skill in the world, there will never be a 'complete' edition of Plath's *Journals*.

Plath's published journals end on 15 November 1959 (with the exception of notes she made about her neighbours, and 'The Inmate', which tells of her stay in hospital in February of 1961). Hughes has made contradictory statements about the last, unpublished volumes of Plath's journals. In particular, he has spoken of two 'maroon-backed ledgers … from late '59 to within three days of her death'. Hughes says of the last of these ledgers, 'I destroyed it because I didn't want her children to have read it', and tells us that the penultimate one 'disappeared'.[129] Referring to these same two journal volumes in another 1982 piece, Hughes writes: 'The second of these two books her husband destroyed, because he did not want her children to have read it … The earlier one disappeared more recently (and may, presumably, still turn up)'.[130]

While similar, Hughes's two accounts of what happened to the last ledger nonetheless differ in important ways. First, as Janet Malcolm has observed, there is Hughes's shift from first person to third person. The distancing effect of his rhetorical pose suggests that he has no personal involvement in all of this.[131] Such a pretence is probably counter-productive, and only reinforces the reader's awareness of the fact that Hughes *is*, or was, 'her husband'. To Malcolm's point we can add Hughes's equally strange attachment of the children to Plath alone. He uses the pronoun 'her' before 'children', where we would expect 'our'. Hughes is at once, or syntactically, nothing to do with the couple's daughter and son. Yet in this protective gesture, he is everything to do with them.

I make these points not to criticise Hughes, but to acknowledge the very difficult position in which he has been placed. It is not surprising that Hughes's attempts to talk about the editing of Plath's work, as if at a professional distance, rupture. The syntax is disrupted again and again, probably with some degree of self-consciousness on Hughes's – the poet's – part. The other significant difference between the two accounts of what happened to the journals is Hughes's parenthetical '(and may, presumably, still turn up)'. One feels that Hughes, within the parentheses that imply relative unimportance, is dryly teasing the Plath scholars, or 'crazy club',[132] as he call them, whom he sees as the enemy. Given what Hughes has been through at the hands of critics, many may sympathise with his impulse to toy with them. Hughes dangles hope that, as Malcolm puts it, 'the journal is in fact … in his hands'.[133] Yet in the same essay, Hughes can also write, maddeningly, because as if innocently, 'we certainly have lost a valuable appendix to all that later writing'.[134] Again the pronoun shift is revealing, and probably intentional. It is as if Hughes suffers the loss with us, and had nothing to do with causing the deprivation. It is as if, also, he wishes to rub it in.

Hughes himself has admitted his own fallibility in accounting for Plath's missing work. He speaks of stories that he 'remembered her having written', stories that he assumed she had 'lost or destroyed as failures', only to find they had turned up at the Lilly Library, 'acquired … from … the writer's mother'.[135] Again, Hughes's language is notable for the way it both involves and distances him. He remembers Plath writing the stories because he was there, intimately, under the same roof, day after day for seven years as her lover and husband. At the same time, she is, formally, 'the writer', not Sylvia, as if there was never any personal relation at all (and he never met her mother).

As Hughes makes clear, what can be made to disappear, or is assumed lost, can potentially (though not necessarily) be recovered. I am not sure we should take him at his word that he destroyed her last journal. True as Hughes's claim may have been, it may also have constituted an understandable ruse along the lines of leave me alone, don't bother me, I have nothing more to give you, I'll say anything if you will just go away. Notably, the American edition of *Johnny Panic* (published in 1979) contains a piece whose full title is 'The Smiths: George, Marjorie (50), Claire (16) (*From Notebooks, Spring 1962*)'[136] (this was reprinted as an appendix to the 2000 edition of the *Journals*, with the family's real name, the Tyrers, restored[137]). According to this parenthetical description (supplied by the editor of *Johnny Panic*), 'The Smiths' is from the period of the lost earlier notebook, or the final one that Hughes destroyed. (So is Plath's 1961 piece about her stay in hospital, 'The Inmate', which appeared in the first edition of the published journals in 1982.) Plath writes acidly of her dislike for 'The Smiths', and her suspicion that their daughter wished to have an affair with Hughes.

Given the relatively late date of 'The Smiths', and the angry, critical nature of the piece, I wondered whether it came from the allegedly destroyed last notebook. If it had, this might be evidence that the last notebooks still existed. Unfortunately, I discovered in the archives that Plath typed this sketch of her neighbours (and numerous others) on separate, loose, extra long, lined sheets of paper. Smith College owns the originals; they are not part of the supposedly destroyed or lost journals. However, the fact that Hughes did leave extant papers that are so closely related to the destroyed journals may indicate that he did not actually annihilate Plath's other private writing of the period. When he comes to write his 1978 Introduction to *Johnny Panic and the Bible of*

Dreams, Hughes speaks of the absent journals in the present tense, as if they still exist. 'Much of this journal either describes people still alive or is very private to her ... A few of the ... later entries have been selected'.[138] Implicitly, if later entries have been 'selected', they have been extracted from a matrix of other work from the same period. You cannot select if you have lost or destroyed all other options. The dated entries of the Smith family piece, like the 'Rose and Percy B' and 'Charlie Pollard and the Beekeepers' pieces that appear in both editions of *Johnny Panic*, mimic the format for headings and dates that Plath often used in her journals. Hughes's 1982 statement that the earlier notebook disappeared 'recently' makes it seem unlikely that he destroyed the later one during the three years that passed between the appearance of *Johnny Panic* and his accounts of what happened to the journals. Why wait until between fifteen and nineteen years after Plath's death to destroy the journals, at a time when one might suppose that grief, while still present, had lost its initial intensity, and emotions were under greater control? Why didn't he do it earlier, if he did it at all?

Moreover, Anne Stevenson tells us in *Bitter Fame* that 'An entry Olwyn remembers from Sylvia's lost journal strikes a poignant note: '"We answer the door together. They step over me as though I were a mat, and walk straight into [Ted's] heart"'.[139] Does Hughes's sister have a photographic memory, so that she remembers word for word a text that supposedly no longer exists? If not and she is paraphrasing, she is doing an excellent job of mimicking words that Plath wrote during the spring of 1962. Or, more likely, does the journal still exist, so that Olwyn Hughes was able to dip into it in the late 1980s and bring along the quotation for Stevenson?

The published letters are cut and edited in such a way that it is impossible to track Plath's references to her novels. The effect is not to downplay Plath's possible novels, but to make the reader all the more curious, because we are so teased and frustrated, about how many she wrote, when she wrote them, and what they were about. The confusion is intensified by Plath's silence about *The Bell Jar* in her letters to her mother, and her wish to keep the novel secret from her.[140] Hughes has alluded to Plath's last novel, 'provisionally titled *Double Exposure*'.[141] In 1971, he spoke of this novel as having 'got lost – along with quite a few other things – in the traffic terminal confusion ... just after her death'.[142] Six years later, he wrote (with what must surely be disingenuous casualness): 'That manuscript disappeared somewhere around 1970'.[143] 1970 is not '*just* after' Plath's death. 1970 is seven years after her death. Plath's mother notes that there were three novels: *The Bell Jar*; the sequel to it that Plath burned during the summer of 1962 while Mrs Plath watched (or witnessed Plath burning *something*); and a third, set in Plath's Devon village and concerning a love triangle.[144] These contradictions are hopeful ones. Something 'lost' might be found. The situation is more open to remedy than one in which something has 'disappeared'.

Hughes has written, fairly enough, of the blur that followed Plath's death, and the period during which he published or withheld her writing, 'I no longer remember why I did many things'.[145] His inconsistent descriptions of what happened to *Double Exposure* are the statements of a man besieged and under terrible pressure. So too is his statement about his editing of *Ariel*, made in his Introduction to the *Collected Poems*. Hughes tell us: 'It omitted some of the more personally aggressive poems from 1962, and might have omitted one or two more if she had not already published them'.[146] Again, we are confronted with that familiar pronoun trick, as if *Ariel* selected and published its own poems, while Hughes was entirely absent from the process. This shift, like the one concerning the maroon journal ledgers, is a corrective to an earlier and less widely disseminated account, in which Hughes does take responsibility for the *Ariel* omissions. He writes, using the first person: 'I also kept out one or two that were aimed too nakedly'.[147] What we have in these statements is, for me, reassuring, not depressing. Hughes's admissions that he would wish to hide poems that are 'personally aggressive' or 'aimed too nakedly' imply that there may be more such poems, somewhere. If there are, they may well come to light.

Admittedly, Hughes's treatment of Plath's work can be frustrating for her readers; the omissions, the misplaced manuscripts, the inconsistent accounts of what actually happened to her work. Yet his actions are themselves worthy of study; they are part of a unique publishing history, the still-unfolding stories of two of the twentieth century's most important bodies of work. In April 2000, Emory University opened its archive of Hughes's personal papers. These are available to scholars. However, there is one exception: a sealed trunk that Hughes stipulated must remain locked for twenty-five years after his death.[148] We can only guess at what this contains; perhaps one or both of Plath's lost journals, perhaps her missing novel, perhaps poems by Plath and Hughes that nobody has ever seen. The story continues.

Notes

1. Hughes, *New Selected Poems*, 1995: 298.
2. Hughes, *Birthday Letters*, 1998: inside front cover.
3. For instance, the line 'Her blacks crackle and drag' (*Collected Poems*, 273), from Plath's 'Edge', appears in a slightly modified version in Hughes's 'Night-Ride on Ariel' as 'Crackling and dragging their blacks' (*Birthday Letters*, 1998: 175). For a detailed discussion of the links between Plath's poems and *Birthday Letters*, see Wagner, *Ariel's Gift*, 2000.
4. Glaister, 'The Rise and Rise of Ted Hughes, Deceased', 1999: 3.
5. Faas, 'Ted Hughes and *Gaudete*', 1980: 213.
6. We learn that *Wodwo* appeared 'four years after' Plath's death and was described by Hughes as ' "a descent into destruction of some sort" ': Bishop, *Re-making Poetry*, 1991: 88. Bishop is quoting Hughes from an interview with Ekbert Faas, 'Ted Hughes and *Crow*'. *London Magazine* 10 (10 Jan. 1971): 5–20, at 15. Reprinted in Faas, *Ted Hughes: The Unaccommodated Universe*, 1980: 197–208, at 205.
7. Sagar, *The Art of Ted Hughes*, 1975: 57, 62.
8. Bishop, *Re-making Poetry*, 1991: ix.
9. Faas, *Ted Hughes: The Unaccommodated Universe*, 1980: 11.
10. Neill, 'The Fire That Still Burns After Sylvia', 1998: 12.
11. Faas, 'Chapters of a Shared Mythology', 1983: 124.
12. *Ibid.*, 120.
13. *Ibid.*, 115.
14. *Ibid.*, 115–16.
15. *Ibid.*, 108.
16. *Ibid.*, 110.
17. *Ibid.*, 114.
18. *Ibid.*, 115.
19. *Ibid.*, 111.
20. Rosenthal, 'Sylvia Plath and Confessional Poetry', 1970: 71.
21. West, *Ted Hughes*, 1985: 14.
22. Scigaj, *Ted Hughes: Form and Imagination*, 1986: 87. Scigaj writes: ' "Snow" … was published before the move to Devon; "The Rescue" … appeared in print before the marital breakdown; and *The Wound*, "Bowled Over," and "The Green Wolf" all antedate Plath's suicide' (87).
23. Scigaj, *Ted Hughes: Form and Imagination*, 1986: 236.
24. *Ibid.*, 196. Along these lines, Scigaj tells us: ' "The Angel," the final poem of *Remains of Elmet*, is a revision of "Ballad from a Fairy Tale" in *Wodwo*. Both poems recount dream premonitions of Sylvia Plath's death some two years before the event. In the dream the white square of satin foreshadowed the white square of satin covering Sylvia's face when Hughes first viewed the body' (253). For the source of this information,

Scigaj cites conversations with Ted and Olwyn Hughes in August of 1979 (335).

25. A particularly absurd example of biographical irrelevance occurs in an 'About the Author' blurb attached to a review of *Birthday Letters*. Hughes, we learn, 'was once so beautiful that some women were physically sick when they saw him'. Hensher, 'Some Home Truths About Sylvia Plath', 1998: 36.

26. Walder, *Ted Hughes*, 1987: 19.

27. *Ibid.*, 20–1. Walder is quoting Plath from A. Alvarez, ed., *The New Poetry*. Harmondsworth: Penguin, 1965: 28.

28. Walder, *Ted Hughes*, 1987: 21.

29. In *Remains of Elmet* (1979).

30. Walder, *Ted Hughes*, 1987: 84.

31. Neill, 'The Fire That Still Burns After Sylvia', 1998: 12.

32. Carey, 'Fatal Attraction', 1998: 1.

33. Hughes, *Birthday Letters*, 1998: inside front cover.

34. Eagleton, *The Rape of Clarissa*, 1982: 43.

35. Hughes, 'Fulbright Scholars', *Birthday Letters*, 1998: 3.

36. Hughes, 'Caryatids (I)', *Birthday Letters*, 1998: 4.

37. Hughes, *Birthday Letters*, 1998: 65.

38. *Ibid.*, 69. Hughes here revisits Plath's poems 'Child's Park Stones' and 'Table of the Rhododendron Stealers'. Childs Park, without an apostrophe and named after the Childs family, is an actual park near Smith College where Hughes and Plath often walked.

39. Hughes, *Birthday Letters*, 1998: 135.

40. I am unable to quote from 'Fidelity'. In a fax sent from the Permissions Controller at Faber & Faber to the publishers of this book, the following was explained:

> We cannot grant permission for any material to be reprinted from … the poem 'Fidelity' which appears in *Birthday Letters*. The author asked that certain poems from *Birthday Letters* were not taken out of context of the work as a whole and we adhere to his wishes today. I have listed the poems that cannot be reprinted from this collection below … 'Fidelity', 'Dreamers', 'The Inscription', 'The Cast', 'The Ventriloquist', 'Life after Death'.

Fax dated 22 August 2000, from Sally Robson, Permissions Controller at Faber & Faber, to Michele Kemp at Pearson Education.

41. Hughes, '18 Rugby Street', *Birthday Letters*, 1998: 24.

42. Hughes, 'God Help the Wolf after Whom the Dogs Do Not Bark', *Birthday Letters*, 1998: 26.

43. Hughes, 'St Botolph's', *Birthday Letters*, 1998: 15.

44. Hughes, *Birthday Letters*, 1998: 134.

45. Hensher, 'Some Home Truths About Sylvia Plath', 1998: 36.

46. Anne Stevenson suggests that readers could use her biography 'as a guide

to *Birthday Letters* as well as to Plath's *Collected Poems*'. Stevenson, 'New Preface, 1998' to *Bitter Fame*, 1989: xi.

47. Wagner, *Ariel's Gift*, 2000: 25.

48. Glaister, 'The Rise and Rise of Ted Hughes, Deceased', 1999: 3.

49. Hughes, 'Visit', *Birthday Letters*, 1998: 9.

50. Hughes, *Birthday Letters,* 1998: 17.

51. Eagleton, *The Rape of Clarissa*, 1982: 48.

52. Pearson Education sent a typescript of *The Other Sylvia Plath* to Faber & Faber, who publish Hughes and Plath in England, and to whom all requests to quote their work must be directed. Faber granted permission for me to quote the extracts from Plath's and Hughes's work that I wished to use in this book, and did so unconditionally and with no interference in my argument. However, their Permissions Controller explained, 'We cannot grant permission for any material to be reprinted from *Howls and Whispers*'. (See also note 40 above.)

53. SMITH. Box: Plath – Letters (A–Z). Folder: Letters, Beuscher, Ruth. T.L.s. 26 Sept. 1962.

54. Hughes, 'The Offers'. *The Sunday Times*. 18 Oct. 1998: Books Section, pp. 8–9.

55. Maguire, 'An Old Fresh Grief', 1998: 11.

56. Neill, 'The Fire That Still Burns After Sylvia', 1998: 12.

57. Hensher, 'Some Home Truths About Sylvia Plath', 1998: 36.

58. Miller, 'Et in America Ego', 1998: 3.

59. Longley, 'Obfuscating Myths', 1998: 30.

60. Glaister, 'The Rise and Rise of Ted Hughes, Deceased', 1999: 3.

61. Evans is quoted in *ibid*.

62. Cunningham, 'For Better or Verse?', 1998: 21.

63. Sagar, *The Art of Ted Hughes*, 1975: 10–11.

64. 'Secretary' and 'Fallgrief's Girl-friends' appeared in the *St Botolph's Review* that Hughes and his Cambridge friends published in 1956. 'Secretary', untitled when it first appeared, was reprinted in *The Hawk in the Rain* (1957).

65. Sagar, *The Art of Ted Hughes*, 1975: 11. Of the three poems Sagar lists here, only 'The Green Wolf' appeared in *Wodwo* (1967). 'View of a Pig' was first published in the *Times Literary Supplement*, 7 Aug. 1959, and reprinted in *Lupercal* (1960) (Sagar 1975: 184). 'Out' was recorded 29 Aug. 1962; 'The Green Wolf' appeared as 'Dark Women', in *The Observer*, 6 Jan. 1963 (Sagar 1975: 186).

66. Lucas Myers, in Appendix I to Stevenson, *Bitter Fame*, 1989: 312.

67. *The Journals of Sylvia Plath*, 1982: 111. *The Journals of Sylvia Plath*, 2000: 211.

68. Gifford and Roberts, *Ted Hughes: A Critical Study*, 1981: 22.

69. Scigaj, *Ted Hughes: Form and Imagination*, 1986: 187. The quotation from *Gaudete* can be found in Hughes, *Gaudete*, 1977: 104.

70. Reprinted in Hughes, *Woduo*, 1967: 104–46.

71. *Ibid.*, 184.

72. 'Crow's Song About England', in Sagar (ed.), *The Achievement of Ted Hughes* (Part 3, 'Uncollected and Unpublished Poems'), 1983: 338.

73. *Collected Poems*, 209.

74. 'Crow's Song About England', in Sagar (ed.), *The Achievement of Ted Hughes* (Part 3, 'Uncollected and Unpublished Poems'), 1983: 338.

75. Nathalie Anderson, 'Ted Hughes and the Challenge of Gender', 1994: 91.

76. Hughes, Introduction to *Johnny Panic*, 1977, 1979: 2 (American first edition).

77. *Ibid.*, 5.

78. *Ibid.*, 7; Faber edition, 12.

79. Hughes, Introduction to *Johnny Panic*, 1977, 1979: 2. (American first edition).

80. Faas, 'Ted Hughes and *Gaudete*', 1980: 214.

81. *Ibid.*, 213.

82. Hughes, 'Dylan Thomas', 1966: 182.

83. These are: 'Chaucer', 'You Hated Spain', 'The Earthenware Head', 'The Tender Place', 'Black Coat', 'Being Christlike', 'The God', and 'The Dogs Are Eating Your Mother'.

84. Armitage, 'Between Consciousness and Cosmos', 1995: 23.

85. In Hughes, *Flowers and Insects*, 1986: 9; 38–9; 52–5.

86. Walder, *Ted Hughes*, 1987: 27.

87. In Hughes, *Wolfwatching*, 1989: 26–32.

88. Nathalie Anderson, 'Ted Hughes and the Challenge of Gender', 1994: 112.

89. Scigaj, 'Ted Hughes and Ecology', 1994: 178.

90. Brandes, 'Hughes, History and the World in Which We Live', 1994: 152.

91. Hughes, *Wolfwatching*, 1989: 30.

92. *Ibid.*, 29.

93. Hughes, *Birthday Letters*, 1998: 138.

94. Walder, *Ted Hughes*, 1987: 54.

95. 'Bawdry Embraced' was published in *Recklings*, 'a limited edition of 150 copies in 1966' (Bishop, 'Neglected Auguries in "Recklings"', 1994: 11). It first appeared in *Poetry* LXXXVIII, 5 Aug. 1956 (Sagar, *The Art of Ted Hughes*, 1975: 182). Nathalie Anderson notes that it was 'explicitly dedicated to Plath' (Anderson, 'Ted Hughes and the Challenge of Gender', 1994: 96).

96. Bishop, 'Neglected Auguries in "Recklings"', 1994: 17.

97. Stan Smith, *Inviolable Voice*, 1982: 166.

98. Hughes, *Cave Birds*, 1978: 14.

99. Stevenson discusses Plath's 'implacability' to Lucas Myers, and her spurning of his and Hughes's efforts to '"make amends"' after a visit to the pub. Stevenson, *Bitter Fame*, 1989: 185. She refers to Hughes's 'ordeal'

after a visit by his sister and her friend Janet Crosbie-Hill during which Plath supposedly demonstrated 'seething aggression' and caused 'acute embarrassment' to all by 'addressing neither look nor word to Janet' (186).

100. Malcolm, *The Silent Woman*, 1994: 8.

101. *Collected Poems*, 221.

102. Hughes, *Cave Birds*, 1978: 56.

103. *Collected Poems*, 222.

104. Hughes, *Cave Birds*, 1978: 56.

105. *Collected Poems*, 222.

106. Hughes, *Cave Birds*, 1978: 56.

107. Hughes, *Woduo*, 1967: 107.

108. *Ibid.*, 127.

109. *Ibid.*, 104.

110. *Ibid.*, 106.

111. *Collected Poems*, 221.

112. Hughes, *Wodwo*, 1967: 109.

113. *Collected Poems*, 221.

114. Hughes, *Wodwo*, 1967: 122–3.

115. Rose, *The Haunting of Sylvia Plath*, 1991: 159, 160.

116. Hughes, *Wodwo*, 1967: 145.

117. *Ibid.*, 146.

118. *Collected Poems*, 222.

119. SMITH. Box: Plath – Ariel Poems. A Birthday Present – Cut. Folder: Ariel Poems, 'Burning the Letters', Draft 1, page 1.

120. SMITH. Box: Plath – Ariel Poems. A Birthday Present – Cut. Folder: Ariel Poems, 'Burning the Letters', Draft 1, page 2.

121. *Ibid.*

122. Van Dyne, *Revising Life*, 1993: 34, 40.

123. SMITH. Box: Plath – Ariel Poems. A Birthday Present – Cut. Folder: Ariel Poems, 'Burning the Letters', Draft 1, page 2.

124. LILLY. Plath MSS. 1961, 16 May. 'Widow'; Hughes, *Meet My Folks!*, 1987: 57.

125. Hughes, *Meet My Folks!*, 1987: 58.

126. *Collected Poems*, 164.

127. *Ibid.*, 165.

128. *Ibid.*, 164.

129. Hughes, Foreword to *The Journals of Sylvia Plath*, 1982: xiii.

130. Hughes, 'Sylvia Plath and Her Journals', 1994, 1995: 177.

131. Malcolm, *The Silent Woman*, 1994: 5–6.

132. Hughes, 'Publishing Sylvia Plath', 1994: 163.

133. Malcolm, *The Silent Woman*, 1994: 5.

134. Hughes, 'Sylvia Plath and Her Journals', 1994, 1995: 178.

135. Hughes, Introduction to *Johnny Panic*, Faber edition, 1977, 1979: 11.

136. *Johnny Panic*, 1977, 1979: 36–51 (American first edition).

137. *The Journals of Sylvia Plath,* 2000: 630–43.
138. Hughes, Introduction to *Johnny Panic* (American first edition), 1977, 1979: 7–8; Faber edition, 13.
139. Stevenson, *Bitter Fame,* 1989: 241.
140. In a 20 Nov. 1961 letter to her mother, Plath refers casually and imprecisely to a 'finished … batch of stuff … tied up in four parcels' for her Saxton grant. This 'stuff' is, in fact, *The Bell Jar. Letters Home,* 437.
141. Hughes, Introduction to *Johnny Panic,* Faber edition, 1977, 1979: 11.
142. Hughes, 'Publishing Sylvia Plath', 1994, 1995: 168.
143. Hughes, Introduction to *Johnny Panic,* Faber edition, 1977, 1979: 11.
144. LILLY. Plath MSS. II, Writings, *Letters Home* – Part Seven. Box 9, folder 10.
145. Hughes, 'Publishing Sylvia Plath', 1994, 1995: 167.
146. Hughes, Introduction to *Collected Poems* (Aug. 1980): 15.
147. Hughes, 'Publishing Sylvia Plath', 1994, 1995: 167.
148. See Wagner, 'At Last, Justice for Hughes', 2000: 6. See Bone, 'Hughes Papers Reveal Devotion to Plath', 2000: 10.

BIBLIOGRAPHY

By Sylvia Plath

Lucas, Victoria. *The Bell Jar.* London: William Heinemann, 1963. First English edition.

Lucas, Victoria. *The Bell Jar.* London: Contemporary Fiction William Heinemann, 1964.

Plath, Sylvia. *Ariel.* London: Faber and Faber, 1965. First English edition.

Plath, Sylvia. *Ariel.* New York: Harper & Row, 1966. First US edition.

Plath, Sylvia. *The Bell Jar.* London: 1963; Faber and Faber, paperback first published 1966.

Plath, Sylvia. *The Bell Jar.* New York: Harper & Row, 1971. First US edition.

Plath, Sylvia. *The Bell Jar.* New York: 1971; Bantam Books paperback edition, 1972.

Plath, Sylvia. *The Bell Jar.* London: Faber and Faber, 1963. Faber Library hardcover edition, 1996.

Plath, Sylvia. *The Bell Jar.* New York: HarperCollins, 1971. Twenty-Fifth Anniversary hardcover edition published 1996.

Plath, Sylvia. *The Collected Poems*, ed. Ted Hughes. London: Faber and Faber Limited, 1981.

Plath, Sylvia. *The Colossus and Other Poems.* New York: Alfred A. Knopf, 1962. First US edition.

Plath, Sylvia. *The Colossus and Other Poems.* London: Faber and Faber, 1967 (Reissue).

Plath, Sylvia. *Crossing the Water.* London: Faber and Faber, 1971. First English edition.

Plath, Sylvia. *Crossing the Water.* New York: Harper & Row, 1971. First US edition.

Plath, Sylvia. *Johnny Panic and the Bible of Dreams and Other Prose Writings.* London: Faber and Faber, 1977, 1979.

Plath, Sylvia. *Johnny Panic and the Bible of Dreams: Short Stories, Prose, And Diary Excerpts.* New York: Harper & Row, 1977, 1979. First US edition.

Plath, Sylvia. *The Journals of Sylvia Plath*, ed. Frances McCullough, consulting ed. Ted Hughes. New York: The Dial Press, 1982.

Plath, Sylvia. *The Journals of Sylvia Plath, 1950–1962*, ed. Karen V. Kukil. London: Faber and Faber, 2000.

Plath, Sylvia. *Letters Home*, ed. Aurelia Schober Plath. London: Faber and Faber, 1975.

Plath, Sylvia. *Sylvia Plath*. Selected by Diane Wood Middlebrook. Everyman's Library Pocket Poets. New York: Alfred A. Knopf, 1998.

Plath, Sylvia. *Winter Trees*. London: Faber and Faber, 1971. First English edition.

Plath, Sylvia. *Winter Trees*. New York: Harper & Row, 1972. First US edition.

Rare or Limited Editions

Ackerman, Diane, *et al*. *About Sylvia*. Wallingford, Pennsylvania: The Elm Press, 1996.

Hughes, Ted. *Howls & Whispers*. Etchings by Leonard Baskin. Rockport, Maine: The Gehenna Press, 1998. Limited edition of 110 numbered copies. Eleven *Birthday Letters* poems not published in *Birthday Letters* (published August 1998).

Plath, Sylvia. *A Day in June*. Ely: Embers Handpress, 1981. Consists of a single short story, 'A Day in June', written in 1952. First edition of 160 copies. Also printed in the British edition of *Johnny Panic and the Bible of Dreams*, but omitted from the American edition.

Plath, Sylvia. *Child*. Exeter: The Rougemont Press, 1971. Limited edition of 325 copies, the first 300 copies only for distribution.

Plath, Sylvia. *Crystal Gazer and Other Poems by Sylvia Plath*. London: Rainbow Press, 1971. Limited edition of 400 numbered copies.

Plath, Sylvia. *The Green Rock*. Ely: Embers Handpress, 1982. Consists of a single short story, 'The Green Rock', written in 1949. First edition of 160 copies. Also printed in the British edition of *Johnny Panic and the Bible of Dreams* published by Faber, but omitted from the American edition.

Plath, Sylvia. *Lyonnesse*. London: Rainbow Press, 1971. Limited edition of 400 numbered copies.

Plath, Sylvia. *Million Dollar Month*. Farnham: The Sceptre Press, 1971. Consists of a single poem, 'Million Dollar Month', written in the early 1950s, while Sylvia Plath was at Smith College. Issue of 150 copies.

Plath, Sylvia. *Pursuit*. London: The Rainbow Press, 1973. With an etching and drawings by Leonard Baskin. Limited edition of 100 copies.

Plath, Sylvia. *Stings*. Original Drafts of the Poem in Facsimile. Reproduced from the Sylvia Plath Collection at Smith College. Easthampton: The Pioneer Valley Printing Company, 1982. Edition of 5000 copies.

Plath, Sylvia. *Three Women*. London: Turret Books, 1968. With an

Introductory Note by Douglas Cleverdon. First broadcast on the BBC
Third Programme, 19 August 1962. Limited edition of 180 numbered
copies (of which only 150 are for sale).

On Sylvia Plath or Her Work

Alexander, Paul. *Rough Magic: A Biography of Sylvia Plath.* New York: Viking
Penguin, 1991.

Alvarez, A. *The Savage God: A Study of Suicide.* Harmondsworth: Penguin,
1971.

Alvarez, A. 'Sylvia Plath' (1963). *Tri-Quarterly.* Number Seven, Fall 1966:
65–74.

Ames, Lois. 'Sylvia Plath: A Biographical Note'. In Sylvia Plath, *The Bell Jar.*
New York: Harper & Row, 1971: 277–96. First US edition.

Anderson, Steven W. (ed.). *The Great American Bathroom Book (Volume II).*
Salt Lake City: Compact Classics, 1993: 283–4.

Axelrod, Steven Gould. *Sylvia Plath: The Wound and the Cure of Words.*
Baltimore: Johns Hopkins University Press, 1990.

Bassnet, Susan. *Sylvia Plath.* London: Macmillan, 1987.

Bloom, Harold (ed.). *Sylvia Plath.* Modern Critical Views series. New York:
Chelsea House Publishers, 1989.

Bone, James. 'Hughes Papers Reveal Devotion to Plath'. *The Times.* 8 April
2000: 10.

Bronfen, Elisabeth. *Sylvia Plath.* Plymouth: Northcote House (in
Association with the British Council), 1998.

Butscher, Edward. *Sylvia Plath: Method and Madness.* New York: Seabury
Press, 1976.

Byatt, A. S. 'Sylvia Plath: *Letters Home*' (1976). In A. S. Byatt. *Passions of the
Mind: Selected Writings.* London: Vintage, 1991: 250–4.

Coles, Joanna. 'Film Teams Jostle for Poetic Justice'. *The Times.* 5 December
1998: 15.

Corroll, Rory. 'Discovery of Plath's Forgotten Teenage Poems Dismays
Friends'. *The Guardian.* 20 November 1998: 2.

Couzyn, Jeni (ed.). *The Bloodaxe Book of Contemporary Women Poets: Eleven
British Writers.* Newcastle upon Tyne: Bloodaxe, 1985.

Cunningham, Valentine. 'For Better or Verse?' *The Times Higher Education
Supplement.* 27 November 1998: 20–1.

Ellmann, Mary. '*The Bell Jar:* An American Girlhood'. In Charles Newman
(ed.), *The Art of Sylvia Plath: A Symposium.* London: Faber and Faber, 1970:
221–6.

'Eroticism and Wit Restored in New Edition of Sylvia Plath Diaries'. *Independent on Sunday*. 1 February 1998: 1 (author unnamed).

Faas, Ekbert. 'Chapters of a Shared Mythology: Sylvia Plath and Ted Hughes'. In Keith Sagar (ed.), *The Achievement of Ted Hughes*. Manchester: Manchester University Press, 1983: 107–24.

Gilbert, Sandra. 'In Yeats' House: The Death and Resurrection of Sylvia Plath'. In Linda W. Wagner, *Critical Essays on Sylvia Plath*. Boston: G. K. Hall, 1984: 204–22.

Hall, Caroline King Barnard. *Sylvia Plath, Revised*. New York: Twayne's United States Author Series (No. 702), 1998.

Hardwick, Elizabeth. 'On Sylvia Plath'. In Paul Alexander (ed.), *Ariel Ascending*. New York: Harper & Row, 1985: 100–15.

Hargrove, Nancy D. *The Journey Toward Ariel: Sylvia Plath's Poems of 1956–1959*. Lund, Sweden: Lund University Press, 1994.

Hayman, Ronald. *The Death and Life of Sylvia Plath*. New York: Birch Lane Press, 1991.

Heaney, Seamus. 'The Indefatigable Hoof-taps: Sylvia Plath'. In Heaney, *The Government of the Tongue*. London: Faber, 1988: 148–70.

Holbrook, David. *Sylvia Plath: Poetry and Existence*. London: Athlone Press, 1976.

Hughes, Ted. 'The Art of Poetry LXXI'. (Drue Heinz, interviewer.) *The Paris Review*. 134. Spring 1995: 55–94.

Hughes, Ted. 'Introduction' (dated May 1978) to Sylvia Plath, *Johnny Panic and the Bible of Dreams: Short Stories, Prose, And Diary Excerpts*. New York: Harper & Row, 1977, 1979: 1–9. First US edition.

Hughes, Ted. 'Publishing Sylvia Plath' (1971). In Ted Hughes, *Winter Pollen: Occasional Prose* (ed. William Scammell). London: Faber, 1994, 1995: 163–9.

Hughes, Ted. 'Sylvia Plath and Her Journals' (1982). In *ibid.*: 177–90.

Hughes, Ted. 'Sylvia Plath: The Evolution of "Sheep in Fog"' (1988). In *ibid.*: 191–211.

Kazin, Alfred. *Bright Book of Life: American Novelists and Storytellers from Hemingway to Mailer*. Notre Dame: University of Notre Dame Press, 1971.

Kendall, Tim. 'Showing Off to an Audience of One'. *Times Literary Supplement*. 5 May 2000: 12.

Kenner, Hugh. 'Sincerity Kills' (1979). In Harold Bloom (ed.), *Sylvia Plath*. New York: Chelsea House Publishers, 1989: 67–78.

Kirkham, Michael. 'Sylvia Plath' (first published in 1984). In Linda W. Wagner (ed.), *Sylvia Plath: The Critical Heritage*. London and New York: Routledge, 1988: 276–91.

Lerner, Laurence. 'New Novels'. First published in *The Listener*, 31 January 1963: 215. Reprinted in Linda W. Wagner (ed.), *Sylvia Plath: The Critical Heritage*. London and New York: Routledge, 1988: 53–4.

Lowell, Robert. 'Foreword' to *Ariel*. In Sylvia Plath, *Ariel*. London: Faber and Faber, 1965: ix–xi. First English edition.

Macpherson, Pat. *Reflecting on The Bell Jar.* London: Routledge, 1991.

Malcolm, Janet. *The Silent Woman: Sylvia Plath and Ted Hughes.* New York: Alfred A. Knopf, 1994. First published in *The New Yorker*. 23 & 30 August 1993: 94–159.

Markey, Janice. *A Journey into the Red Eye: The Poetry of Sylvia Plath – A Critique.* London: The Women's Press, 1993.

Marsack, Robyn. *Sylvia Plath.* Buckingham: Open University Press, 1992.

McClatchy, J. D. 'Short Circuits and Folding Mirrors' (1979). In Harold Bloom (ed.), *Sylvia Plath*. New York: Chelsea House Publishers, 1989: 79–93.

McCullough, Frances. 'Foreword to the Twenty-Fifth Anniversary Edition'. In Sylvia Plath, *The Bell Jar*. New York: HarperCollins, 1971. Twenty-Fifth Anniversary hardcover edition published 1996: ix–xviii.

Middlebrook, Diane Wood. *Everyman's Library Pocket Poets: Sylvia Plath.* New York: Alfred A. Knopf, 1998.

Newman, Charles (ed.). *The Art of Sylvia Plath.* Bloomington and London: Indiana University Press, 1970.

Oates, Joyce Carol. 'The Death Throes of Romanticism: The Poetry of Sylvia Plath'. In Joyce Carol Oates. *New Heaven, New Earth: The Visionary Experience in Literature.* London: Victor Gollancz, 1976: 111–40.

Orr, Peter. *Plath Reads Plath* (interview with Peter Orr). Cambridge: Credo Records, 1975. Recorded 30 October 1962. Transcription from recording: mine.

Orr, Peter. *The Poet Speaks.* London: Routledge, 1966.

Ostriker, Alicia. 'The Americanization of Sylvia'. In Linda W. Wagner (ed.), *Critical Essays on Sylvia Plath.* Boston: G. K. Hall, 1984: 97–109.

Ostriker, Alicia Suskin. *Stealing the Language: The Emergence of Women's Poetry in America.* London: The Women's Press, 1986.

Pearson, Allison. 'Trapped in Time: Sylvia Plath'. *The Daily Telegraph* (Arts & Books Section). 1 April 2000: A1–A2.

Pereira, Malin Walther. 'Be(e)ing and "Truth": *Tar Baby's* Signifying on Sylvia Plath's Bee Poems'. *Twentieth Century Literature.* Winter 1996. Volume 42, Number 4: 526–34.

Perloff, Marjorie. 'Sylvia Plath's *Collected Poems*' (1981). In Linda W. Wagner (ed.), *Sylvia Plath: The Critical Heritage.* London and New York: Routledge, 1988: 293–303.

Perloff, Marjorie. 'The Two *Ariels*: The (Re)making of the Sylvia Plath Canon'. *American Poetry Review* 13. November–December 1984: 10–18.

Reimann, Aribert. *Six Poems by Sylvia Plath for Soprano and Piano* (musical score). New York: Schott, 1987.

Rorem, Ned. *Ariel: Five Poems of Sylvia Plath, for Soprano, Clarinet and Piano* (musical score). New York: Boosey & Hawkes, 1974.

Rose, Jacqueline. *The Haunting of Sylvia Plath.* London: Virago Press, 1991.

Rose, Jacqueline. 'So Many Lives, So Little Time'. *The Observer* (Review Section). 2 April 2000: 11.

Rosenthal, M. L. 'Sylvia Plath and Confessional Poetry' (1967). In Charles Newman (ed.), *The Art of Sylvia Plath.* Bloomington and London: Indiana University Press, 1970: 69–76.

Rowley, Rosemarie. 'Electro-Convulsive Treatment in Sylvia Plath's Life and Work'. *Thumbscrew* 10, Spring 1998: 87–99.

Sambrook, Hana. *York Notes: Sylvia Plath: Selected Works.* Harlow: Longman York Press, 1990.

Sheldon, Michael. 'The "Demon" that Killed Sylvia'. *The Daily Telegraph.* 13 March 2000: 9.

Shulamit, Ran. *Music of Ran Shulamit* (includes *Apprehensions, for Voice, Clarinet and Piano*). New York: CRI, 1991 (CD).

Smith, Stan. *Inviolable Voice: History and Twentieth-Century Poetry.* Dublin: Gill and Macmillan, 1982.

Steiner, George. 'Dying is an Art'. In Charles Newman (ed.), *The Art of Sylvia Plath: A Symposium.* London: Faber and Faber, 1970: 211–18.

Steiner, Nancy Hunter. *A Closer Look at Ariel: A Memory of Sylvia Plath.* London: Faber, 1974.

Stevenson, Anne. *Bitter Fame: A Life of Sylvia Plath.* London: Viking, 1989.

Stevenson, Anne. 'Sylvia Plath's Word Games'. *Poetry Review.* Volume 86, No. 4, Winter 1996/7: 28–34.

'Under the Skin' (unsigned review). First published in the *Times Literary Supplement.* 25 January 1963: 53. Reprinted in Linda W. Wagner (ed.), *Sylvia Plath: The Critical Heritage.* London and New York: Routledge, 1988: 52.

Van Dyne, Susan R. ' "More Terrible Than She Ever Was": The Manuscripts of Sylvia Plath's Bee Poems'. In Sylvia Plath, *Stings.* Original Drafts of the Poem in Facsimile. Reproduced from the Sylvia Plath Collection at Smith College. Easthampton: The Pioneer Valley Printing Company, 1982: 3–12.

Van Dyne, Susan R. *Revising Life: Sylvia Plath's Ariel Poems.* Chapel Hill: University of North Carolina Press, 1993.

Voices & Visions: Sylvia Plath. New York: Mystic Fire Video, 1988.

Wagner, Erica. *Ariel's Gift: Ted Hughes, Sylvia Plath and the Story of Birthday Letters.* London: Faber and Faber, 2000.

Wagner, Erica. 'At Last, Justice for Hughes'. *The Times.* 10 April 2000: 6–7.

Wagner, Erica. 'Love That Passed All Understanding'. *The Times.* 18 March 2000: 21.

Wagner, Linda W. (ed.). *Critical Essays on Sylvia Plath.* Boston: G. K. Hall and Co., 1984.

Wagner, Linda W. (ed.). *Sylvia Plath: The Critical Heritage*. London and New York: Routledge, 1988.

Wagner-Martin, Linda W. *Sylvia Plath: A Biography*. London: Cardinal, 1987.

Other Literary Works Cited

Atwood, Margaret. *The Edible Woman* (1969). London: Virago, 1980.

Brontë, Charlotte. *Villette* (1853). Oxford: Oxford University Press, 1984, 1990.

Byatt, A. S. *Babel Tower*. London: Chatto & Windus, 1996.

Byatt, A. S. *Possession: A Romance*. London: Chatto & Windus, 1990.

Carson, Rachel L. *The Sea Around Us*. London: Staples Press, 1951.

Carson, Rachel L. *Silent Spring*. London: Penguin, 1962. First appeared in *The New Yorker*, 16 June 1962: 35–99; 23 June 1962: 31–89; 30 June 1962: 35–67.

Carson, Rachel L. *Under the Sea Wind: A Naturalist's Picture of Ocean Life*. London: Staples Press, 1952.

Dunn, Sara (ed.). *Beneath the Wide Wide Heaven: Poetry of the Environment from Antiquity to the Present*. London: Virago, 1991.

Grimm, Jacob and Wilhelm. *The Complete Fairy Tales of the Brothers Grimm*. Translated by Jack Zipes. London and New York: Bantam Books, 1987, 1992.

Hardy, Thomas. *The Well-Beloved*. London: Macmillan, 1975.

Hughes, Ted. *Birthday Letters*. London: Faber, 1998 (published February 1998).

Hughes, Ted. *Cave Birds: An Alchemical Cave Drama*. Drawings by Leonard Baskin. New York: The Viking Press, 1978.

Hughes, Ted. *Crow*. London: Faber, 1970, 1972. Faber Library edition (with seven additional poems), 1995.

Hughes, Ted. 'Dylan Thomas' (1966). Excerpt reprinted in Ekbert Faas, *Ted Hughes: The Unaccommodated Universe*. Santa Barbara: Black Sparrow Press, 1980: 182–3.

Hughes, Ted. *Elmet*. Photographs by Fay Godwin. London: Faber, 1994. (Many of the poems in *Elmet* were first published as *Remains of Elmet* in 1979.)

Hughes, Ted. 'The Environmental Revolution' (1970). In Ted Hughes, *Winter Pollen: Occasional Prose* (ed. William Scammell). London: Faber, 1994: 28–35.

Hughes, Ted. *Flowers and Insects.* Drawings by Leonard Baskin. London: Faber, 1986.

Hughes, Ted. *Gaudete.* London: Faber, 1977.

Hughes, Ted. *The Iron Woman.* London: Faber, 1993.

Hughes, Ted. *Meet My Folks!* London: Faber, 1961. Revised edition, 1987.

Hughes, Ted. *Moortown.* London: Faber, 1979.

Hughes, Ted. *New Selected Poems 1957–1994.* London: Faber, 1995.

Hughes, Ted. 'The Offers'. *The Sunday Times.* 18 October 1998: Books Section, pp. 8–9. (First published in *Howls & Whispers*; see Rare and Limited Editions, above.)

Hughes, Ted. *Three Books: Remains of Elmet* (1979), *Cave Birds* (1978), *River* (1983). London: Faber, 1993.

Hughes, Ted. *Winter Pollen: Occasional Prose.* Edited by William Scammell. London: Faber, 1995.

Hughes, Ted. *Wodwo.* London: Faber, 1967.

Hughes, Ted. *Wolfwatching.* London: Faber, 1989.

James, Henry. *The American* (1877). New York: Rinehart & Co., 1949, 1953.

Joyce, James. *Ulysses* (1922). Harmondsworth: Penguin, 1969.

Lawrence, D. H. *Selected Poems.* Harmondsworth: Penguin, 1950.

Sexton, Anne. *The Complete Poems.* Boston: Houghton Mifflin Co., 1981.

Woolf, Virginia. *The Complete Shorter Fiction of Virginia Woolf.* Edited by Susan Dick. New York: Harcourt Brace Co., 1989.

Woolf, Virginia. *Congenial Spirits: Selected Letters.* Edited by Joanne Trautmann Banks. London: Hogarth Press, 1989.

Woolf, Virginia. *Mrs Dalloway* (1925). Oxford: Oxford University Press, 1992.

Woolf, Virginia. *Orlando* (1928). Oxford: Oxford University Press, 1992.

Woolf, Virginia. 'Professions for Women' (1931). In Michèle Barrett (ed.), *Virginia Woolf: On Women and Writing.* London: Women's Press, 1979: 57–63.

Woolf, Virginia. *A Room of One's Own* (1929). Oxford: Oxford University Press, 1992.

Woolf, Virginia. *To the Lighthouse* (1927). Oxford: Oxford University Press, 1992.

Woolf, Virginia. *The Voyage Out* (1915). Oxford: Oxford University Press, 1992.

Woolf, Virginia. *The Waves* (1931). Oxford: Oxford University Press, 1992.

Woolf, Virginia. *A Writer's Diary.* Edited by Leonard Woolf. Oxford: Oxford University Press, 1953.

Other Critical Works Cited

Abel, Elizabeth. *Virginia Woolf and the Fictions of Psychoanalysis.* London: University of Chicago Press, 1989.

Ahmad, Aijaz. 'The Politics of Literary Postcoloniality'. *Race & Class.* Vol. 36, No. 3, January–March 1995: 1–20.

Anderson, Benedict. *Imagined Communities.* London: Verso, 1991.

Anderson, Nathalie. 'Ted Hughes and the Challenge of Gender'. In Keith Sagar (ed.), *The Challenge of Ted Hughes.* London and Basingstoke: Macmillan, 1994: 91–115.

Armitage, Simon. 'Between Consciousness and Cosmos' (review of *New Selected Poems*). *Times Literary Supplement.* 21 April 1995: 23.

Bate, Jonathan. *Romantic Ecology: Wordsworth and the Environmental Tradition.* London: Routledge, 1991.

Bentley, Paul. *The Poetry of Ted Hughes: Language, Illusion and Beyond.* London: Addison Wesley Longman, 1998.

Bhabha, Homi K. 'Postcolonial Authority and Postmodern Guilt'. In Lawrence Grossberg *et al.* (eds), *Cultural Studies.* New York: Routledge, 1992: 56–68.

Biehl, Janet. *Rethinking Ecofeminist Politics.* Boston: South End Press, 1991.

Bishop, Nicholas. 'Neglected Auguries in "Recklings"'. In Keith Sagar (ed.), *The Challenge of Ted Hughes.* London and Basingstoke: Macmillan, 1994: 11–39.

Bishop, Nicholas. *Re-making Poetry: Ted Hughes and a New Critical Psychology.* Hemel Hempstead: Harvester Wheatsheaf, 1991.

Braidotti, Rosi, *et al.* *Women, the Environment and Sustainable Development: Towards a Theoretical Synthesis.* London and New Jersey: Zed Books, 1994.

Brandes, Rand. 'Hughes, History and the World in Which We Live'. In Keith Sagar (ed.), *The Challenge of Ted Hughes.* London and Basingstoke: Macmillan, 1994: 142–59.

Brooks, Paul. *The House of Life: Rachel Carson at Work, With Selections from her Writings Published and Unpublished.* London: George Allen & Unwin, 1972.

Brown, Ron. *Beekeeping: A Seasonal Guide.* London: B. T. Batsford, 1985.

Bull, John and Farrand, John, Jr. *The Audubon Society Field Guide to North American Birds.* New York: Knopf, 1977, 1993.

Byerly, Alison. 'The Uses of Landscape: The Picturesque Aesthetic and the National Park System'. In Cheryll Glotfelty and Harold Fromm (eds), *The Ecocriticism Reader: Landmarks in Literary Ecology.* Athens and London: University of Georgia Press, 1996: 52–68.

Cady, Michael, *et al.* (eds). *The Complete Book of British Birds.* Basingstoke and Bedfordshire: The Automobile Association and the Royal Society for the Protection of Birds, 1992.

Carey, John. 'Fatal Attraction' (review of *Birthday Letters*). *The Sunday Times* (*Books*, Section 8). 25 January 1998: 1–2.

Deitering, Cynthia. 'The Postnatural Novel: Toxic Consciousness in Fiction of the 1980s'. In Cheryll Glotfelty and Harold Fromm (eds), *The Ecocriticism Reader: Landmarks in Literary Ecology*. Athens and London: University of Georgia Press, 1996: 196–203.

Eagleton, Terry. 'Capitalism, Modernism and Postmodernism' (first published in 1985). In David Lodge (ed.), *Modern Criticism and Theory: A Reader*. London: Longman, 1988: 384–98.
Eagleton, Terry. *The Rape of Clarissa: Writing, Sexuality and Class Struggle in Samuel Richardson*. Oxford: Basil Blackwell, 1982.

Faas, Ekbert. 'Ted Hughes and *Crow*' (1970 interview with Ted Hughes). In Ekbert Faas, *Ted Hughes: The Unaccommodated Universe*. Santa Barbara: Black Sparrow Press, 1980: 197–208.
Faas, Ekbert. 'Ted Hughes and *Gaudete*' (1977 interview with Ted Hughes). In *ibid.*: 208–15.
Faas, Ekbert. *Ted Hughes: The Unaccommodated Universe*. Santa Barbara: Black Sparrow Press, 1980.
Freud, Sigmund. 'The Infantile Genital Organization' (1923). In *The Essentials of Psycho-Analysis*, ed. Anna Freud, trans. James Strachey. Harmondsworth: Penguin, 1986: 390–4.
Freud, Sigmund. 'The "Uncanny"' (1919). In *The Penguin Freud Library*, *vol.* 14: 335–81.
Friedan, Betty. *The Feminine Mystique*. London: Penguin, 1963.

Gifford, Terry. *Green Voices*. Manchester: Manchester University Press, 1995.
Gifford, Terry and Roberts, Neil. *Ted Hughes: A Critical Study*. London: Faber and Faber, 1981.
Glaister, Dan. 'The Rise and Rise of Ted Hughes, Deceased'. *The Guardian*. 12 January 1999: 3.
Graham, Frank. *Since Silent Spring*. London: Hamish Hamilton, 1970.

Heinzel, Hermann, *et al*. *The Birds of Britain and Europe*. London: Collins, 1972, 1974.
Hensher, Philip. 'Some Home Truths About Sylvia Plath' (review of *Birthday Letters*). *Night & Day*. 1 February 1998: 36.
Hey, D. H. (ed., *et al.*). *Kingzett's Chemical Encyclopaedia: A Digest of Chemistry & Its Industrial Applications*. London: Baillière, Tindall and Cassell, 1966.

Hirschberg, Stuart. *Myth in the Poetry of Ted Hughes*. Totowa: Barnes and Noble Books, 1981.
Hobsbawm, E. J. *Nations and Nationalism Since 1780: Programme, Myth, Reality*. Cambridge: Cambridge University Press: 1990.

Hynes, Patricia H. *The Recurring Silent Spring.* New York and Oxford: Pergamon Press, 1989.

Jouve, Nicole Ward. *White Woman Speaks with Forked Tongue.* London: Routledge, 1991.

Klein, Melanie. 'A Study of Envy and Gratitude' (1956). In *The Selected Melanie Klein,* ed. Juliet Mitchell. London: Penguin, 1986: 211–29.

Kristeva, Julia. 'About Chinese Women' (1974). In *The Kristeva Reader,* ed. Toril Moi. Oxford: Blackwell, 1986: 138–59.

Kristeva, Julia. 'The Adolescent Novel' (1990). In *Abjection, Melancholia and Love: the Work of Julia Kristeva,* ed. John Fletcher and Andrew Benjamin. London: Routledge, 1990.

Kristeva, Julia. *Desire in Language: A Semiotic Approach to Literature and Art.* Oxford: Blackwell, 1980.

Kristeva, Julia. *Powers of Horror: An Essay on Abjection* (first published in 1980). New York: Columbia University Press, 1982.

Kristeva, Julia. *Revolution in Poetic Language* (first published in 1974), trans. Margaret Waller. New York: Columbia University Press, 1984.

Legler, Gretchen T. 'Ecofeminist Literary Criticism'. In Karen J. Warren (ed.), *Ecofeminism: Women, Culture, Nature.* Bloomington and Indianapolis: Indiana University Press, 1997: 227–38.

Longley, Edna. 'Obfuscating Myths' (review of *Birthday Letters*). *Thumbscrew* 10, Spring 1998: 27–30.

Maguire, Sarah. 'An Old Fresh Grief' (review of *Birthday Letters*). *The Guardian* (Books). 22 January 1998: 11.

Marco, Gino J. et al. (eds). *Silent Spring Revisited.* Based on a symposium on the topics posed in Rachel Carson's *Silent Spring,* held in Philadelphia, 1984. Washington DC: American Chemical Society, 1987.

Merchant, Carolyn. *The Death of Nature.* San Francisco: Harper & Row, 1989.

Miller, Karl. 'Et in America Ego' (review of *Birthday Letters*). *Times Literary Supplement.* 6 February 1998: 3–4.

Neill, Heather. 'The Fire That Still Burns After Sylvia' (review of *Birthday Letters*). *Times Educational Supplement.* 30 January 1998: 12.

Pero, Thomas. 'Poet, Pike and a Pitiful Grouse' (interview with Ted Hughes). *The Guardian.* 9 January 1999: (*Saturday Review* Section) 1–2.

Plumwood, Val. *Feminism and the Mastery of Nature.* London: Routledge, 1993.

Robinson, Craig. *Ted Hughes as Shepherd of Being.* London and Basingstoke: Macmillan, 1989.

Roe, Sue. *Writing and Gender: Virginia Woolf's Writing Practice.* Hemel Hempstead: Harvester Wheatsheaf, 1990.

Sagar, Keith (ed.). *The Achievement of Ted Hughes*. Manchester: Manchester University Press, 1983.

Sagar, Keith. *The Art of Ted Hughes*. Cambridge: Cambridge University Press, 1975.

Sagar, Keith (ed.). *The Challenge of Ted Hughes*. London and Basingstoke: Macmillan, 1994.

Sagar, Keith. *Ted Hughes*. Harlow: Longman, 1972.

Schlesinger, Philip. 'Europeanness: A New Cultural Battlefield?' (first published 1992). In John Hutchinson and Anthony D. Smith (eds), *Nationalism*. Oxford: Oxford University Press, 1994: 316–25.

Schmitt, Peter J. *Back to Nature: The Arcadian Myth in Urban America*. Baltimore and London: John Hopkins University Press, 1969, 1990.

Scigaj, Leonard M. 'Ted Hughes and Ecology: A Biocentric Vision'. In Keith Sagar (ed.), *The Challenge of Ted Hughes*. London and Basingstoke: Macmillan, 1994: 160–81.

Scigaj, Leonard M. *Ted Hughes: Form and Imagination*. Iowa City: University of Iowa Press, 1986.

Slicer, Deborah. 'Toward an Ecofeminist Standpoint Theory: Bodies as Grounds'. In Greta Gaard and Patrick D. Murphy (eds), *Ecofeminist Literary Criticism: Theory, Interpretation, Pedagogy*. Urbana and Chicago: University of Illinois Press, 1998: 49–73.

Slovic, Scott. 'Nature Writing and Environmental Psychology'. In Cheryll Glotfelty and Harold Fromm (eds), *The Ecocriticism Reader: Landmarks in Literary Ecology*. Athens and London: University of Georgia Press, 1996: 351–70.

Smith, Anthony D. *National Identity*. London: Penguin, 1991.

Walder, Dennis. *Ted Hughes*. Milton Keynes: Open University Press, 1987.

Warren, Karen J. 'Taking Empirical Data Seriously: An Ecofeminist Philosophical Perspective'. In Karen J. Warren (ed.), *Ecofeminism: Women, Culture, Nature*. Bloomington and Indianapolis: Indiana University Press, 1997: 3–20.

Warwick, Ronald. 'A Common Wealth'. *The Times Higher Education Supplement*. 5 May 1995: 27.

West, Thomas. *Ted Hughes*. London: Methuen, 1985.

Woods, Richard. 'Hughes Saw Ghost of Plath on the Tube'. *The Sunday Times*. 18 October 1998: 6.

INDEX